The Aims of Argument

The Aims
of Argument

A BRIEF RHETORIC

Second Edition

Timothy W. Crusius / Carolyn E. Channell

Southern Methodist University

Mayfield Publishing Company
Mountain View, California
London • Toronto

LIBRARY OF CONGRESS CATALOGING–IN–PUBLICATION DATA
Crusius, Timothy W.,
    The aims of argument : a brief rhetoric / Timothy W. Crusius,
Carolyn E. Channell.—2nd ed.
      p.   cm.
    Includes index.
    ISBN 1-55934-933-6
    1. English language—Rhetoric.   2. Persuasion (Rhetoric).   3. Report writing.
I. Channell, Carolyn E.   II. Title.
PE1431.C778   1997
808'.042—dc21   97-1161
                                                               CIP

Manufactured in the United States of America
10   9   8   7   6   5   4   3   2

Mayfield Publishing Company
1280 Villa Street
Mountain View, CA 94041

Sponsoring editor, Thomas V. Broadbent; production editor, Julianna Scott Fein; manuscript editor, Andrea McCarrick; design and art manager, Susan Breitbard; text designer, David Bullen; cover designer, Susan Breitbard; manufacturing manager, Randy Hurst. The text was set in 10½/12 Bembo by Thompson Type and printed on acid-free 45# Chromatone Matte by Banta Book Group.

Cover art: Kenneth Noland, *Comet,* 1994. Kenneth Noland/VAGA, New York.

Acknowledgments and copyrights continue at the back of the book on pages 275–276, which constitute an extension of the copyright page.

For W. Ross Winterowd

In 1980 an author could justify a new argumentation textbook for first-year college students simply by saying that it filled a void; now prospective authors must ask themselves, Does the profession really need yet another book on argumentation? Moreover, they had better have a good answer to a question that experienced instructors of argument will surely ask: How, specifically, is your text different from—and better than—the one I am using?

People write textbooks for many reasons, but probably the most important reason—the one that keeps authors going long after the initial enthusiasm (and advances) are spent—is the chance of satisfying a need. With over thirty years of teaching experience between us, we have tried most of the argumentation texts currently available. Some of them are quite good, and we have learned from them. However, we found ourselves adopting a text not so much out of genuine enthusiasm but rather because it had fewer liabilities than any of the others under consideration. True, all textbook selection involves comparisons of the "lesser evil" sort. But we wondered why we were so lukewarm about even the best argumentation textbooks. What was it exactly that put us off?

We found many problems, both major and minor. But our dissatisfaction boiled down to a few major criticisms:

Most treatments were too formalistic and prescriptive.

Most failed to integrate class discussion and individual inquiry with written argumentation.

Apart from moving from simple concepts and assignments to more complicated ones, no book offered a learning sequence.

Despite the fact that argument, like narrative, is clearly a mode or means of development, not an end in itself, no book offered a well-developed view of the aims or purposes of argument.

We thought that these shortcomings had many undesirable results in the classroom, including the following:

The overemphasis on form confused students with too much terminology, made them doubt their best instincts, and drained away energy and interest from the process of inventing and discovering good arguments. Informal argumentation is not cut-and-dried but open-ended and creative.

The separation of class discussion from the process of composition created a hiatus (rather than a useful distinction) between oral and written argument so that students had difficulty seeing the relation between the two and using the insights learned from each to improve the other.

The lack of a learning sequence—of assignments that begin by refining and extending what students can do without help and that then build on these capacities with each subsequent assignment—meant that courses in argumentation were less coherent and less meaningful than they could be. Students did not understand why they were doing what they were doing and could not envision what might reasonably come next.

Finally, inattention to what people actually use argument to accomplish resulted in too narrow a view of the functions of argument and thus in unclear purposes for writing. Because instruction was mainly limited to what we call arguing to convince, too often students saw argument only as a monologue of advocacy. Even when their viewpoint was flexible, too often they assumed a pose of dogmatism and ignored any true spirit of inquiry.

We set out consciously to solve these problems—or at least to render them less problematical. The result is a book different in notable respects from any other argument text currently available. In Chapter 1 we define and explain four aims of argument:

Arguing to inquire, the process of questioning opinions
Arguing to convince, the process of making cases
Arguing to persuade, the process of appealing to the whole person
Arguing to negotiate, the process of mediating between or among conflict-
ing positions

We have found that instructors have certain questions about these aims, especially in terms of how they relate to one another. No doubt we have yet to hear all the questions that will be asked but hope that by answering the ones we have heard, we can clarify some of the implications of our approach.

1. *What is the relative value of the four aims? Since negotiation comes last, is it the best or most valued?* Our answer is that no aim is "better" than any other aim. Given certain needs or demands for writing and certain audiences, one aim can be more appropriate than another for the task at hand. We treat negotiation last because it involves inquiry, convincing, and persuading and thus comes last in the learning sequence.

2. *Must inquiry be taught as a separate aim?* Not at all. We have designed the text so that it may be taught as a separate aim (the use of argument Plato and Aristotle called *dialectic*), but we certainly do not intend this "may" to be interpreted as a "must." We do think that teaching inquiry as a distinct aim has certain advantages. Students need to learn how to engage in con-

structive dialogue, which is more disciplined and more focused than class discussion usually is. Once they see how it is done, students seem to enjoy dialogue with one another and with texts. Dialogue helps students think through their arguments and imagine reader reaction to what they say, both of which are crucial to convincing and persuading. Finally, as with the option of teaching negotiation, teaching inquiry offers instructors the option to make assignments in addition to the standard argumentative essay.

3. *Should inquiry come first?* For a number of reasons, inquiry has a certain priority over the other aims. Most teachers are likely to approach inquiry as a prewriting task, preparatory to convincing or persuading. And very commonly we return to inquiry when we find something wrong with a case we are trying to construct, so the relation between inquiry and the other aims is as much recursive as it is a matter of before and after.

However, we think inquiry also has psychological, moral, and practical claims to priority. When we are unfamiliar with an issue, inquiry comes first psychologically, often as a felt need to explore existing opinion. Regardless of what happens in the "real world," convincing or persuading without an open, honest, and earnest search for the truth is, in our view, immoral. Finally, inquiry goes hand-in-hand with research, which, of course, normally precedes writing in the other aims of argument.

In sum, we would not defend Plato's concept of the truth. Truth is not simply "out there" in some wordless place waiting to be discovered; rather, our opinion is what we discover or uncover as we grapple with a controversial issue and results largely from how we interpret ourselves and our world. We agree, therefore, with Wayne Booth that truth claims ought to be provisional and subject to revision, held for good reasons until better ones change our minds. Moreover, we agree with Plato that rhetoric divorced from inquiry is dangerous and morally suspect. The truth (if always provisional—some person's, some group's, or some culture's version of the truth) must count for more than sheer technical skill in argumentation.

4. *Isn't the difference between convincing and persuading more a matter of degree than of kind?* Fairly sharp distinctions can be drawn between inquiry and negotiation and between either of these two aims and the monologues of advocacy: convincing and persuading. But convincing and persuading do shade into one another, so that the difference is only clear at the extremes, with carefully chosen examples. Furthermore, the "purest" appeal to reason—a lawyer's brief, a philosophical or scientific argument—appeals in ways beyond the sheer cogency of the case being made. Persuasive techniques are typically submerged but not absent in arguing to convince.

Our motivation for separating convincing from persuading is not so much theoretical as pedagogical. Students usually have so much difficulty with case-making that individual attention to the logical appeal by itself is justified. Making students focally conscious of the appeals of character, emotion, and style while they are struggling to cope with case-making is too much to ask and can overburden them to the point of paralysis.

Regardless, then, of how sound the traditional distinction between convincing and persuading may be, we think it best to take up convincing first and then persuasion, especially since what students learn in the former can be carried over more or less intact into the latter. And, of course, it is not only case-making that carries over from convincing into persuading. Since one cannot make a case without unconscious appeal to character, emotional commitments (such as values), and style, teaching persuasion is really a matter of exposing and developing what is already there in arguing to convince.

The central tenets of an approach based on aims of argument may be summarized as follows:

> *Argumentation is a mode or means of discourse, not an aim or purpose of discourse;* consequently, our task is to teach the aims of argument.
>
> *The aims of argument are linked in a learning sequence, so that convincing builds on inquiry, persuasion on convincing, and all three contribute to negotiating;* consequently, we offer this learning sequence as an aid to conceiving a course or courses in argumentation.

We believe in the learning sequence as much as we do in the aims of argument. We think that anyone giving it an honest chance will come to prefer this way of teaching argument over any other ordering currently available.

At the same time, we recognize that textbooks are used selectively, as teachers and programs need them for help in achieving their own goals. As with any other text, this one can be used selectively, ignoring some parts, playing up others, designing other sequences, and so on. If you want to work with our learning sequence, it is there for creative adaptation. If not, the text certainly does not have to be taught as a whole and in sequence to be useful and effective.

Some reviewers and users have called our approach innovative. But is it better? Will students learn more? Will instructors find the book more satisfying and more helpful than what they currently use? Our experience—both in using the book ourselves and in listening to the responses of those who have read it or tested it in the classroom for us—is that they will. Students complain less about having to read this book than they do about having to read others used in our program. They do seem to learn more. Teachers claim to enjoy the text and find it stimulating, something to work with rather than around. We hope your experience is as positive as ours has been. We invite your comments and will use them in the process of perpetual revision that constitutes the life of a text and of our lives as writing teachers.

NEW TO THE SECOND EDITION

The major changes from the first edition are the following:

In Chapter 3, Anna Quindlen's "Making the Mosaic" replaces Susan Brownmiller's "Pornography Hurts Women." Less polemical than Brownmiller's, Quindlen's essay should help students retain sharper focus on the goal of the chapter—learning how to read an argument.

In Chapter 6, we offer now, with commentary designed to highlight crucial aspects of the process, a detailed, phase-by-phase development of a student essay, from initial exploration to final draft. The advantages are obvious for helping students cope successfully with arguing to convince.

In Appendix A, "Researching Arguments," we have included advice on accessing and evaluating data from on-line services and examples of how to document electronic sources. Clearly students should use computers and use them skillfully and responsibly. This new material should help.

There are, of course, thousands of other changes, small but not unimportant, many of them the result of excellent work by our copyeditor, Andrea McCarrick. Large and small, we think the changes have made *Aims* a better book while not altering its fundamental character.

All authors whose textbooks reach a second edition owe the most to teachers who gave a new and unfamiliar book a chance. Thanks for using *Aims,* for helping to make others aware of it, and for your comments and suggestions.

Here at SMU Gary Kriewald's advice and student papers were especially helpful. Marcella Stark, of our central library, helped with the material on computer sources in Appendix A.

We wish to acknowledge the work of the following reviewers: Elizabeth Howard Borczon, University of Kansas; Margaret Cullen, Ohio Northern University; Richard Fulkerson, Texas A&M University, Commerce; Matthew Hearn, Valdosta State University; James L. Kastely, University of Houston; William Keith, Oregon State University; and Judith Gold Stitzel, West Virginia University.

At Mayfield the insight, patience, and sagacity of Drake Bush was helpful indeed.

NOTE TO STUDENTS

Our goal in this book is not just to show you how to construct an argument but to make you more aware of why people argue and the purposes that argument serves in our society. Consequently, this book introduces four specific aims that people may have in mind when they make arguments: to inquire, to convince, to persuade, and to negotiate. Preceding the chapters on each specific aim of argument, however, are four relatively short chapters that offer an overview of the four aims and prepare you for working with assignments in the aims.

Chapter 1 explains the aims and how they fit into the larger concept of *rhetoric,* the persuasive use of language.

Chapter 2 explains what a writer's notebook is and how it can help you cope with writing assignments in any college course.

Chapter 3 offers an approach to reading any argument.

Chapter 4 shows you, step-by-step, how to analyze the logic of any argument.

Because critical reading and analysis prepare you for the first aim, arguing to inquire, Chapters 3 and 4 lead directly into Chapter 5, and each subsequent chapter on the aims assumes and builds on the previous one.

This book concludes with two appendixes, each a reference that you will want to consult repeatedly as you work through the assignments in the main parts of the text. Appendix A offers advice about how to do library and field research and how to handle formal documentation. We see such research as a vital component of preparing to write convincingly on any topic, unless you take an extremely personal approach and have had first-hand experiences to draw upon for support. Try not to think of your writing assignments as research papers; instead, think of how even a brief argument can gain strength from facts or opinions taken from one or two well-selected sources. Appendix B focuses on editing, the art of polishing and refining prose, and on proofreading for some common errors.

Arguing well is difficult for anyone. For many college students it is especially challenging because they have had little experience writing arguments. We have tried to write a text that is no more complicated than it has to be, and we welcome your comments so that we may improve future editions. Please write us at the following address:

The Rhetoric Program
Dallas Hall
Southern Methodist University
Dallas, Texas 75275

You may also e-mail your comments to the following address:

cchannel@post.cis.smu.edu.

CONTENTS

The Aims of Argument

CHAPTER ONE

An Overview
of Key Terms

Commonly, the word *argument* refers to a verbal conflict, a dispute involving two or more people. In this book we will use the word in a sense closer to that of the Latin verb from which it derives: *arguere,* "to make clear."

WHAT IS ARGUMENT?

Argument is the process of making what we think clear to ourselves and to others. It takes us from a vague, private viewpoint to a clearly stated position that we can defend publicly in speech or writing. Like any journey, the process provides us with discoveries and new knowledge. If we undertake this process in a spirit of honesty and openness, we can compare it to a search for truth.

Argument in this sense of seeking clarity has a two-part form or structure: (1) the statement of an opinion and (2) the statement of one or more reasons for holding that opinion. If you say, for example, "Student loans for college ought to be more widely available," you have stated an opinion. In doing so, you have made one thing clear—namely, your position on the issue of student loans. But as yet you have not made an argument in our particular sense of the word. Not until you add to your opinion a reason for holding it—for example, "because rising costs are preventing too many capable but impoverished students from attending"—do you construct an argument. By adding your reason you have made something else clear—namely, *why* you take the position you do.

As we will see in detail in later chapters, arguments require more than simply an opinion coupled with a reason. But this basic form is fundamental to accomplishing any of the aims of argument.

WHAT ARE THE AIMS OF ARGUMENT?

Argument is not in itself an end or a purpose of communication. It is rather a *means* of discourse, developing what we have to say. In this book we use the term *aims of argument* to refer to the various purposes that argument helps us accomplish.

We all know people who seem to argue just for the sake of argument, who would argue with a post, so to speak. But even these people have an aim beyond argument itself. It may be to vent hostility or resentment or outrage. Or it may be to show off, to display what they know, or to dominate (or enliven) a discussion. We may feel that such contentious people are arguing inappropriately, but they are clearly not arguing just to argue. They are arguing to express themselves.

An argument may be almost entirely self-expression. Some speakers and writers are satisfied just to have their say; they don't care about winning their opponents over to their side. Consider the letters to the editor in your local paper. A few attempt to influence the viewpoints of others, but most only state an opinion, offering perhaps some minimal justification. Newspaper editors appropriately give these sections titles such as "Sounding Off."

In fact, all arguments are expressive to some degree. Nothing tells us more about people than the opinions they hold and their reasons for holding them. Our opinions play a large role in making us what we are: conservative, liberal, or middle-of-the-road in politics; a believer, an atheist, or an agnostic in religion; and so on. Because what we think is so much what we are, we typically hold our opinions with deep conviction and genuine passion—so much so that we often fail to question our own opinions or to listen to the arguments of other people who disagree with us.

In societies that value freedom of speech, argument as self-expression is common. It is also quite spontaneous: we learn it much as we learned our first language, by just attempting it, with little thought about the form of the argument or the process that brought us to our position. For this reason we have not singled out argument as expression for special concern in this book.

We assume most of your arguments will be expressive, or at least will begin as self-expression. But when you examine your own opinions or the opinions of someone who disagrees with you, when you try to get others to change their positions, when you explore avenues of compromise between competing positions, you are moving beyond self-expression to one of the following four aims of argument, on which we will focus.

Arguing to Inquire

The ancient Greeks called argument as inquiry *dialectic;* today we might think of it as *dialogue,* or serious conversation. But arguing to inquire can also be done in writing and may in fact work best when we can scrutinize our thoughts "out there" on the page.

Arguing to inquire helps us to form opinions, to question opinions we already have, and to reason our way through conflicts or contradictions. It is how we decide what we will accept as the truth about a given issue. It requires an attitude of patient questioning under nonthreatening circumstances and is therefore something we most often do alone or among trusted friends and associates.

In everyday life we most commonly argue to inquire when we face a complicated decision, such as buying just the right car or deciding which major to take in college. We want to make an intelligent decision, one that seems reasonable to ourselves and to others whose opinions we respect. What do we do? We argue with ourselves, we try out arguments on our friends, we offer a tentative opinion to someone more knowledgeable (the parent who helps pay for the car or college tuition, for example).

We also use argument as inquiry when we think through dilemmas, whether personal or public—when one voice inside says one thing and another says something that conflicts with the first. For example, we have been taught to be tolerant of others, to respect the opinions of people who disagree with us. But when we encounter opinions that are themselves intolerant, that are racist or sexist in an aggressive and even potentially violent way, we are confronted with a dilemma: How much tolerance is too much tolerance? Where do we draw the line between differences that must be respected, even encouraged, and opinions that are dangerous and should be actively opposed, even suppressed? Should we protest a Nazi group's demonstration on Main Street? Should we support or challenge a campus group that destroys every issue of a school-supported newspaper it finds offensive?

Sometimes college courses ask us to confront such basic philosophical dilemmas as the limits of tolerance. More commonly, though, the purpose of inquiry in college is to help us form opinions about issues requiring some kind of research. We become acquainted with an issue through lectures and assigned reading; then, to assess what we have heard and read, we must seek out additional information and opinions. Argument as inquiry helps us read and listen more critically so that we can arrive at our own position with confidence. Because inquiry engages us in dialogues with others and with ourselves, its success depends on the art of asking questions, which is the principal concern of Chapter 4.

Finally, argument as inquiry plays a role in our professional lives. A research scientist may devote years, even a lifetime, to formulating, testing, and reformulating hypotheses that explore a single set of phenomena—black holes, for example. Businesspeople must find solutions to practical problems (How can we increase sales in our southern region?), resolve dilemmas based on changing societal and political attitudes (How can we achieve our goals for affirmative action and still hire the best people?), and meet new and often unanticipated challenges that have a direct impact on success or failure (How should we respond to the evolving economic and political conditions in Eastern Europe?). Basic to such research and decision-making is arguing to inquire.

Arguing to Convince

Some inquiry never stops, remaining permanently open-ended; the goal of most inquiry, however, is to reach some kind of conclusion. This conclusion can go by many names, but we'll call it a *conviction* and define it as "an earned opinion, achieved through careful thought, research, and discussion." Once we arrive at a conviction, we ordinarily want others to share it—that is, the aim of further argument is to secure the assent of people who do not share our conviction (or who do not share it fully). Such assent is an agreement of minds secured by reason rather than by force.

Arguing to inquire centers on asking questions; we use argument as inquiry to expose and examine what we think. Arguing to convince centers on making a case, which, as we shall see in Chapter 6, involves an elaboration of the basic structure "x because y"; we use argument as convincing in an effort to get others to agree with what we think. Inquiry is the search for what is true; convincing is the attempt to get others to accept the truths we claim to have reached.

Examples of arguing to convince are all around us. The purest may be found in scholarly and professional writing (for example, when a historian interprets the causes of an event in the past and makes a case for his or her interpretation or when a judge writes up a justification for a particular ruling). But we see examples in everyday life as well: on editorial pages, where writers make a case for their position on local issues or candidates for office, and even at school, when a student tries to appeal a grade.

Whenever we encounter a stance supported by reasons that asks for our assent to the position being argued, we are dealing with argument as convincing. Whenever our intent as writers is primarily to gain the intellectual assent of our reader (when we want a reader to respond with "I agree" or "You're right"), we are arguing to convince.

Arguing to Persuade

Persuasion, as we will consider it, is convincing *plus*. More than simply to earn the assent of readers, its aim is to influence their behavior as well, to move them to act upon the conviction to which they have assented. An advertisement for Mercedes-Benz aims not only to convince us that the company makes a high-quality car, but also to go out and buy one. A Sunday sermon asks for more than agreement with some interpretation of a biblical passage; the minister wants the congregation to apply the message to their lives. Persuasion asks us to *do* something—spend money, live a certain way, cast a vote, join a movement. Because we don't always act on our convictions, persuasion cannot rely on reasons alone; it must appeal in broader and deeper ways.

Usually persuasion appeals to the reader's emotions. We may be convinced by an argument that starving children deserve our help, but actually getting us to send money may require a photograph of a child with skeletal limbs and a hunger-bloated stomach. The intent of such tactics is clear: to reinforce reasons with pity, the better to move us to action.

To a greater extent than convincing, persuasion also relies on the personal appeal of the writer. To convince, a writer must earn the reader's respect and trust; to persuade, a writer must get the reader to identify his or her own interests with those of the writer. A writer's personal charm may help, but such identification requires much more than the reader liking the writer. Any good feeling must be joined to something "higher" or "larger" than the writer, to something that the writer represents and that the reader would like to be associated with. A majority of Americans identified with Ronald Reagan, for example; his appeal combined personal likeableness with a larger antigovernment sentiment, deeply rooted in American history. Similarly, Lee Iacocca managed for a time to get many Americans to identify with him as standing for the revival of American industry. Of course, few of us have the persuasive advantage of being a public figure. Nevertheless, we can ally ourselves with causes and values that our readers find sympathetic. Chapter 7 investigates the resources of identification in more detail.

Finally, in addition to relying on emotional and personal appeals, persuasion exploits the resources of language more fully than convincing does. To convince, our language must be clear and cogent so that readers can follow our case; to persuade, we need language that readers will remember and that will appeal by its sound and by the images it creates. In Chapter 7 we will also explore the persuasive resources of language, traditionally called *style*.

Arguing to Negotiate

By the time we find ourselves in a situation where our aim is to negotiate, we will have already attempted to convince an opponent of our case and to persuade that opponent to settle a conflict or dispute to our satisfaction. Our opponent will no doubt also have used convincing and persuading in an attempt to move us similarly. Yet neither side will have been able to secure the assent of the other, and "agreeing to disagree" is not a practical solution because the participants must come to some mutual agreement in order to pursue a necessary course of action.

In most instances of negotiation, the parties involved try to work out the conflict themselves because they have some relationship they wish to preserve— as employer and employee, business partners, family members, neighbors, even coauthors of an argument textbook. Common differences requiring negotiation include the amount of a raise or the terms of a contract, the wording of a bill in a congressional committee, and trade agreements among nations. In private life, negotiation helps roommates live together and families decide on everything from budgets to vacation destinations.

Just like other aims of argument, arguing to negotiate requires sound logic and the clear presentation of positions and reasons. However, negotiation challenges our interpersonal skills more than do the other aims. Each side must listen closely to understand not just the other side's case but also the other side's emotional commitments and underlying values. Initiating such a conversation and keeping it going can sometimes be so difficult that an outside party, a mediator, must assist in the process. With or without a mediator, when negotiation works, the opposing sides begin to converge. Exchanging viewpoints and information and building empathy enable all parties to make concessions,

THE AIMS OF ARGUMENT: A SUMMARY

Argument (the assertion of an opinion, supported by a reason or reasons) is not an end in itself; rather, we construct arguments to achieve something else. The major ends or aims of argument are:

Inquiry: *forming our opinions or questioning those we already have.* The purpose of inquiry is to find and articulate what is true for us. Genuine classroom discussions are good examples of argument as inquiry.

Convincing: *gaining assent from others through case-making.* In inquiry we look for reasons that convince us; in convincing we look for reasons that will gain the assent of our audience or readership. Good examples of convincing are a lawyer's brief or the justification a newspaper offers for supporting a political candidate.

Persuasion: *moving others to action through rational, emotional, personal, and stylistic appeals.* Persuasion is convincing *plus;* that is, it uses reasons integrated with the other forms of appeal. Political speeches, sermons, and advertising are instances of arguing to persuade.

Negotiation: *exploring differences of opinion in the hope of reaching agreement and/or cooperation.* The aim of negotiation is to build consensus, usually by making and asking for concessions. Argument as negotiation is typical of diplomacy, labor relations, and organizational decision-making. It is also common in private life to reduce or eliminate conflict between friends and family members.

to loosen their hold on their original positions, and finally to reach consensus—or at least a resolution that all participants find satisfactory.

As Chapter 8 makes clear, this final aim of argument brings us full circle, back to *dialogue,* to the processes involved in arguing to inquire. The major difference is that in negotiation we are less concerned with our own claims to truth than we are with overcoming conflict, with finding some common ground that will allow us to live and work together.

WHAT IS RHETORIC?

In this book we will be looking at argument as a rhetorical art. *Rhetoric* originally meant "the art of persuasive *speaking,*" but the term has come to include written discourse as well. Whether oral or written, rhetoric always aims to influence an audience. By *art* we mean not "fine art" (painting, sculpture, music, and so on) but the principles underlying some activity that require education, experience, and judgment—the art of medicine, for example. Like medicine, rhetoric is a practical art: the art of speaking or writing well.

Studying rhetoric involves learning and applying a body of knowledge that originated in ancient Greece and has existed for about 2,400 years. Like all academic and professional fields, this body of knowledge has changed over time as our understanding of language and human nature has evolved. However, in his early analysis of persuasion, the Greek philosopher Aristotle identified three basic types of appeals that have remained useful to the study of rhetoric through the centuries: _logos,_ the use of logic, which appeals to the audience's reason and intellect; _ethos,_ the speaker's attempts to project his or her own character as wise, ethical, and practical; and _pathos,_ the appeal to the emotions or sympathies of the audience.

In addition to these basic concepts, more specific sets of principles have appeared as rhetoric responded to developments in psychology, literature, and philosophy: principles for inventing and organizing arguments, for anticipating the needs of audiences, for building logical cases, and for polishing style and language. Rhetoric has also been influenced by historical developments, such as the spread of democracy and the rise of electronic media. This book combines current principles with classical tradition to present a contemporary rhetoric for argument.

To a degree, you have been practicing the art of rhetoric all your life. For example, even as a small child you figured out how to convince your parents that you should be able to stay up an hour later or that you "deserved" a certain new toy. Formal rhetoric builds on your aptitudes and experiences, allowing you to develop a more conscious and therefore more discriminating awareness of what you can achieve with argument.

Some people who speak or write well claim to have taught themselves. But most of us need more than our natural ability and experience, and even the talented few can improve by joining natural talents with conscious knowledge and informed, helpful feedback from others. For the purposes of this book, learning rhetoric means consciously applying formal knowledge about arguments and the aims of argument to what you already understand based on your experiences arguing informally. You will become more critical of what you do when you argue. You will also become a more critical listener to and reader of the arguments of others.

We want to stress that arguing well is an ethical act, for the authentic art of rhetoric is, in fact, ethical. The principles of rhetoric oblige a speaker or writer to make the best possible case and to respect the audience, rather than pander to or manipulate it. Too many public speakers and writers today practice an insincere rhetoric that has given the term negative connotations. As we will show, all of the aims of argument require sensitivity to questions of right and wrong.

Each of the major aims of argument has its own rhetoric—its own focus, principles, and methods—and in Chapters 5 through 8 we will take them up one by one, as though they were separate from one another. But we will also explore how they connect with each other and how they often work together in practice. Moreover, we will see how convincing builds on inquiry, how persuasion builds on convincing, and how negotiation integrates inquiry, convincing, and persuading.

Following Through

Recall a recent argument you made, either spoken or written. What was your point? Who was your audience? What was your main aim in arguing? Merely to express your opinion? to convince your audience to assent to your view on the issue? to get your audience to take some action? to negotiate a compromise? Can you think of another recent argument in which your aim was different?

CHAPTER TWO

Keeping a Writer's Notebook

In the past you may have kept a journal, a diary, a lab notebook, or some other written record with daily or weekly entries. A writer's notebook is like these in that it records experiences and activities; it differs from them, however, in that it primarily records preparations for writing something else, such as a major essay or a term paper for one of your courses. You may have turned in a lab notebook for a grade, for example, but a writer's notebook has no other function than to help you sort out what you learn, accomplish, and think as you go through the stages of creating a finished piece of writing. A writer's notebook contains the writing you do before you write; it is a place to sketch out ideas, assess research, order what you have to say, and determine strategies and goals for writing.

WHY KEEP A NOTEBOOK?

Short, simple, and routine kinds of writing—personal letters, notes to friends, memos, and the like—require little preparation. We just sit down and write them. But much writing in college and professionally demands weeks, months, or—in the case of a book—even years of work. Some projects require extensive research and consultation, which involve compiling and assessing large amounts of data and working one's way through complex chains of reasoning. Under such conditions even the best memory must fail without the aid of a notebook. Given life's distractions we often forget too much and recall imprecisely what we do manage to remember. With a writer's notebook we can preserve the idea that came to us as we were walking across campus or staring into space over our morning coffee. Throughout this book we will encourage you to use a writer's notebook extensively as you criticize and create arguments.

WAYS OF USING A NOTEBOOK

What sort of notebook entries might be appropriate? The simple answer is anything that helps, whatever you want to write down for future reference. Following are some more specific possibilities for using a writer's notebook.

To Explore Issues You Encounter in and out of Class

Your notebook is a place for freewriting—that is, private exploration for your eyes only. Such writing should not be judged as good or bad. Don't worry about organization, spelling, grammar, or any of the things that might concern you if someone else were to read your entries.

If you have been assigned a topic, write down your first impressions and opinions about it. If you will be choosing some of your own topics in a course, use the notebook to respond to controversial issues in the news or on campus. Your notebook can then become a source of ideas for your essays. Bring it with you to each class session so you can record ideas that come up during class discussions. In fact, a notebook can make you a better contributor to class discussion because it's easier to share your ideas publicly if you have roughed them out in writing first; use your notebook to respond to ideas presented in class and in every reading assignment.

To Copy down and Analyze Assignments

If your instructor gives you a handout explaining an assignment, staple it to a page in the notebook. If not, write down the assignment word for word from the board or as it is dictated to you. In addition, take notes as your instructor explains the assignment. After class, take time to look over the assignment more carefully. What are the key words? Circle them and make sure you know exactly what they mean. Underline due dates and such information as paper length and format. Record any questions you have about the assignment, and ask your instructor for clarification at the first appropriate opportunity; you may also want to note down your instructor's answers.

To Work out a Timetable for Completing an Assignment

One way to avoid procrastination is to divide the time you have for completing an assignment into blocks: preparation, writing and rewriting, editing, making a final copy, and proofreading. Work out in your notebook how many days you can devote to preparation and research, how many to writing a first draft, how many to revising, how many to editing, and how many to the final typing and proofreading. Draft a tentative schedule for yourself. Your schedule will probably change as you complete the assignment, but mapping one out and attempting to stick to it should help you make steady progress and avoid scrambling at the last moment to get your paper in on time.

To Make Notes as You Research

No matter the type of research, you should have a place to record ideas, questions, and preliminary conclusions that occur to you as you read, discuss your ideas with others, conduct experiments, compile surveys and question-naires, consult with experts, and pursue other types of information about your topic. Keep your notebook handy at all times, and write down as soon as possible whatever comes to mind, no matter how promising or unpromising it may initially seem. You can assess the value of your notes later when you have completed your research, but there will be nothing to assess if you do not keep a written record of your thoughts during the process.

To Respond to Arguments You Hear or Read

Your most immediate written responses to what you read are likely to be brief comments in a book's margins. Marginal annotation is a good habit to develop, but an equally good habit is to follow up your reading by jotting down more extended responses in your notebook. You might evaluate a text's strengths and weaknesses, compare the argument with other arguments you have read on the same topic, and make notes about how you might use material in the text to build your own argument (noting down page numbers at this point will make it easier to use such information in your paper later). We'll make more specific suggestions in Chapter 3 about how to read arguments.

To Write a Rhetorical Prospectus

A prospectus details a plan for a proposed work. A rhetorical prospectus gets you thinking not just about *what* you want to say but about the rhetorical context in which you will say it: *to whom, how,* and—most importantly—*why* you are writing. In real-life arguments these elements are simply a given, but to write a successful argument for a class assignment, you usually have to create a rhetorical situation for yourself. In your notebook, explore

> Your *thesis:* What are you claiming?
> Your *aim:* What do you want to accomplish?
> Your *audience:* Who should read this? Why? What are these people like?
> Your *persona:* What is your relationship to the audience? How do you want them to perceive you?
> Your *subject matter:* What does your thesis obligate you to discuss? What do you need to learn more about? How do you plan to get the information?
> Your *organizational plan:* What should you talk about first? Where might that lead? What might you end with? (This need not be a complete outline; an overview will suffice.)

If you have trouble with the prospectus, discuss it with your instructor at a conference or with a tutor at the writing center, if your school has one.

To Record Useful Feedback

A student writer has at least two sources of feedback on ideas and drafts—other students and the instructor. Many writing classes are now designed to encourage such interaction. Throughout this book we will suggest points in the writing process when seeking feedback may be a good idea. Examples of such times are:

> When your *initial ideas* have taken shape. Seeking feedback now helps you discover how well you can explain your ideas to others and how they respond.
>
> After you and other students have *completed research* on common or similar topics. Feedback at this point allows you to share information and to compare evaluations of the sources.
>
> At the completion of a *first draft.* At this point feedback uncovers what you need to do in a second draft in order to accommodate readers' needs, objections, and questions.
>
> At the end of the *revising process.* This sort of feedback helps eliminate surface problems, such as awkward sentences, usage errors, misspellings, and typos.

You will benefit most from feedback opportunities if you prepare yourself with specific questions to ask your instructor or classmates. What concerns *you* about how the project is going? Use your notebook to jot down such questions, and leave room to sum up the comments you receive. The suggestion that seems too good to forget during a conference may elude your recall a day or two later at your word processor.

To Assess a Graded Paper

We seldom learn all we can from the comments of instructors. If the comments are positive, we tend to bask in the warmth of praise; if not, we tend to be embarrassed, frustrated, even angry. Neither response is likely to make us better writers.

The best approach is to let the feelings play themselves out: bask when you can, and feel discouraged when you have to. Then resolve to sit down and look over the comments carefully, writing down in your notebook what you find useful for future reference. On the positive side, what did you do well? What did you learn that might carry over to the next assignment? On the not-so-positive side, can you detect any pattern in the shortcomings and errors your instructor has pointed out? If so, list the types of problems you discover, and refer to them at an appropriate time when revising or editing or when composing your next essay. If, for example, you did not develop and support your points well, revise with this in mind or devote special attention to this issue as you plan and draft in the future. If you have a tendency to misplace the apostrophe in plural possessives, check all plural possessive apostrophes in subsequent final drafts.

It is natural to want to be done with a paper once you have turned it in, to get a grade and forget about it. Resist this desire long enough to record anything you can learn from your instructor's comments. The self-assessment preserved in your notebook will help you apply what you have learned to future assignments in future semesters.

Following Through

What issues do you currently have strong opinions about? Although you can look to today's newspaper or the evening news for inspiration, think as well about events you've noticed on campus, at your job, or around your town—a change in course requirements for your planned major, a conflict over some aspect of your work environment, or a proposed land development near your house. Write a notebook entry in which you list several possible topics for written arguments. Then pick one or two, and create the briefest of arguments—a statement of your position followed by a statement of your best reason for holding that position. Think about who the audience for such an argument could be. Think also about your aim: Would you be arguing to inquire, convince, persuade, or negotiate?

CHAPTER THREE

Reading an Argument

Throughout this book you will be reading both professional and student-written arguments that exemplify ways to argue. Many also offer multiple viewpoints on contemporary issues—conversations you will join when you write arguments of your own. You should read these arguments *critically*, taking on the role of a critic by *analyzing* (to see how the argument is put together) and by *evaluating* (to decide how well the argument achieves its aim and whether it advances a position that merits respect). Critical reading is not casual and should not be undertaken by a tired or distracted mind. Critical reading skills are essential to understanding the aims and methods of argument; we focus now on some specific methods for you to practice.

BEFORE YOU READ

Experts have found that readers who have the greatest success comprehending the ideas in any text meet two criteria: (1) they have some *prior knowledge* of the subject matter, and (2) they are able to see a piece of writing in its *rhetorical context*. Such readers can use context to determine the meaning of unfamiliar words, and they are often able to read between the lines, recognizing ideas and assumptions that are only implied. Let's look at these two factors with an eye toward argument.

Recalling Prior Knowledge

Virtually every piece of writing about an issue is part of an ongoing conversation, involving a number of participants who represent a range of opinions and who have each contributed a variety of ideas, facts, and authoritative citations to the debate. The greater a reader's familiarity with this background, the easier it is for him or her to approach a new argument from a critical perspective, filling in any gaps of information and recognizing a writer's assumptions and biases.

Therefore, it makes sense to take some time before you start reading to recall what you already know about the topic: the basic issues involved and the perspectives you have read or heard expressed. Use your writer's notebook to record what you remember. And don't neglect to consider your own opinions about the issue. If you are conscious of the attitudes and ideas you bring to your reading, you can better see an argument in its own light and not so much colored by your own biases.

Following Through

You are about to read an argument entitled "Making the Mosaic." What does the title tell you? A mosaic, a design composed of many small pieces of stone or tile, is often used as a metaphor for American society, emphasizing that we are a people with distinct ethnic backgrounds. Many people debate whether the mosaic metaphor is appropriate, since an earlier metaphor, comparing America to a melting pot, suggests a different picture, a society in which ethnic differences melt down and immigrants assimilate to the single identity of "American." There is also debate about whether a common identity is possible or desirable since today's immigrants come from such distant and varied parts of the world.

In your writer's notebook, jot down some arguments you have heard about issues relating to legal immigration. Have you heard arguments for or against putting greater limits on legal immigration? What sort of limits do some people argue for? What reasons are offered? If you have heard arguments for immigrants' either maintaining or losing their ethnic identity, can you recall some of the reasons on either side? How might one's background or personal experience affect one's perspective on these questions? Which metaphor— melting pot or mosaic—fits your own view of America? How might your background affect your view?

Considering the Rhetorical Context

Critical readers breathe life into a written argument by seeing it as part of a dynamic activity. They think of the author as a human being with hopes, fears, biases, ambitions, and—most importantly—a purpose that his or her words on the page are intended to accomplish. The argument becomes an action, aimed at affecting a particular audience in a particular place and time.

Publishers' notes and editorial headnotes often include information and clues that can help you answer the following questions about rhetorical context:

When was this argument written? (If not recently, how might it be helpful to know something about the time it first appeared?)

Why was it written? What prompted its creation?

Who is the author, and what are his or her occupation, personal background, political leanings?

Where does the article appear? If it is reprinted, where did it appear originally?

For whom do you think the author is writing?

What purpose does the author have in writing? What does he or she hope to accomplish through the act of making this argument?

Following Through

Read the following editorial headnote for the argument "Making the Mosaic":

> Anna Quindlen, a novelist and syndicated columnist who won a Pulitzer Prize in 1992, comments on contemporary issues from the perspective of a liberal, a feminist, and a mother. The following column appeared in the *New York Times* in November 1991.

In your writer's notebook, make some notes about what this headnote tells you about the argument's rhetorical context. Do you think that immigration issues were much the same in 1991 as they are today? What do you know about the *New York Times* and its readership? What does it mean to have a liberal perspective in general? What viewpoints would you anticipate finding in the writing of someone with a liberal perspective on immigration?

As you read the essay, you will fill in your understanding of its rhetorical context, and you may revise or correct some of the expectations you had about it based on your prior knowledge and the headnote. All reading involves the revision of preconceptions, but it is better to define some initially rather than to begin with none or only vague ones.

AS YOU READ

Critical reading never involves reading a text only once. In fact, critical reading should take you through a text at least three times. Here we will suggest some goals for each of these three readings, but you are likely to have your own way of noting ideas and making connections. Be ready to record whatever thoughts come to mind.

The First Reading

Your first reading of any text is an exploration of new territory. You might prefer to start at the beginning and simply read the selection straight through. But it's a good idea to look first at the opening and closing paragraphs, where you will often find explicit statements of the author's thesis and additional clues to help you construct the rhetorical context. You might also scan the text, looking at major headings (if any) and the first sentences of paragraphs. Then read through the essay at a moderate pace.

During this first reading, don't feel compelled to make marks in the text, beyond circling words to look up; but don't hesitate to make marginal notes if thoughts or questions occur to you.

Following Through

Before you read "Making the Mosaic," look at the first and last paragraphs and at the first sentence of each body paragraph. Try to determine Quindlen's main point and purpose, as well as her intended audience—those whom she is trying to persuade. Then, after you have read through the essay once, use your writer's notebook to record your responses to the six questions on rhetorical context listed on pages 17–18.

ANNA QUINDLEN

Making the Mosaic

THERE IS some disagreement over which wordsmith first substituted "mosaic" for "melting pot" as a way of describing America, but it is undoubtedly a more apt description. And it undoubtedly applies in Ms. Miller's third-grade class and elsewhere in the Lower East Side's Public School 20.

The neighborhood where the school is located is to the immigrant experience what Broadway is to actors. Past Blevitzky Bros. Monuments ("at this place since 1914"), past Katz's Delicatessen with its fan mail hung in the window, past the tenement buildings where fire escapes climb graceful as cat burglars, P.S. 20 holds the corner of Essex and Houston.

Its current student body comes from the Dominican Republic, Cambodia, Bangladesh, Puerto Rico, Colombia, mainland China, Vietnam and El Salvador. In Ms. Miller's third-grade class these various faces somehow look the same, upturned and open, as though they were cups waiting for the water to be poured.

There's a spirit in the nation now that's in opposition to these children. It is not interested in your tired, your poor, your huddled masses. In recent days it has been best personified by a candidate for governor and the suggestion in his campaign that there is a kind of authentic American. That authentic American is white and Christian (but not Catholic), ethnic origins lost in the mists of an amorphous past, not visible in accent, appearance or allegiance.

This is not a new idea, this resilient form of xenophobia. "It is but too common a remark of late, that the American character has within a short time been sadly degraded by numerous instances of riot and lawless violence," Samuel F. B. Morse wrote in an 1835 treatise called "Imminent Dangers to the Free Institutions of the United States through Foreign Immigration," decrying such riffraff as Jesuits.

Times are bad, and we blame the newcomers, whether it's 1835 or 1991. Had Morse had his way, half of me would still be in Italy; if some conservatives had their way today, most of the children at P.S. 20 would be, in that ugly phrase, back where they came from. So much for lifting a lamp beside the golden door.

They don't want to learn the language, we complain, as though the old neighborhoods were not full of Poles and Italians who kept to their mother tongue. They don't want to become American, we say, as though there are not plenty of us who believe we lost something when we renounced ethnicity. "Dagos," my mother said the American kids called them, American being those not Italian. "Wops." How quickly we forget as we use pejoratives for the newest newcomers.

Our greatest monument to immigration, the restored Ellis Island, seems to suggest by its display cases that coming to America is a thing nostalgic, something grandparents did. On the Lower East Side it has never been past tense, struggling with English and poverty, sharing apartments with the bathroom in the hall and the bathtub in the kitchen.

They send their children to school with hopes for a miracle, or a job, which is almost the same thing. This past week the School Volunteer Program, which fields almost 6,000 volunteer tutors, sponsored the first citywide Read Aloud: 400 grown-ups reading to thousands of kids in 90 schools. In P.S. 20, as so many have done before, the kids clutched their books like visas.

It is foolish to forget where you come from, which, in the case of the United States, is almost always somewhere else. The true authentic American is a pilgrim with a small "p," armed with little more than the phrase "I wish. . . ." New ones are being minted in Ms. Miller's class, bits of a mosaic far from complete.

10

The Second Reading

The goals for your second reading are to recognize the structure of the argument and to wrestle with any difficult passages.

Analyzing Structure

By structure we mean the writer's plan or arrangement. Arguments seldom divide into anything like the formulaic "five-paragraph essay" with thesis and reasons in predetermined places. Arrangements for arguments are practically infinite, and good writers make their own decisions about what should go where in any given situation. But in a well-written argument, it should be clear that different parts have different jobs to do. These may include:

Providing background
Offering and developing a reason
Giving an opposing view
Rebutting an opposing view

If the writer's case has been tightly crafted, breaking the essay into its parts can be like breaking a Hershey's bar into its already well-defined segments. Other arguments are more loosely structured, however, and their divisions less readily discernible; even with these, though, close analysis will generally reveal some fault lines that indicate specific divisions, and it will be possible to see the roles played by the various chunks. As you read a second time, draw lines between the paragraphs where you detect dividing points. (Some chunks may be single paragraphs, and others may be groups of as many as five or more paragraphs.) Then, drawing on your understanding of the author's purpose and audience, try to describe the function of each part.

This brief essay by Quindlen seems informal and loosely structured, but a careful look reveals that it is a well-crafted argument with a structure of four main parts, each with its own role to play. Paragraphs 1, 2, and 3 form the introduction. They work together to open with a positive and sympathetic look at an ethnically diverse immigrant community, but notice that they do not present Quindlen's main point. Paragraph 4 introduces an opposing view that current trends in immigration may bring too much poverty and too much ethnic diversity. Paragraphs 5, 6, 7, 8, and 9 offer reasons and evidence for rejecting this opposing view, and paragraph 10 concludes with Quindlen's main point, that America ought to be a country where people with nothing can have an opportunity to fulfill their dreams.

Quindlen's audience most likely consists of educated professionals who read the *New York Times* over their morning coffee. They would probably be aware that there is some debate about how an influx of poor and ethnically diverse immigrants will affect American society. She knows her readers don't want to be lectured to, so she makes her case in an indirect and even entertaining way. Looking in more detail at the four subdivisions of her essay, we can appreciate her strategy in appealing to this audience.

1. Paragraphs 1, 2, and 3 serve to introduce the argument by giving a lively and colorful description of an immigrant neighborhood. Quindlen wants to emphasize the continuity of the immigrant experience, so she reminds the reader that the Lower East Side of New York has historically been the home of poor immigrants (nothing new or threatening here). And the immigrants she puts in her picture are a class of hopeful third-graders.
2. Paragraph 4 introduces an opposing view, that the U.S. should not continue to admit large numbers of poor and ethnically diverse people. Quindlen's presentation of this view shows that she wants to discredit it. To emphasize how unfair it is, she has placed it in sharp juxtaposition to her description of the children's "upturned and open" faces. Notably, she doesn't name the politician who personifies this viewpoint because that would aim the argument too directly at a single individual.
3. Paragraphs 5, 6, 7, 8, and 9 really are the heart of the argument, as they offer reasons and evidence for rejecting what she calls the "conservative" opposing view. You may notice that Quindlen presents the reasons indirectly. She does not say "This fear of difference is unfair and irrational

because first, second, and third." Instead of spelling them out, she presents the reasons *through* the details. A careful reader extracts the reasons—a skill known commonly as reading between the lines. We have paraphrased the reasons in italics below. You can decide what the essay would have gained—or lost—if Quindlen had been more explicit about spelling them out.

> In paragraphs 5 and 6 she offers one reason: *Similar arguments against ethnic groups in the past now appear as examples of obvious bigotry and paranoia.* As evidence, she offers Samuel Morse's quotation from 1835, and she cites examples of the Jesuits and her own Italian grandparents.
>
> A second reason comes in paragraph 7: *The belief that there is only one true kind of American makes immigrants give up their cultural heritage.* This idea makes three appearances in the essay, here and in paragraphs 5 and 10, but largely it goes without concrete support. Perhaps she believes that her readers, if they are Americans with an "amorphous past," will regret that they have lost touch with some part of their heritage too.
>
> Finally, in paragraphs 8 and 9, Quindlen offers a final reason: *Today's immigrants have the same determination to achieve the American dream that all earlier waves of immigrants had.* As evidence, she cites some of the hardships of daily life for poor immigrant families and shows their children's eagerness to learn how to read.

4. Paragraph 10 sums up what she is really arguing for: It shouldn't matter where immigrants come from; wanting to make something of yourself through hard work is the only requirement for being a true American.

Working through Difficult Passages

In every text or piece of writing, a reader will find some passages that are less accessible than others. As you read another person's writing, you may feel a little shaky about what the author means. You may encounter words new to your vocabulary, which you simply have to look up, yet there are several other factors outlined in the following sections that contribute to comprehension difficulty. In many cases, paraphrasing—putting the passage into your own words—can increase your reading comprehension and your confidence about understanding something new. Paraphrasing is a useful skill for any writer working with other written texts; therefore, in Appendix A, "Researching Arguments," we offer more detailed advice on how to paraphrase.

Metaphors   One obstacle to reading comprehension may result from a writer's use of metaphors. A metaphor is a way of seeing one thing in terms of something else. For example, we commonly describe the act of beginning to love someone in terms of "falling in love." The meanings we associate with literal falling—loss of control, being a victim of circumstance—are carried over into the new context of describing an emotional state. We tend not to notice such common metaphors (and similes, which employ the words *like* or *as* to make the comparison more plainly), but a new metaphor in an unfamiliar context will make a reader stop and think.

We have already pointed out that Quindlen uses the metaphors "melting pot" and "mosaic," which are common enough in our culture to pose no barrier to most readers' understanding. The term "dead metaphor" is sometimes used to describe metaphorical expressions that are so common we do not even think of them as metaphors. But we *should* think about them because, in a very concise but powerful way, all metaphors are arguments. That is, they argue for a particular perspective on something, just as the "falling" metaphor argues that we should view love as a condition beyond our control. Dead metaphors are particularly dangerous because we do not even think about how they shape our attitudes.

Consider how the common metaphors "America is a melting pot" and "America is a mosaic" make different arguments about how immigrants should act and how they should be treated. Appreciating the full impact of these metaphors will help your critical reading of Quindlen's essay.

In the last sentence of paragraph 4, Quindlen uses metaphors that are fresh and unusual: Some Americans' ethnic origins, she says, are "lost in the mists of an amorphous past." "Mists" is a metaphor for the vague sense some people have of their ancestors; they cannot see their pasts clearly. To speak of the past as amorphous, or shapeless, is also metaphorical: Can the past, an abstract concept, ever have a shape? She is saying that a shapeless past has nothing distinctive, nothing to mark it from everyone else's. In both metaphors, Quindlen uses concrete terms as a way of seeing something abstract. Something is lost by putting the idea into nonmetaphorical words of our own, but it helps us appreciate the persuasive effects of Quindlen's phrasing.

Remember that metaphors are everywhere, not just in poetry and fiction. You may find a passage of argumentative writing difficult if you try to read a literal meaning into a metaphorical passage.

Unusual Syntax   *Syntax* simply means the order of words in a sentence. In English, readers expect something close to a subject-verb-object sequence, with some modifiers here or there. But as you know, writers vary syntax to avoid monotony or to get a certain effect. They use fragments. They create long, long sentences with many modifiers. They invert the expected order. And they leave out words they think the reader can fill in: To err is human, to forgive divine. Sometimes a sentence is long and complicated because the idea it expresses is long and complicated. In all these cases, paraphrasing can help. Casting an idea into plainer syntax will make it clearer to you; in particular, it is a good idea to break a long sentence into several shorter ones of your own. Let's look again at the last sentence of Quindlen's fourth paragraph:

> That authentic American is white and Christian (but not Catholic), ethnic origins lost in the mists of an amorphous past, not visible in accent, appearance or allegiance.

This sentence starts out simply enough, but after the comma, Quindlen makes an unusual grammatical choice—an absolute phrase. That's a phrase containing a noun and modifiers, but the phrase does not modify anything itself. Here is a clearer but also less dramatic way of saying this same idea:

> Authentic Americans are white Protestants whose looks and speech show no trace of their ethnic origins and who have no feelings of loyalty toward any ethnic group.

Multiple Voices   Most texts include quotations, either direct or indirect, from other speakers or written texts. With direct quotations, if the speaker is clearly named, readers will not be confused; however, indirect quotations can be tricky. For example, in paragraph 5, Quindlen quotes Samuel Morse both directly and indirectly. When she describes the Jesuits as "riffraff," this is clearly not her own opinion but Morse's that she is presenting. On your second reading of any argument, you might notice passages where you are uncertain whose point of view is being represented. These problems clear up on repeated readings and through discussions with other readers.

Allusions   Many arguments contain brief references to people, events, songs, art, anything in the culture that the author assumes he or she shares with the readers. Such allusions are one way for the author to form a bond with the readers—that is, provided the readers' and the author's opinions are the same about what is being alluded to. For example, most Americans are proud of the Statue of Liberty and familiar with the words that appear on its base, the closing lines of Emma Lazarus's 1883 poem "The New Colossus":

> Give me your tired, your poor,
> Your huddled masses yearning to breathe free.
> The wretched refuse of your teeming shore.
> Send these, the homeless, tempest-tost to me,
> I lift my lamp beside the golden door.

Notice how Quindlen borrows freely from this poem in paragraphs 4 and 6, clearly assuming her readers' familiarity with it. You might consider how directly mentioning Lazarus or the Statue of Liberty would have changed the effect.

Following Through

Paragraph 5 is a difficult passage, partly because of vocabulary but also because of the nineteenth-century wording in the quotation from Morse. Paraphrase this entire paragraph, quoting Morse indirectly and using your own diction and syntax as much as possible. Make it clear that Morse is connecting lawlessness with immigration.

READING ARGUMENTS CRITICALLY

Note the *main claim,* or *thesis,* of the argument, if it appears explicitly. If it does not, paraphrase it in the margin.

Pick out and mark the *main reasons* in support of the thesis. (Don't expect to find many major reasons; in a good argument, much space and effort may go toward developing and supporting even one reason.)

Consider the *evidence* offered, and write marginal comments about the reasons themselves and how well they are supported. Question evidence in terms of both quantity and quality.

Note *key terms* and how the writer defines (or fails to define) them. Would most readers agree with the definitions? How would you define or illustrate key terms that need clarification?

If the writer presents any *analogies,* are the things being compared truly similar? Note any problems.

Are there any *contradictions?* Does any evidence cited in the text contradict other evidence in the text or other evidence you know about that is not cited?

Upon what *assumptions* are the thesis and reasons based? Does the argument, or any of its reasons, rest upon an assumption that all readers may not share?

Where, if at all, are *opposing views* represented? Do you think they are depicted fairly?

What is your *personal response?* What do you agree with? What seems true to you? What do you disagree with? Why?

The Third Reading

Chapter 5 of this book explores and explains in depth how a reader can enter into a dialogue with the writer of an argument—by posing questions to the writer and using the text itself as a basis for imagining the writer's responses. Such an extended dialogue is the best inquiry into a written argument, but a faster alternative is to raise questions and note the anticipated objections of those with opposing views directly in the margins of the printed text. In your third reading you should raise such questions even if you agree with the writer's argument. It may be easier (and more fun) to challenge arguments you disagree with, but if you are studying arguments as claims to truth, it is even more important to challenge the views you find most sympathetic.

Even if you oppose a writer's position, be open in your third reading to recognizing valid points and good reasoning. This kind of critical reading will enlarge your understanding of an issue and open your mind to new perspectives. In fact, it may cause you to change your mind. The box "Reading Arguments Critically" lists some things to look for when annotating an argument.

We have annotated the first four paragraphs as an example.

ANNA QUINDLEN

Making the Mosaic

THERE IS some disagreement over which wordsmith first substituted "mosaic" for "melting pot" as a way of describing America, but it is undoubtedly a more apt description. And it undoubtedly applies in Ms. Miller's third-grade class and elsewhere in the Lower East Side's Public School 20.

So she favors preserving differen—

The neighborhood where the school is located is to the immigrant experience what Broadway is to actors. Past Blevitzky Bros. Monuments ("at this place since 1914"), past Katz's Delicatessen with its fan mail hung in the window, past the tenement buildings where fire escapes climb graceful as cat burglars, P.S. 20 holds the corner of Essex and Houston.

Analogy suggests all pass through their wa— to succe—

I think this would pose a language problem.

Its current student body comes from the Dominican Republic, Cambodia, Bangladesh, Puerto Rico, Colombia, mainland China, Vietnam and El Salvador. In Ms. Miller's third-grade class these various faces somehow look the same, upturned and open, as though they were cups waiting for the water to be poured. *Metaphor suggests optimism.*

Like my own.

There's a spirit in the nation now that's in opposition to these children. It is not interested in your tired, your poor, your huddled masses. In recent days it has been best personified by a candidate for governor and the suggestion in his campaign that there is a kind of authentic American. That authentic American is white and Christian (but not Catholic), ethnic origins lost in the mists of an amorphous past, not visible in accent, appearance or allegiance.

But is fair to that her opponent are agai— the child

shapeless

Following Through

Read "Making the Mosaic" a third time, writing marginal annotations as you go (refer to the illustration of marginal annotations above). Use the suggestions listed in the box "Reading Arguments Critically." In addition, make a special effort to consider the following: We have offered paraphrases of the main point and the reasons. How would you put them into your own words? Would you add anything to Quindlen's definition of "authentic American"? How thoroughly and fairly has she presented the opposing view? What is Quindlen assuming about the chances for success for this new wave of immigrants? Has she given enough evidence to suggest that the public schools can handle the variety of ethnic groups she describes? Does Quindlen need more evidence to show that earlier waves of immigrants also learned English only reluctantly?

AFTER YOU READ

A person who invests time and effort in critical reading usually becomes engaged enough in the text and the issue it deals with to be curious about others' reactions to the same argument. As a student in a college course, you will be able to compare your responses to arguments with the responses of other students and your instructor. Thus, critical reading is a way for you to enter the ongoing conversation that serves to create knowledge itself. For professionals in all fields, conversations about one another's arguments go on all the time—orally, in meetings and at conferences, and in writing, through informal critiques as well as articles in popular and professional journals. Ultimately, such conversations establish and refine the bodies of knowledge that constitute the various disciplines and professions.

Finally, any reading should point you in the direction of further reading. For example, you might find references to other books or articles on the topic; many scholarly arguments conclude with a bibliography showing works the author consulted. Or you can use the research methods described in Appendix A to find other articles and arguments.

Following Through

In your writer's notebook, respond to Quindlen's argument. Do you accept her position? Do you find the argument convincing? If you do, why? If not, why not? Much of the debate today about legal immigration centers on a change in immigration policy that occurred in 1965 and its effects over the last three decades. What more would you need to know before you could arrive at the best position, the position closest to the truth, on U.S. immigration policy?

CHAPTER FOUR

Analyzing an Argument: A Simplified Toulmin Method

In Chapter 3 we discussed the importance of reading arguments critically: breaking them down into their parts to see how they are put together, noting in the margins key terms that are not defined, raising questions about the writer's claims or evidence. Although these general techniques are sufficient for analyzing many arguments, sometimes—especially with intricate arguments and with arguments we sense are faulty but whose weaknesses we are unable to define—we need a more systematic technique.

In this chapter we explain and illustrate such a technique based on the work of Stephen Toulmin, a contemporary philosopher who has contributed a great deal to our understanding of argumentation. This method will allow you to analyze the logic of any argument, whether written or spoken; you will also find it useful in examining the logic of your own arguments as you draft and revise them. Keep in mind, however, that because it is limited to the analysis of logic, the Toulmin method provides an incomplete basis for evaluating an argument. It is also important to question an argument through dialogue (see Chapter 5) and to look at the appeals of character, emotion, and style (see Chapter 6).

A PRELIMINARY CRITICAL READING

Before we consider the Toulmin method, let's first explore the following argument carefully, using the general process for critical reading we described in Chapter 3.

WILLIAM F. MAY

Rising to the Occasion of Our Death

> *William F. May (b. 1927) is a distinguished professor of ethics at Southern Methodist University. The following essay appeared originally in* The Christian Century *(1990).*

FOR MANY parents, a Volkswagen van is associated with putting children to sleep on a camping trip. Jack Kevorkian, a Detroit pathologist, has now linked the van with the veterinarian's meaning of "putting to sleep." Kevorkian conducted a dinner interview with Janet Elaine Adkins, a 54-year-old Alzheimer's patient, and her husband and then agreed to help her commit suicide in his VW van. Kevorkian pressed beyond the more generally accepted practice of passive euthanasia (allowing a patient to die by withholding or withdrawing treatment) to active euthanasia (killing for mercy).

Kevorkian, moreover, did not comply with the strict regulations that govern active euthanasia in, for example, the Netherlands. Holland requires that death be imminent (Adkins had beaten her son in tennis just a few days earlier); it demands a more professional review of the medical evidence and the patient's resolution than a dinner interview with a physician (who is a stranger and who does not treat patients) permits; and it calls for the final, endorsing signatures of two doctors.

So Kevorkian-bashing is easy. But the question remains: Should we develop a judicious, regulated social policy permitting voluntary euthanasia for the terminally ill? Some moralists argue that the distinction between allowing to die and killing for mercy is petty quibbling over technique. Since the patient in any event dies—whether by acts of omission or commission—the route to death doesn't really matter. The way modern procedures have made dying at the hands of the experts and their machines such a prolonged and painful business has further fueled the euthanasia movement, which asserts not simply the right to die but the right to be killed.

But other moralists believe that there is an important moral distinction between allowing to die and mercy killing. The euthanasia movement, these critics contend, wants to engineer death rather than face dying. Euthanasia would bypass dying to make one dead as quickly as possible. It aims to relieve suffering by knocking out the interval between life and death. It solves the problem of suffering by eliminating the sufferer.

The impulse behind the euthanasia movement is understandable in an age when dying has become such an inhumanly endless business. But the movement may fail to appreciate our human capacity to rise to the occasion of our death. The best death is not always the sudden death. Those forewarned of death and given time to prepare for it have time to engage in acts of reconciliation. Also, advanced grieving by those about to be bereaved may ease some of their pain. Psychiatrists have observed that those who lose a loved one accidentally have a more difficult time recovering from the loss than those who have suffered through an extended period of illness before the death. Those who have lost a close relative by accident are more likely to experience what Geoffrey Gorer has called limitless grief. The community, moreover, may need its aged and dependent, its sick and its dying, and the virtues which they sometimes evince—the virtues of humility, courage, and patience—just as much as the community needs the virtues of justice and love manifest in the agents of care.

On the whole, our social policy should allow terminal patients to die but it should not regularize killing for mercy. Such a policy would recognize and respect that moment in illness when it no longer makes sense to bend every effort to cure or to prolong life and when one must allow patients to do their own dying. This policy seems most consonant with the obligations of the community to care and of the patient to finish his or her course.

Advocates of active euthanasia appeal to the principle of patient autonomy—as the use of the phrase "voluntary euthanasia" indicates. But emphasis on the patient's right to determine his or her destiny often harbors an extremely naïve view of the uncoerced nature of the decision. Patients who plead to be put to death hardly make unforced decisions if the terms and conditions under which they receive care already nudge them in the direction of the exit. If the elderly have stumbled around in their apartments, alone and frightened for years, or if they have spent years warehoused in geriatrics barracks, then the decision to be killed for mercy hardly reflects an uncoerced decision. The alternative may be so wretched as to push patients toward this escape. It is a huge irony and, in some cases, hypocrisy to talk suddenly about a compassionate killing when the aging and dying may have been starved for compassion for many years. To put it bluntly, a country has not earned the moral right to kill for mercy unless it has already sustained and supported life mercifully. Otherwise we kill for compassion only to reduce the demands on our compassion. This statement does not charge a given doctor or family member with impure motives. I am concerned here not with the individual case but with the cumulative impact of a social policy.

I can, to be sure, imagine rare circumstances in which I hope I would have the courage to kill for mercy—when the patient is utterly beyond human care, terminal, and in excruciating pain. A neurosurgeon once showed a group of physicians and an ethicist the picture of a Vietnam casualty who had lost all four limbs in a landmine explosion. The catastrophe had reduced the soldier to a trunk with his face transfixed in horror. On the battlefield I would hope that I would have the courage to kill the sufferer with mercy.

But hard cases do not always make good laws or wise social policies. Regularized mercy killings would too quickly relieve the community of its obligation to provide good care. Further, we should not always expect the law to provide us with full protection and coverage for what, in rare circumstances, we may morally need to do. Sometimes the moral life calls us out into a no-man's-land where we cannot expect total security and protection under the law. But no one said that the moral life is easy.

A STEP-BY-STEP DEMONSTRATION OF THE TOULMIN METHOD

The Toulmin method requires an analysis of the claim, the reasons offered to support the claim, and the evidence offered to support the reasons, along with an analysis of any refutations offered.

Analyzing the Claim

Logical analysis begins with identifying the *claim,* the thesis or central contention, along with any specific qualifications or exceptions.

Identify the Claim

First ask yourself, *What statement is the author defending?* In "Rising to the Occasion of Our Death," for example, William May spells out his claim in paragraph 6:

> Our social policy should allow terminal patients to die but it should not regularize killing for mercy.

In his claim, May supports passive euthanasia (letting someone die by withholding or discontinuing treatment) but opposes "regularizing" (making legal or customary) active euthanasia (administering, say, an overdose of morphine to cause a patient's death).

Much popular argumentation is sometimes careless about what exactly is being claimed: untrained arguers too often content themselves with just taking sides ("Euthanasia is wrong."). Note that May, a student of ethics trained in philosophical argumentation, makes a claim that is both specific and detailed. Whenever an argument does not include an explicit statement of its claim, you should begin your analysis by stating the writer's claim yourself. Try to state all claims fully and carefully in sentence form, as May's claim is stated.

Look for Qualifiers

Next ask, *How is the claim qualified?* Is it absolute, or does it include words or phrases to indicate that it may not hold true in every situation or set of circumstances?

May qualifies his claim with the phrase "on the whole" (paragraph 6), indicating that he recognizes possible exceptions to the application of his claim. Other possible qualifiers include "typically," "usually," and "most of the time." Careful arguers are generally wary of making absolute claims. While unqualified claims are not necessarily faulty in themselves, they do insist that there be no cases or circumstances in which the claim might legitimately be contradicted. Qualifying words or phrases are often used to restrict a claim and improve its defensibility.

Find the Exceptions

Finally ask, *In what cases or circumstances would the writer not press his or her claim?* Look for any explicit exceptions the writer offers to qualify the claim.

May, for example, is quite clear in paragraph 8 about when he would not press his claim:

> I hope I would have the courage to kill for mercy—when the patient is utterly beyond human care, terminal, and in excruciating pain.

Once he has specified these conditions in abstract terms, he goes further and offers a chilling example of a case when he believes mercy-killing would be appropriate. Nevertheless, he insists that such exceptions are rare and thus do not justify making active euthanasia legal or allowing it to become common social policy.

Critical readers respond to unqualified claims skeptically—by hunting for exceptions. With qualified claims they look to see what specific exceptions the writer will admit and what considerations make restrictions necessary or desirable.

Summarize the Claim

At this point it is a good idea to write out the claim, its qualifiers, and its exceptions in your writer's notebook so that you can see all of them clearly. For May they look like this:

> (qualifier) "On the whole,"
> (claim)   "our social policy should allow terminal patients to die but it should not regularize killing for mercy."
> (exception) "when the patient is utterly beyond human care, terminal, and in excruciating pain."

Record the claim and its qualifiers and exceptions in whatever way helps you see them best, but do not skip this step. Not only will it help you remember the results of your initial claim analysis, you will also be building on this summary as you go on to analyze the argument in more detail.

Analyzing Reasons

Once you have analyzed the claim, you should next identify and evaluate the reasons offered for the claim.

List the Reasons

Begin by asking yourself, *Why is the writer advancing this claim?* Look for any statement or statements that are used to justify the thesis. May groups all of his reasons in paragraph 5:

The dying should have time to prepare for death and to reconcile with relatives and friends.

Those close to the dying should have time to come to terms with the impending loss of a loved one.

The community needs examples of dependent but patient and courageous people who sometimes do die with dignity.

The community needs the virtues ("justice and love") of those who care for the sick and dying.

When you list reasons, you need not preserve the exact words of the arguer; often doing so is impossible, since reasons are not always explicit but may have to be inferred. Be very careful, however, to adhere as closely as possible to the writer's language; otherwise, your analysis can easily go astray, imposing a reason of your own that the writer did not have in mind.

Note that reasons, like claims, can be qualified. May does not say, for instance, that "the aged and dependent" *always* show "the virtues of humility, courage, and patience." He implicitly admits that they can be ornery and cowardly as well. But for May's purposes, it is enough that they sometimes manifest the virtues he admires.

Use your writer's notebook to list the reasons following your summary of the claim, qualifiers, and exceptions. One possibility is to list them beneath the summary of the claim in the form of a tree diagram (see the diagram on page 34).

Examine the Reasons

There are two questions to ask as you examine the reasons you have listed. First, *Are they really good reasons?* A reason is only as good as the values it invokes or implies. A value is something we think is good, worth pursuing for its own sake or because it leads to attaining other goods. For each reason you should specify the values involved and then determine whether you accept those values as generally binding.

Second ask, *Is the reason relevant to the thesis?* In other words, does the relationship between the claim and the reason hold up to examination? For example, the claim "You should buy a new car from Fred Freed" cannot be supported by the reason "Fred is a family man with three cute kids" unless you accept a relationship between an auto dealer's having cute children and his or her reliability in dealing with customers.

Be careful and deliberate as you examine whether reasons are good and whether they are relevant. No other step is as important in assessing the logic of an argument, and no other can be quite as tricky.

To illustrate, consider May's first reason: Those who know they are about to die should have time to prepare for death and to seek reconciliation with people from whom they have become estranged. Is this a good reason? Most of us would probably think so, valuing the chance to prepare for death and to reconcile ourselves with estranged friends or family members. Not to do so would seem immature, irresponsible, unforgiving.

A Toulmin Model for Analyzing Arguments

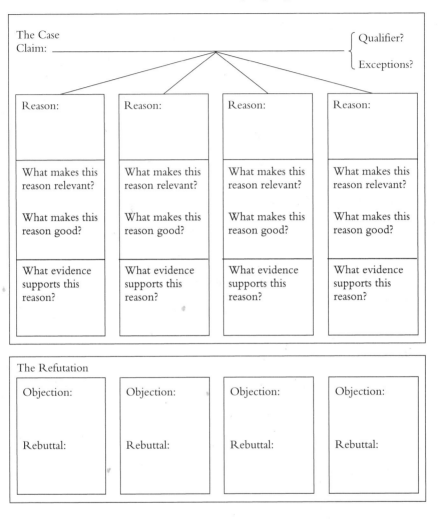

The Case

Claim: _____ Qualifier?

                                                  Exceptions?

Reason:	Reason:	Reason:	Reason:
What makes this reason relevant? What makes this reason good?	What makes this reason relevant? What makes this reason good?	What makes this reason relevant? What makes this reason good?	What makes this reason relevant? What makes this reason good?
What evidence supports this reason?	What evidence supports this reason?	What evidence supports this reason?	What evidence supports this reason?

The Refutation

Objection: Rebuttal:	Objection: Rebuttal:	Objection: Rebuttal:	Objection: Rebuttal:

But is the reason relevant? May seems to rule out the possibility that a dying person seeking active euthanasia would be able to prepare for death and reconcile with others. But this is obviously not the case. Terminally ill people who decide to arrange for their own deaths may make any number of preparations beforehand, so the connection between this reason and May's claim is really quite weak. To accept a connection, we would have to assume that active euthanasia necessarily amounts to a sudden death without adequate preparation; since we cannot do so, we are entitled to question the relevance of the reason, no matter how good it might be in itself.

Following Through

Now examine May's second, third, and fourth reasons on your own, as we have just examined the first one. Make notes about each reason, evaluating how good each is in itself and how relevant it is to the thesis. In your notebook, create your own diagram based on the model on page 34.

Analyzing Evidence

Once you have finished your analysis of the reasons, the next step is to consider the evidence offered to support any of those reasons.

List the Evidence

Ask, *What kinds of evidence (data, anecdotes, case studies, citations from authority, and so forth) are offered as support for each reason?* Some arguments advance little in the way of evidence. May's argument is a good example of a moral argument from and about principles; such an argument does not require much evidence to be effective. Lack of evidence, then, is not always a fault. For one of his reasons, however, May does offer some evidence: after stating his second reason in paragraph 5—the chance to grieve before a loved one dies can be helpful for those who must go on living after the patient's death—he invokes authorities who agree with him about the value of advanced grieving.

Examine the Evidence

Two questions apply. First, *Is the evidence good?* That is, is it sufficient, accurate, and credible? Second, *Is it relevant to the reason it supports?* Clearly, the evidence May offers in paragraph 5 is sufficient; any more would probably be too much. We assume his citations are accurate and credible as well. We would generally also accept them as relevant, since apart from our own experience with grieving, we have to rely on expert opinion for such information. (See Chapter 6 for a fuller discussion of estimating the adequacy and relevance of evidence.)

Noting Refutations

A final—and optional—step is to assess an arguer's refutations, his or her effort to anticipate objections and answer them in advance. In a refutation a writer raises a potential objection to his or her position and tries to show why it does not undermine the basic argument. Refutations do not relate directly to claims, reasons, and evidence. A skilled arguer uses them not as part of the main logic of an argument but as a separate step to deal with any obvious objections a reader is likely to have.

First ask, *What refutations does the writer offer?* Summarize all refutations and list them on your tree diagram of claims, reasons, and evidence. Then ask, *How does the writer attack each objection?* May's refutation occupies paragraph 7. He recognizes that the value of free choice lends weight to the pro-euthanasia position, and so he relates this value to the question of "voluntary euthanasia." Because in our culture individual freedom is so strong a value, May doesn't attack the value itself; rather, he forces us to question whether voluntary euthanasia is in fact a matter of free choice. He suggests that unwanted people may be subtly coerced into "choosing" death or may simply be so isolated and neglected that death becomes preferable to life. In this way he refutes the objection that dying people should simply have freedom of choice where death is concerned.

Summarizing Your Analysis

Once you have completed your analysis, it is a good idea to summarize the results in a paragraph or two. Be sure to set aside your own position on the issue, and confine your summary to the argument the writer makes. In other words, whether you agree with the author or not, attempt to assess his or her logic fairly.

While May's logic is strong, it doesn't, in our view, seem fully compelling. He qualifies his argument and uses exceptions effectively, and his single use of refutation is skillful. However, he fails to acknowledge that active euthanasia need not be a sudden decision leading to sudden death. Consequently, his reasons for supporting passive euthanasia can be used to support at least some cases of active euthanasia as well. It is here—in the linkage between his reasons and his claim—that May's argument falls short. Furthermore, we may question whether the circumstances under which May would permit active euthanasia are in fact as rare as he suggests. Experience tells us that many people are beyond human care, terminal, and in pain, and many others suffer acute mental anguish for which they might legitimately seek the relief of death.

Following Through

Following is a student-written argument on capital punishment. Read it through once, and then use the Toulmin method as described in this chapter to analyze its logic systematically.

Student Sample: An Argument for Analysis

AMBER YOUNG

Capital Punishment: Society's Self-Defense

JUST AFTER 1:00 A.M. on a warm night in early June, Georgeann, a *1* pretty college student, left through the back door of a fraternity house to walk the ninety feet down a well-lighted alley to the back door of her sorority house. Lively and vivacious, Georgeann had been an honor student, a cheerleader, and Daffodil Princess in high school, and now she was in the middle of finals week, trying to maintain her straight A record in college. That evening several people saw Georgeann walk to within about forty feet of the door of her sorority house. However, she never arrived. Somewhere in that last forty feet, she met a tall, handsome young man on crutches, his leg in a cast, struggling with a brief case. The young man asked Georgeann if she could help him get to his car which was parked nearby. Georgeann consented. Meanwhile, a housemother sleeping by an open window in a nearby fraternity house was awakened by a high-pitched, terrified scream that suddenly stopped. That was the last anyone ever heard or saw of Georgeann Hawkins. Her bashed skull and broken body were dumped on a hillside many miles away, along with the bodies of several other young female victims who had also been lured to their deaths by the good looking, clean-cut, courteous, intelligent, and charming Ted Bundy.

By the time Ted Bundy was caught in Utah with his bashing bar and other homemade tools of torture, he had bludgeoned and strangled to death at least thirty-two young women, raping and savaging many of them in the process. His "hunting" trips had extended into at least five Western states, including Washington, Oregon, Idaho, Utah, and Colorado, where he randomly selected and killed his unsuspecting victims.

Bundy was ultimately convicted of the attempted kidnapping of Carol DeRonche and imprisoned. For this charge he probably would have been paroled within eighteen months. However, before parole could be approved, Bundy was transferred to a jail in Colorado to stand trial for the murder of Caryn Campbell. With Bundy in jail, no one died at his hands or at the end of his savagely swung club. Young women could go about their lives normally, "safe" and separated from Ted Bundy by prison walls. Yet any number of things could have occurred to set Bundy free—an acquittal, some sympathetic judge or parole board, a psychiatrist pronouncing him rehabilitated and safe, a state legislature passing shorter sentencing or earlier parole laws, inadequate prison space, a federal court ruling abolishing life in prison without any possibility for parole, or an escape.

In Bundy's case, it was escape—twice—from Colorado jails. The first time he was immediately caught and brought back. The second time Bundy made it to Florida, where fifteen days after his escape he bludgeoned and strangled Margaret Bowman, Lisa Levy, Karen Chandler, and Kathy Kleiner in their Tallahassee sorority house, tearing chunks out of Lisa Levy's breast and buttock with his teeth. Ann Rule, a noted crime writer who became Bundy's confidant while writing her book *The Stranger Beside Me,* described Bundy's attack on Lisa Levy as like that of a rabid animal. On the same night at a different location, Bundy sneaked through an open window and so savagely attacked Cheryl Thomas in her bed that a woman in the apartment next door described the clubbing as seeming to reverberate through the whole house for about ten seconds. Then, three weeks later, less than forty days after his escape from the Colorado jail, Bundy went hunting again. He missed his chance at one quarry, junior high school student Leslie Ann Parmenter, when her brother showed up and thwarted her abduction. But Bundy succeeded the next day in Lake City, where he abducted and killed twelve-year-old Kimberly Diane Leach and dumped her strangled, broken body in an abandoned pig barn.

The criminal justice system and jails in Utah and Colorado did not keep Margaret Bowman, Lisa Levy, Karen Chandler, Kathy Kleiner, Cheryl Thomas, Leslie Ann Parmenter, or little Kimberly Leach safe from Ted Bundy. The state of Florida, however, with its death penalty, has made every other young woman safe from Ted Bundy forever. Capital punishment is society's means of self-defense. Just as a person is justified in using deadly force in defending herself or himself against a would-be killer, so society also has a right to use deadly force to defend itself and its citizens from those who exhibit a strong propensity to kill whenever the opportunity and the urge arise.

However, while everyone wants a safe society, some people would say that capital punishment is too strong a means of ensuring it. Contemporary social critic Hendrick Hertzberg often attacks the death penalty, using arguments that are familiar, but not compelling, to those who do not share his absolute value-of-life position. For example, in one article he tries to paint a graphic picture of how horrible and painful even the most modern execution methods, such as lethal injection, are to the prisoner ("Premeditated"). Elsewhere he dismisses the deterrence argument as "specious," since "[n]o one has ever been able to show that capital punishment lowers the murder rate" ("Burning" 4). But the Florida death penalty has, in fact, made certain that Ted Bundy will never again go on one of his hunting trips to look for another young woman's skull to bash or body to ravage. A needle prick in the arm hardly conjures up images of excruciating pain so great as to be cruel and unusual. Thousands of good people with cancer and other diseases or injuries endure much greater pain every day until death. Therefore, waiting for death, even in pain, is more a part of a common life experience than a cruel or unusual punishment.

Of course, the possibility of mistakenly executing an innocent person is a serious concern. However, our entire criminal justice system is tilted heavily toward the accused, who is protected from the start to the end of the criminal justice procedure by strong individual-rights guarantees in the Fourth, Fifth, Sixth, and Seventh Amendments of the U.S. Constitution. The burden of proof in a criminal case is on the government, and guilt must be proved beyond a reasonable doubt. The chances of a guilty person going free in our system are many times greater than those of an innocent person being convicted. Those opposed may ask, "How do we know that the number of innocent people found guilty is really that low?" The number must be low because when the scandal of an innocent person being convicted comes to light, the media covers it from all angles. The movie *The Thin Blue Line* is an example of such media attention. In addition, the story of *The Thin Blue Line* is illustrative in that the U.S. Supreme Court caught the error and remanded the case, and Randall Adams is no longer subject to the death penalty.

If, however, such a mistake should occur in spite of all the protections guaranteed to the accused, such an innocent death would certainly be tragic, just as each of the nearly 50,000 deaths of innocent people each year on our highways are tragic. As much as we value human life, we inevitably weigh and balance that value against social costs and benefits, whether we like to admit it or not. If the rare, almost nonexistent, chance that an innocent person might be executed is such a terrible evil as to require abolition of capital punishment, then why don't we also demand the abolition of automobiles as well? Because we balance the value of those lives lost in traffic accidents against the importance of automobiles in society. In doing so, we choose to accept the thousands of automobile deaths per year in order to keep our cars. It is interesting to note that even opponents of capital punishment, like Hertzberg, do not demand abolition of the automobile, which leads to the observation that even they may not be at the extreme, absolute end of the life-value scale, where preservation of life takes precedence over *all* other social concerns.

Just as we, as a society, have decided that the need for automobiles outweighs their threat to innocent life, we can decide that capital punishment is necessary for the safety and well-being of the general populace. The most legitimate and strongest reason for capital punishment is not punishment, retribution, or deterrence, but simply society's right to self-defense. Society has a right to expect and demand that its government remove forever those persons who have shown they cannot be trusted to circulate in society, even on a limited basis, without committing mayhem. First degree murderers, like Bundy, who hunt and kill their victims with premeditation and malice aforethought must be removed from society permanently as a matter of self-defense.

Having made that decision, there are only two alternatives available— 10
life in prison or death. We base our approval or disapproval of capital punishment as an option on fundamental values and ideals relating to life itself, rather than on statistics or factual evidence. Most of us are a long way from the extreme that considers life to have no value; instead, we crowd more closely to the other side, where life is viewed as inviolable. However, few in our society go so far as to believe that life is sacrosanct, that its preservation is required above all else. Our founding fathers wrote in the Declaration of Independence that all men are endowed by their Creator with unalienable rights, including "life, liberty, and the pursuit of happiness." However, there is no indication that life was more sacred to them than liberty. In fact, Patrick Henry, who would later be instrumental in the adoption of the Bill of Rights to the U.S. Constitution, is most famous for his defiant American Revolutionary declaration "I know not what course others may take, but as for me, give me liberty or give me death!"

The sentiment that some things are worse than death remains pervasive in this country where millions of soldiers and others have put themselves in harm's way and even sacrificed their lives to preserve and defend freedom for themselves or for the people they leave behind. Many people will readily or reluctantly admit to their willingness to use deadly force to protect themselves or their families from a murderer. The preservation of life, any life, regardless of everything else, is not an absolute value that most people in this country hold.

In fact, many prisoners would prefer to die than to languish in prison. While some might still want to read and expand their minds even while their bodies are confined, for those who are not intellectually or spiritually oriented, life in prison would be a fate worse than death. Bundy himself, in his letters from prison to Ann Rule, declared, "My world is a cage," as he tried to describe "the cruel metamorphosis that occurs in captivity" (qtd. in Rule 148). After his sentencing in Utah, Bundy described his attempts to prepare mentally for the "living hell of prison" (qtd. in Rule 191). Thus, some condemned prisoners, including Gary Gilmore, the first person to be executed after the U.S. Supreme Court found that Utah's death penalty law met Constitutional requirements, refused to participate in the appeals attempting to convert his death sentence to life in prison because he preferred death over such a life. In our society, which was literally founded and sustained on the principle that liberty is more important than life, the argument that it is somehow less cruel and more civilized to deprive someone of liberty for the rest of his or her life than just to end the life sounds hollow. The Fifth Amendment of the U.S. Constitution prohibits the taking of either life or liberty without due process of law, but it does not place one at a higher value than the other.

The overriding concerns of the Constitution, however, are safety and self-defense. The chance of a future court ruling, a release on parole, a pardon, a commutation of sentence, or an escape—any of which could turn the murderer loose to prey again on society—creates a risk that society should not have to bear. Lisa Levy, Margaret Bowman, Karen Chandler, Kathy Kleiner, Cheryl Thomas, and Kimberly Leach were not protected from Bundy by the courts and jails in Utah and Colorado, but other young women who were potential victims are now absolutely protected from Bundy by the Florida death penalty.

The resolutions of most great controversies are, in fact, balancing acts, and capital punishment is no exception. There is no perfect solution; rather, the best answer lies on the side with the greatest advantages. It comes down to choosing, and choosing has a price. Capital punishment carries with it the slight risk that an innocent person will be executed; however, it is more important to protect innocent, would-be victims of already convicted murderers. On balance, society was not demeaned by the execution of Bundy in Florida, as claimed by Hertzberg ("Burning" 49). On the contrary, society is, in fact, better off with Ted Bundy and others like him gone.

WORKS CITED

Hertzberg, Hendrick. "Burning Question." *The New Republic* 20 Feb. 1989: 4+.

———. "Premeditated Execution." *Time* 18 May 1992: 49.

Rule, Ann. *The Stranger Beside Me.* New York: Penguin, 1989.

The Thin Blue Line. Dir. Errol Morris. HBO Video, 1988.

FROM ANALYSIS TO INQUIRY

No method for analyzing arguments is perfect, and no method can guarantee that everyone using it will assess an argument the same way. Uniform results are not especially desirable anyway. What would be left to talk about? The point of argumentative analysis is to step back and examine an argument carefully, to detect how it is structured, to assess the cogency and power of its logic. The Toulmin method helps us move beyond a hit-or-miss approach to logical analysis, but it does not yield a conclusion as compelling as mathematical proof.

Convincing and persuading always involve more than just logic, and, therefore, logical analysis alone is never enough to assess the strength of an argument. For example, William May's argument attempts to discredit those like Dr. Jack Kevorkian who assist patients wishing to take their own lives. May depicts Kevorkian as offering assistance without sufficient consultation with the patient. Is his depiction accurate? Clearly, we can answer this question only by finding out more about how Kevorkian and others like him work. Because such questions are not a part of logical analysis, they have not been of concern to us in this chapter. But any adequate and thorough analysis of an argument must also address questions of fact and the interpretation of data.

Logical analysis as we have been discussing it here is a prelude to arguing to inquire, the focus of the following chapter. Analysis helps us find some of the questions we need to ask about the arguments we read and write. Such "stepping back" is good discipline, but we think you will agree that "joining in," contributing to dialogue over arguments, is both more fun and more rewarding. So, not forgetting what we have learned in this chapter, let's move on to the more interesting and more human art of *dialogue*.

CHAPTER FIVE

Preparing to Write: Arguing to Inquire

In Chapter 1 we distinguished four aims or uses of argument: inquiring, convincing, persuading, and negotiating. Argument as inquiry, the focus of this chapter, has the following characteristics.

Its end or purpose is truth. Truth is a claim about what we believe or ought to believe—what we take to be right or correct. When we argue to inquire, we are not attempting to support a belief or position we hold already; rather, we are seeking to define our position on an issue or examining a tentatively held position to discover if it is really the one we should take. Inquiry is a means of finding the position on some issue that both satisfies us personally and holds up under the scrutiny of others.

Its audience is primarily the inquirer along with fellow inquirers concerned with the same controversial issue. In inquiry we argue with ourselves or with other people whose minds are open and who share our interest in some question. Such people might include friends, classmates, counselors, parents, teachers—anyone who will cooperate with us in a patient questioning of opinion.

Its medium is dialogue. Why does inquiry require participating in a conversation instead of simply doing research? Because no claim to truth about a topic exists outside of human conversation, free of opinions and values. Even a factual news report of an event—for example, an assisted suicide—comes to our attention in a way that challenges a set of values, complete with quoted opinions from involved parties and interested authorities. Our opinions result partly from our responses to these other opinions. When we go on to do library research, we extend the conversation as we question and interpret information and arguments in books and articles. Inquiry is interactive, a question-and-answer process that can take a variety of forms. The most common forms are one-on-one dialogues and small-group discussions, but inquiry can also take the form of imaginary dialogues that you carry on with yourself. Further, when you base your inquiry on a written text, you should also engage in "conversation"—listening to what the text says and trying to detect its strengths and weaknesses.

Its art consists of discovering the right questions and the best answers. Inquiry is the process through which we form and test our opinions and earn our claims to truth, our convictions. Therefore, the "right" questions are those that improve our understanding and that reveal weak or misleading parts of an argument. The best answers in inquiry are those that are direct and honest, not evasively convoluted or defensively dogmatic. Inquiry is friendly interrogation: its aim is not to prove that we are right and someone else is wrong; rather, it is a disinterested examination of opinion to discover truth.

In sum, then, argument as inquiry is a dialogue with oneself, a person, or a text—a way of examining competing claims of truth through a process of questioning and answering.

THE IMPORTANCE OF INQUIRY

We begin with argument as inquiry for several reasons. First, inquiry is often where we must start a writing project, especially when we know relatively little about the topic at hand. Even when we know enough to have formed an opinion about the topic, we still need to examine what we claim to know and the stance we want to take.

More important, we start with inquiry because, alone among the aims of argument, it has truth as its single goal. Before trying to move an audience toward a position we advocate, we have a moral responsibility to first examine that position and why we hold it. Convincing and persuading become immoral when people have no regard for the truth—when they set out to gain advantage by glossing over or distorting what they know to be true or when they make no effort to distinguish truth from error in the first place. Of course, there is nothing wrong with the desire to influence other people. But we need only look around us to see a world full of irresponsible advocacy. Advertising agencies agree to promote products without questioning their effectiveness or even their safety. Politicians appeal to voters' prejudices and willingly change their positions with the shifting winds of public opinion. Television preachers take advantage of the gullible and uneducated, persuading them to send money in return for prayers and miracles. Special interest groups thwart the public interest by coercing votes from policymakers fearful of their influence and dependent on their campaign contributions.

Less obviously, perhaps, as individuals we shirk our moral responsibility when we accept uncritically as received truth the beliefs of others—whether parents, teachers, or so-called experts. Questioning received truths takes effort and may make us uncomfortable, but we must do it if we are to earn our convictions and responsibly exercise our right to free speech.

No amount of thoughtful inquiry can prevent us from being mistaken some of the time; what we take to be true will often turn out to be false or only partly true. But at least if we commit ourselves to serious inquiry we can avoid unethical argumentation, the kind that has no regard for the truth.

Finally, inquiry is fundamental to the academic environment in which you now find yourself. No other contemporary institution is dedicated to inquiry to the extent that higher education is. Here people are valued not only for what they know but also, and more importantly, for the searching questions they ask. Research methods in the various fields of study differ greatly, but all claims to knowledge are arguments, and all arguments are subject to question, to inquiry. Consequently, what we are about to discuss—argument as inquiry—applies to anything you might study in college as well as to the arguments you encounter elsewhere.

QUESTIONS FOR INQUIRY

How do we go about inquiring into our own or someone else's position on an issue? There is no single procedure to follow, because a conversation is a natural act and does not run according to a script or pattern. But while every conversation may take its own course, the quality of the dialogue will depend on the kinds of questions posed. The following list suggests what you should ask when you want to open an argument to scrutiny.

Ask if you have understood the arguer's position on the issue. The best way to do this is to restate, paraphrase, or summarize the thesis. (Face-to-face you might say, "I believe that you are saying. . . . Am I understanding you?") Be sure to note how strongly the claim is made. Has the arguer qualified it by suggesting conditions or exceptions? If you are inquiring into your own argument, ask if you have stated your own position clearly. Do you need to qualify it in any way?

Ask about the meaning of any words that seem central to the argument. You can do this at any point in a conversation and as often as it seems necessary. When dealing with a written text, try to discern the meaning from context. For instance, if an author's case depends on the fairness of a proposed solution, you'll need to ask what "fair" means, since the word has a range of possible applications. You might ask, "Fair to whom?"

Ask what reasons support the thesis. Paraphrasing reasons is a good way to open up a conversation to further questions about assumptions, values, and definitions.

Ask about the assumptions on which the thesis and reasons are based. Most arguments are based on one or more unstated assumptions. For example, if a college recruiter argues that the school he or she represents is superior to most others (thesis) because its ratio of students to teachers is low (reason), the unstated assumptions are (1) that students there will get more attention, and (2) that more attention results in a better education. As you inquire into an argument, note the assumptions and ask if they are reasonable.

Ask about the values expressed or implied by the argument. For example, if you argue that closing a forest to logging operations is essential even at the cost of dozens of jobs, you are valuing environmental preservation over the livelihoods of the workers who must search for other jobs.

Ask how well the reasons are supported. Are they offered as opinions only, or are they supported with evidence? Is the evidence recent? Sufficient? What kind of testimony is offered? Who are the authorities cited? What are their credentials and biases? Are there other facts or authoritative statements that might weaken the argument?

Consider analogies and comparisons. If the author makes an argument by analogy, does the comparison hold up? For example, advocates of animal rights draw an analogy with civil rights when they claim that just as we have come to recognize the immorality of exploiting human beings, so we should recognize the immorality of exploiting other species. Do you think this analogy is sound?

Ask about the arguer's biases and background. What past experiences might have led the arguer to take this position? What does the holder of this position stand to gain? What might someone gain by challenging it?

Ask about implications. Where would the argument ultimately lead should we accept what the speaker advocates? For example, if someone contends that abortion is murder, asking about implications would result in the question, Are you willing to put women who get abortions on trial for murder and, if they are convicted, to punish them as murderers are usually punished?

Ask whether the argument takes opposing views into account. If it does, are they presented fairly and clearly or with mockery and distortion? Does the author take them seriously or dismiss them? Are they effectively refuted?

Use the preceding questions as a checklist as you inquire into arguments; it is a good idea to memorize them or write them down in your writer's notebook for easy reference. Keep in mind, however, that effective inquiry requires much more than a list of questions. First, you must read or listen attentively, taking in what other arguers have to say without being too anxious to assert your own point of view. Of course, you will almost always have some sort of gut reaction to any argument, but be careful to listen rather than rush to judgment, just as you would want others to hear you out. Inquiry is more than an exchange of opinion; it is an exploration of opinion. Clearly no exploration can occur without first listening.

Second, you must ask thoughtful questions and be genuinely engaged in the argument at hand. Because each argument is unique, you cannot apply a checklist of questions mechanically, the same way in every case. In order to open up a particular argument, you must find the "right" questions to ask, those that reveal the argument's strengths and weaknesses. The art of inquiry, unlike a mechanical process, is a dialogue with one's self, another person, or a text.

INQUIRY AND WRITTEN ARGUMENTS: THE PROCESS OF DIALOGUE

We have said that it is possible to have a "conversation" with writers of written arguments. Doing so requires some imagination on the part of the inquirer, who must not only pose questions but also supply plausible answers from the writer's point of view. Such an imagined dialogue is a good way to evaluate arguments you encounter in your research and to decide which arguments you may want to adapt in support of your own position.

A Preliminary Critical Reading

Suppose you encounter the following argument by Michael Levin while researching the topic of international terrorism and the various antiterrorism policies adopted by nations around the world. First read Levin's argument critically, following the procedure discussed in Chapter 3. Start by skimming, reading the first and last paragraphs and the first sentence or two of each paragraph in between in order to get a quick overall idea of Levin's point. Then read the argument sequentially, at a moderate pace. Finally, after putting it aside for awhile, read the argument a second time, underlining whatever seems most important and writing down your responses in the margins and in your writer's notebook. If you find the argument complicated or if you have trouble following its logic, you may want to subject it to a Toulmin analysis as described in Chapter 4. A full critical analysis will help prepare you to enter into a dialogue with the argument.

MICHAEL LEVIN

The Case for Torture

Michael Levin is a philosophy professor at the City College of New York. This argument was written in 1982 and originally published in Newsweek *magazine.*

IT IS generally assumed that torture is impermissible, a throwback to a   *1* more brutal age. Enlightened societies reject it outright, and regimes suspected of using it risk the wrath of the United States.

I believe this attitude is unwise. There are situations in which torture is not merely permissible but morally mandatory. Moreover, these situations are moving from the realm of imagination to fact.

Death. Suppose a terrorist has hidden an atomic bomb on Manhattan Island which will detonate at noon on July 4 unless. . . . (here follow the usual demands for money and release of his friends from jail). Suppose, further, that he is caught at 10 A.M. of the fateful day, but—preferring death to failure—won't disclose where the bomb is. What do we do? If we follow due process—wait for his lawyer, arraign him—millions of people will die. If the only way to save those lives is to subject the terrorist to the most excruciating possible pain, what grounds can there be for not doing so? I suggest there are none. In any case, I ask you to face the question with an open mind.

Torturing the terrorist is unconstitutional? Probably. But millions of lives surely outweigh constitutionality. Torture is barbaric? Mass murder is far more barbaric. Indeed, letting millions of innocents die in deference to one who flaunts his guilt is moral cowardice, an unwillingness to dirty one's hands. If *you* caught the terrorist, could you sleep nights knowing that millions died because you couldn't bring yourself to apply the electrodes?

Once you concede that torture is justified in extreme cases, you have 5 admitted that the decision to use torture is a matter of balancing innocent lives against the means needed to save them. You must now face more realistic cases involving more modest numbers. Someone plants a bomb on a jumbo jet. He alone can disarm it, and his demands cannot be met (or if they can, we refuse to set a precedent by yielding to his threats). Surely we can, we must, do anything to the extortionist to save the passengers. How can we tell 300, or 100, or 10 people who never asked to be put in danger, "I'm sorry, you'll have to die in agony, we just couldn't bring ourselves to. . . ."

Here are the results of an informal poll about a third, hypothetical, case. Suppose a terrorist group kidnapped a newborn baby from a hospital. I asked four mothers if they would approve of torturing kidnappers if that were necessary to get their own newborns back. All said yes, the most "liberal" adding that she would like to administer it herself.

I am not advocating torture as punishment. Punishment is addressed to deeds irrevocably past. Rather, I am advocating torture as an acceptable measure for preventing future evils. So understood, it is far less objectionable than many extant punishments. Opponents of the death penalty, for example, are forever insisting that executing a murderer will not bring back his victim (as if the purpose of capital punishment were supposed to be resurrection, not deterrence or retribution). But torture, in the cases described, is intended not to bring anyone back but to keep innocents from being dispatched. The most powerful argument against using torture as a punishment or to secure confessions is that such practices disregard the rights of the individual. Well, if the individual is all that important—and he is—it is correspondingly important to protect the rights of individuals threatened by terrorists. If life is so valuable that it must never be taken, the lives of the innocents must be saved even at the price of hurting the one who endangers them.

Better precedents for torture are assassination and preemptive attack. No Allied leader would have flinched at assassinating Hitler, had that been possible. (The Allies did assassinate Heydrich.[1]) Americans would be angered to learn that Roosevelt could have had Hitler killed in 1943—thereby shortening the war and saving millions of lives—but refused on moral grounds. Similarly, if nation A learns that nation B is about to launch an unprovoked attack, A has a right to save itself by destroying B's military capability first. In the same way, if the police can by torture save those who would otherwise die at the hands of kidnappers or terrorists, they must.

Idealism. There is an important difference between terrorists and their victims that should mute talk of the terrorists' "rights." The terrorist's victims are at risk unintentionally, not having asked to be endangered. But the terrorist knowingly initiated his actions. Unlike his victims, he volunteered for the risks of his deed. By threatening to kill for profit or idealism, he renounces civilized standards, and he can have no complaint if civilization tries to thwart him by whatever means necessary.

Just as torture is justified only to save lives (not extort confessions or recantations), it is justifiably administered only to those *known* to hold innocent lives in their hands. Ah, but how can the authorities ever be sure they have the right malefactor? Isn't there a danger of error and abuse? Won't We turn into Them?

10

Questions like these are disingenuous in a world in which terrorists proclaim themselves and perform for television. The name of their game is public recognition. After all, you can't very well intimidate a government into releasing your freedom fighters unless you announce that it is your group that has seized its embassy. "Clear guilt" is difficult to define, but when 40 million people see a group of masked gunmen seize an airplane on the evening news, there is not much question about who the perpetrators are. There will be hard cases where the situation is murkier. Nonetheless, a line demarcating the legitimate use of torture can be drawn. Torture only the obviously guilty, and only for the sake of saving innocents, and the line between Us and Them will remain clear.

There is little danger that the Western democracies will lose their way if they choose to inflict pain as one way of preserving order. Paralysis in the face of evil is the greater danger. Some day soon a terrorist will threaten tens of thousands of lives, and torture will be the only way to save them. We had better start thinking about this.

A Sample Dialogue

Begin your dialogue with Michael Levin by questioning the gist of his position in "The Case for Torture." As with any written argument, you must

[1]Reinhard Heydrich, deputy chief of the Gestapo in Hitler's Germany, was known as "the Hangman of Europe." He was assassinated by Czech patriots.

take special care in doing so because the author is not present to correct you if you go wrong. The questioner should always begin with what the answerer has said, gaining the assent of the answerer at every step in the line of reasoning: "Did I understand you to say . . . ?" "Yes." "And did you also assert . . . ?" "I did." These preliminary questions are important because they set the stage for exploring the argument itself and help ensure the mutual understanding necessary for dialogue.

In "The Case for Torture" you don't have to search for a thesis; Levin states his central position explicitly in the second paragraph: "There are situations in which torture is not merely permissible but morally mandatory." You might begin the dialogue by paraphrasing that main idea:

Q: Professor Levin, the way I hear it, you believe that given certain conditions, the *only* right thing to do is to torture someone.

[At this point, you can feel confident that Levin would agree.]

A: Yes, it would be immoral not to.

[Now you are ready to ask another question to explore more fully the point to which Levin has just assented. Asking for definitions is often a good way to probe more deeply. Does anything in Levin's position statement need clarification?]

Q: I'd like to know what you mean by situations or conditions in which torture must occur.

[Here, again, Levin makes the question relatively easy to answer by stating these conditions explicitly in his essay. You can paraphrase them.]

A: Innocent people would be about to die at the hands of terrorists, and the captured terrorist would have to be obviously guilty and have information that would save their lives.

[You are now ready to ask Levin a question about his reasons.]

Q: Why is it morally mandatory to torture a terrorist under the circumstances you describe above?

[This reason is stated most explicitly in paragraph 5.]

A: The torture will save the lives of innocent people.

[Now that you have elicited Levin's reason, you might ask about the assumptions underlying his position. For example, what is he assuming about the information to be gained through torture?]

Q: Aren't you assuming that the person being tortured will tell the truth? If a person is willing to die for a cause, wouldn't he or she also lie—mislead the authorities until the bomb explodes?

[By challenging this assumption, have you deflated Levin's whole argument? Recall that in inquiry you are not seeking to destroy an argument but rather to examine it. This goal requires that you attempt to find the best response to any question. In this case, you must make an honest effort to answer the question as Levin would.]

A: The torturer does assume that the terrorist will tell the truth in an effort to get the pain over with as soon as possible. Pain weakens a person's will to resist.

[You might press further on this point, particularly if you know something about how the victims of torture generally respond to their captors' demands for information. But you could just as well question at this point the values inherent in Levin's thesis.]

Q: I see that while you value civilized behavior over brutality, you value innocent lives most of all. Is that right?

[Again you should try honestly to respond as Levin would.]

A: Yes. I suggest that we substitute for our current principle "thou shalt never torture" a new principle: "the decision to use torture is a matter of balancing innocent lives against the means needed to save them" (paragraph 5). In other words, the moral principle underlying my argument is essentially "act always to protect the lives of innocent people."

[At this point, remembering that Levin has illustrated his principle with examples—innocent airline passengers and innocent citizens of Manhattan facing nuclear annihilation—you might be ready to say, "Yes, I see that you have a point." But inquiry obligates you to press further: Is it really *right* to accept this principle?]

Q: What about our constitutional right to due process, meaning a trial, which pertains even when accused criminals plead guilty?
A: Torture probably is unconstitutional, but the number of lives saved justifies the violation of constitutional rights.
Q: But in paragraph 6, you suggest that if kidnappers threatened to kill even one newborn baby, torture would be justified. Is the number of lives saved through torture a factor or not?

[Since an argument must be consistent, finding a satisfactory answer to this question is obviously crucial to defending Levin's position. Levin would probably deny that quantity was a factor.]

A: I believe that once you accept the principle that saving innocent lives justifies torture, it does not matter if it is one or one million that you save. I began with the extreme case to persuade you to agree with the principle.

[You might also ask a further question about constitutional rights.]

Q: The Constitution also guards against the use of cruel and unusual punishment. Obviously, torture is cruel. What specific means are you advocating? Only once do you offer any concrete example of what you have in mind, when you refer in paragraph four to applying electrodes. Let's be more concrete. Is any sort of torture allowable? In addition to electric shock, could we also, say, apply acid to the skin? or beat the captured terrorist with a rubber hose, perhaps concentrating on the genitalia? or sever a limb? Furthermore, if one form of torture fails to work, may we try another, more painful one? Exactly how far can we take it? And when do we give up trying to extract the information we want?

[You might assume that Levin would step back a bit from his position at this point and respond with some qualification.]

A: I am not advocating gruesome or disfiguring forms of torture. Electric shock was what I had in mind. And, clearly, we can only take it as far as unconsciousness. We stop when the possibility of saving innocent lives is past.

[But this is not, in fact, consistent with what Levin actually says in paragraph 9, where he suggests that we may use "whatever means necessary" to thwart terrorist activity. To present Levin's position accurately, there is only one consistent response.]

A: I set no limits. We should use any means at our disposal. However, I advocate torture not as a punishment but as a means of preventing the loss of innocent lives.

[Once it is clear that the brutality can be unlimited, your next question might center on the issue of determining guilt.]

Q: But what if we only *believe* the captured terrorist is guilty? Maybe he or she has been mistakenly identified.

[Levin seems to have anticipated this objection. In paragraphs 11 and 12, he answers that we should torture only the "obviously guilty" and claims that terrorists' own desire for publicity makes this error nearly impossible. Accepting Levin's qualification, you might still be troubled by the fact that others— legitimate soldiers in a war, for example—may cause the death of innocent people. How are terrorists more "guilty" than soldiers?]

Q: What are the reasons that terrorists blow up airplanes?

[You can paraphrase Levin's response in paragraph 9.]

A: Terrorists operate for profit or idealism, that is, out of political motives. Often terrorists are attempting to secure the release of "freedom fighters" or the safety of people fighting for their own political views or disputed land.

Q: Is it possible that terrorists see themselves as soldiers at war?

A: Yes, they might see themselves as guerrillas.

Q: If our country were at war and our military captured enemy soldiers who had information about a planned attack on some American city or base, would our military be able to torture these prisoners of war? Would they not be forbidden to do so under Geneva convention rules?

A: Of course, we should treat our enemies in a declared war according to these principles, but terrorists are not ordinary soldiers; terrorists take the lives of innocent civilians, not other soldiers.

Q: Do not soldiers in declared wars sometimes take the lives of innocent civilians? Would you have advocated that the Japanese torture a captured American who could have given them information about the bombing of Hiroshima?

A: No, I would not advocate torture in a declared war.

Q: So you are saying that in some circumstances, it is mandatory to protect the lives of innocents through torture but that in others it is immoral to protect the lives of innocents through torture?

A: Yes, that is what I am saying.

The dialogue with Michael Levin could go on indefinitely, exploring the definition of war and the rights of people who fight and kill for political reasons, assuming that both sides were interested in pursuing the truth about whether torture is indeed ever justified. In your dialogues with texts and other people, try to remember that the point is not to attack or defend but to probe—to uncover the uncomfortable spots that make both questioner and answerer think harder. Such dialogue tends to reveal the full complexity of a topic, which is exactly what is required to find the best position and make the most truthful argument.

Following Through

1. In your writer's notebook, continue the dialogue with Levin. You might pursue one of the following areas of questioning or another that you have in mind yourself.

   Does Levin offer any evidence? What might you ask him about it? What might he have included that he did not?

   In paragraphs 7 and 8, Levin contrasts torture with capital punishment and also compares it with assassination and preemptive attacks. Continue the dialogue, inquiring into the similarities and differences among these.

2. Select one of the two essays from the following list, and do a critical reading as described in Chapter 3 and an analysis as described in Chapter 4. Annotate the text, and make notes in your writer's notebook. With another student or in a small group, create a dialogue with the writer based on the questions outlined on pages 44–45. Then share your questions and answers with the rest of your class, comparing results and focusing on the variety of paths dialogues can take.

EVALUATING AN ARGUMENT: AN ANALYSIS BASED ON INQUIRY

A dialogue can take you in many directions and open up a great deal you may not have thought about carefully before. Writing an essay after you conclude a dialogue can help you summarize and reflect on your total experience and articulate your best insights in order to decide how much of an argument you are willing to accept. Sometimes an informal paragraph or two in your writer's notebook is enough. However, if you want to present your assessment of an argument to other readers, you will need to write a more formal paper, an analysis that evaluates.

The audience for such an evaluation will be other people interested in the issue who, like you, are trying to decide what they think. You may assume that they have read the argument and that they are also trying to evaluate its claim to truth. In other words, think of your audience and yourself as peers, fellow truth-seekers. Your tone should be critical but impartial. Your goal is to evaluate, but you should also be interested in helping your readers understand the argument. There is no lockstep process for an essay evaluating an argument, but we can offer some suggestions.

Preparing to Write

First, of course, read the argument thoroughly and critically, until you feel confident about your own understanding of it. Review the definition of critical reading (page 16) and our other suggestions in Chapter 3.

As you read, you should mark up the text of the argument (make a photocopy for this purpose, if necessary). Identify the claim, the reasons, and any evidence; mark the sections that the essay breaks down into; note how (and whether) terms are defined; and so on. See Chapter 4 for more advice about analyzing arguments.

If the argument is particularly difficult, summarize and paraphrase the parts you find troublesome (refer to the section in Appendix A entitled "Using Sources"). Raise questions about these passages in class or in conference with your instructor.

Next, in addition to discussing the essay with others, you should write out a dialogue with the writer as we have illustrated in this chapter, posing questions and providing careful responses that accurately reflect the writer's position. You will not reproduce the dialogue in your essay, but what you learn and conclude from such dialogue will certainly be useful.

From Dialogue to Draft

Analytical essays are not summaries. You should assume your readers have also read the text you are analyzing; they are looking for your insights into the argument and your assessment of the writer's claim to truth rather than a summary of the text. Your thesis, therefore, will be some statement evaluating the overall worth of the argument you are analyzing. To arrive at it, review your annotations and recall your dialogue with the text. What strengths and weaknesses did you uncover? Try to consider the larger picture: With respect to the given issue, does the argument shed valuable light on the truth?

Support your thesis with comments (either negative or positive) that have resulted from your reading of the argument and your dialogue with it. You may focus your critical reading on key aspects of the argument which will form natural topics for paragraphs or groups of paragraphs in your written analysis. For example, you might build a part of your analysis around an evaluation of the argument's main reason, around an important analogy in the argument, or around an assumption of the writer's that you do not share. One way to discover points to include in your analysis is to recall your dialogue with the writer: What questions proved most fruitful? You will also need to support and develop your comments with specific references to passages in the argument, making use of brief summaries and paraphrases as well as direct quotations.

Remember that you may not be able to include every critical observation in your analysis. Attempting to work in everything can result in an analysis that is more like an inventory or a laundry list—not very readable. It is better to concentrate on related points so that your analysis has unity and focus. Above all, emphasize the main qualities that make the argument succeed or fail in your estimation.

A Sample Analysis

Since we have already illustrated a dialogue with Michael Levin's "The Case for Torture," we follow up with a sample analysis of this argument.

Michael Levin's "The Case for Torture": *A Dangerous Oversimplification*

TORTURE IS one topic about which the truth seems clear. Enlight-   *1* ened people the world over believe that torture is immoral and barbaric. However, Michael Levin in his essay "The Case for Torture" challenges Americans to rethink their position that nothing could ever justify torture. Levin's case is thought-provoking, but his position is not one that we should accept.

Levin's reason for justifying torture appears in paragraph 5: the end, saving innocent people's lives, justifies the means, denying terrorists their right not to be subjected to cruel and unusual punishment. This reason (and therefore his entire case) rests on two assumptions: that authorities will have terror-ists in custody and that torturing them would yield information that would save innocent lives. But if we assent to torture based on these conditions, can we be sure that it will be put into practice only in situations that are equally clear-cut? How would we know, for example, that a "terrorist" was not insane or simply bluffing? What if the terrorist never did speak? And even if he or she did, how would we know that the information was the truth and not a desperate lie aimed at buying time or getting revenge for the torture? No actual situation is likely to be as neat as the one Levin poses, and assenting to torture could result in horrible abuses.

Even if we grant that torture would save lives in such a situation, can we accept Levin's argument? He attempts to win our assent through three hypo-thetical cases (paragraphs 2–6) in which he claims torture would be "morally mandatory." He first tries to get the reader to accept his argument based on millions of lives being at stake. Levin then extends the principle to a situation where hundreds of lives are at stake and finally to one in which just one life, a newborn baby's, is at stake. By the time he gets to the baby in paragraph 6, he seems to have forgotten that he justified torture's barbarity earlier on the grounds that "millions of lives surely outweigh constitutionality" and that "mass murder" is more barbaric than torture (paragraph 4). Is Levin saying that quantity matters—or not? Because of this inconsistency, Levin's argument here relies more upon emotional appeal than good reasoning.

Another major section of Levin's argument turns on the distinction be-tween torture and punishment. We may agree that torture, unlike the death penalty, might save the lives of potential victims (paragraph 7). However, when Levin says torture is like a preemptive military strike (paragraph 8), he exposes his argument to serious questions. If we can torture a terrorist to save innocent lives, why not torture a soldier to accomplish the same ends? Levin would say the difference is one of guilt and innocence, that the soldier is also an innocent.

However, Levin's use of the terms "guilt" and "innocence" can also be questioned. He defines the innocent as those who have not asked to be put in danger, using newborn babies as one example. Certainly, a soldier, at least one who volunteers to fight, is not innocent according to this definition. Levin would probably argue that soldiers put themselves at risk for better reasons than terrorists do. But Levin admits that terrorists kill for "idealism" (para-graph 9) or to win the release of their "freedom fighters" (paragraph 11). This is killing for political reasons, making a terrorist akin to a soldier. And if we try to make a distinction based on the fact that terrorists kill civilians, we must acknowledge that American soldiers have killed civilians, even infants, in many of our wars, most notably in the bombing of Hiroshima and Nagasaki, but also in Vietnam and more recently in Iraq. Suddenly, Levin's goal of keeping the line clear between "Us and Them" (paragraph 11) becomes more compli-cated. Just who is eligible for torture?

Admitting that most terrorists are more like soldiers than they are like crimi-nals does not justify terrorism, but it does help us see the problem of terrorism in its political complexity. It also leads us to examine some implications of the decision that torture can be right. Can we assent to using it in warfare? Is torture right depending on whose "civilization," "idealism," and "order" it preserves?

Ultimately, Levin's argument fails to convince. It raises some interesting issues, but even in the most clear-cut situation he presents, Levin is not able to establish the morality of torture. Torture is something we might wish to use given certain circumstances; but defending it as a moral choice, much less as "morally mandatory," does not work.

Following Through

Find an argument on a topic that you are currently researching. Read the argument critically, annotating the text, and write a dialogue with the author. Rather than just pairing questions and answers, try to make chains of questions and answers that follow naturally from one another, as we did earlier with the Levin argument. While you must find justification in the text for every response you have the writer make, you should also push beyond the surface of the text. The dialogue should dig more deeply into the argument, uncovering what is implied, along with what is stated directly. If you get stuck, consult the list of questions on pages 44–45 to help you start a new chain of questioning.

Look over your dialogue and your annotations for points to make about the argument and how well it stands up to inquiry. Finally, draft an analytical essay based on your inquiry. Before you write, you might want to read student Cindy Tarver's analysis of an argument by William Murchison, both of which follow.

WILLIAM MURCHISON

City Shouldn't Ignore Morality

William Murchison is a syndicated columnist whose work appears often in the Dallas Morning News, *where this argument was originally published.*

AND SO another U.S. city bellies up to the gay rights issue. Dallas' City Council asks: Should we or shouldn't we hire gay cops? The answer up to now has been an automatic no. Police work is public in nature. Public law forbids the sexual practices that define homosexuality: in addition to which, police officers function as role models.

Advocates of homosexual rights are nonetheless voluble and persistent. They want action. Americans are having to think carefully about a moral issue long regarded as settled. How should they think? Here is one view.

The homosexual cop issue, it seems to me, is only superficially about civil rights and hiring policy. Deeper down, it is about the legitimation of homosexuality as just another modern "lifestyle."

It is all part of a great design: claim accredited victim status, repeal the anti-sodomy laws, depict practicing homosexuals as appropriate role models, intimidate doubters by smearing them as "homophobic," drop the very word "homosexual" in favor of the positive, upbeat-sounding "gay."

As heterosexuals acquiesce in this design, out of fear or the desire to 5 be politically correct, they move homosexuality further down the road to legitimation.

The campaign has succeeded in marked degree. Various cities prohibit various kinds of "discrimination" against homosexuals. The ordination of practicing (as distinguished from celibate) homosexuals is a hot issue among Methodists, Presbyterians, Episcopalians, and others. Traditional prohibitions, such as the military's ban on homosexual personnel, are under legal and political attack.

Non-homophobic foes of homosexual "rights" sometimes don't know what to do. They don't want to injure the feelings of homosexual friends, and they don't want to countenance a radical redrafting of the moral laws. And so they worry.

Why? Can't the moral law be changed by a good old democratic vote? To say so evidences a dramatic misreading of the moral law.

The moral law—peculiar to no religious tradition; rather, innate in the human species—is no set of icky-picky prescriptions made up by kill-joys.

The moral law is an owner's manual for the human body—and soul. 10 You follow it for the reason you change (or should change) your automobile's oil every 3,000 miles: because if you don't, things start to happen, things you may not like.

The human "owner's manual" says—always has, actually—that heterosexual monogamy works. It does not work perfectly by the standards of an imperfect world; yet, on the historical record, the alternatives work less satisfactorily and sometimes injuriously. This is as true of, for instance, heterosexual adultery as of other misadventures.

Ten years ago, a well-known homosexual activist paid a call on me to press the case for "gay rights." He grew livid during our visit, all but pounded on the table. Whose business was it, he demanded to know, what sexual preference he evinced? He would do as he wanted. I had never anticipated otherwise. A few years later, he was dead. Of AIDS.

That is not a smug, God-struck-him-dead kind of remark. It is a painful observation about the necessary sequence of cause and effect: If you do "A," expect "B." Or "C." Or "D." Or various permutations and combinations of same.

The great irony of AIDS, the vast majority whose incidences result from anal copulation, is that it occurs in the midst of the ongoing national celebration of the "gay lifestyle." It is like Poe's *Masque of the Red Death*. While inside the nobles whoop it up, the great destroyer enters, unnoticed.

What a waste! My caller of 10 years ago was a talented and probably,   *15*
when he wasn't yelling at me, genial man. The world was better off with than
without him, as could be said of numberless AIDS victims.

Anyone who hates or physically torments practicing homosexuals is, in
theological or secular terms, a swine. The moral law—remember it?—calls
hatred wrong. Wrong likewise is the failure to draw meaningful distinctions
among different species of conduct and conviction. American society is being
offered that precise temptation today. We should resist to the uttermost.

Student Sample: An Analysis Based on Inquiry

CINDY TARVER

An Appeal to Prejudice

HOMOSEXUALITY EXISTED in biblical times and continues to be   *1*
viable today. Indeed, the open expression of homosexuality is now so prevalent
that gay rights have become a major concern of the American public. Evidence of this concern can be seen specifically in the question recently posed
by the Dallas City Council: Should we or shouldn't we drop the ban on gay
police officers?

William Murchison, a columnist for the *Dallas Morning News,* states in
his editorial "City Shouldn't Ignore Morality" that there is no reason homosexuals should be permitted to serve on the Dallas police force. Nevertheless,
Murchison's is not a strong argument as it is based upon faulty reasoning,
distorted evidence, and broad assumptions.

Murchison presents several reasons to justify his stance against homosexual cops. His first and most effective reason deals with the questionable legality
of allowing gays to serve as officers of the law. Murchison cites the state
sodomy law, which declares relations with someone of the same sex a misde-
meanor. In doing so, he argues that gays, who must be considered repeat
offenders under this law, do not qualify to serve as police.

Murchison's second reason deals with his perception of gay police as
poor role models. However, Murchison does not clearly state why he feels
homosexual police would be poor role models. One must assume it is because
he sees homosexuality as wrong and fears that children would become too
accepting of the gay lifestyle were they to embrace gay role models. Moreover,
Murchison may fear that children would actually become gay in an effort to
imitate their role models. If so, he is assuming that an officer's sexual orientation
would be apparent during the performance of his or her professional duties.
Furthermore, scientific evidence has begun to point towards a biological basis
for homosexuality. If this is in fact the case, society need not worry about
children choosing to become homosexual because they think it is "cool."

However, the most destructive flaw in Murchison's argument results from the assumptions upon which he bases his main reason: that homosexuality violates "the moral law." First, Murchison assumes that "moral law" exists. This is a major fault because the existence of moral law cannot be proven. It hinges upon individual beliefs about the human condition. Thus, people who believe that humans are innately good are likely to believe in moral law, while those who believe that humans are innately evil are unlikely to believe in moral law. Thus much of Murchison's argument is ineffective if the audience does not believe in moral law.

Murchison also assumes that all of mankind shares the same moral law. However, this is not necessarily the case. In fact, many would argue that morality is shaped by religion and can thus vary as greatly as do religious beliefs and practices. Another assumption which relates to this concept is the premise that homosexuality is against moral law. If all of humanity does not share the same moral law, then homosexuality may not be against everyone's moral law.

Murchison's final assumption is that homosexuality is a choice, and while that may be, there is mounting evidence that biological factors play a large role in determining sexual orientation. If this is in fact the case and sexual preference is actually determined before birth, then how can homosexuality be considered wrong? Wouldn't it have to become amoral, and of no more consequence than the color of one's eyes?

As evidence to support his point that homosexuality violates the moral law, Murchison argues that AIDS is a logical outcome of engaging in homosexual activities. Evidently, Murchison has forgotten about the tremendous number of people who have contracted AIDS through heterosexual sex, blood transfusions, and sharing needles, as well as the many practicing homosexuals who have not contracted AIDS. The belief that homosexuality and AIDS are intrinsically linked is a massive distortion of the truth.

Thus, what at first appears to be a thoughtful and well executed argument is actually full of weaknesses and contradictions. Murchison's reasoning is faulty, his evidence is distorted, and the assumptions upon which he bases his argument are not necessarily true. It is clear that Murchison designed his argument to appeal to those already entrenched in antihomosexual prejudice. Murchison's argument is nothing more than an emotional appeal, and thus he fails to convince the reader of the validity of his claim.

INQUIRING INTO A RANGE OF POSITIONS

When preparing to write an argument of your own, you should review a variety of published arguments and informative articles about your issue. As you read conflicting points of view, you will discover that the debate surrounding an issue seldom lines up on two distinct sides, for and against. Instead, you will find a range of positions, varying with the particular interests and insights of the participants in the debate. Writers who disagree on some points, for example, will agree on others. In order to determine your own best position, you will need to explore a full range of opinions. But sorting through the many positions can be a challenge. We suggest that as you inquire into the various positions on an issue, you use your writer's notebook or index cards to record your responses based on the following advice.

> *Read the sources critically.* Be sure that they are addressing the same issue, not just the same topic. For example, one issue growing out of the topic of acquaintance rape is whether incidents of acquaintance rape on college campuses should be handled by college judicial boards or turned over to local police; a different issue on the same topic is whether acquaintance rape can be distinguished from other types of rape. Be able to write a clear statement of the issue being addressed.
>
> *Identify the important facts involved in the debate.* Factual information can be verified: names, numbers, locations, dates, and so on. Note if any sources disagree about some of the facts. Which sources seem most reliable?
>
> *Identify the positions.* If your sources are arguments, paraphrase each writer's main claim, or thesis. If you have a source that is an informative article, several positions may be given, including the names of people or groups who hold those positions. Paraphrase each of these positions as well. Extreme contrasts among positions will be readily apparent; but also try to note more subtle differences among positions that are similar.
>
> *Note interactions among the different positions.* As you compare arguments on a common issue, you will find topics addressed by several if not all voices in the debate. Cutting across the arguments, look at how questions raised by one writer are also addressed by other writers. The idea is to note the threads of conversation that weave through the entire debate and see where the writers agree and where they disagree.
>
> As you move back and forth across the arguments, you may want to work with different-colored highlighters to code the major questions of the debate. Another practical method for making comparisons is to use index cards, recording on one card what writer A has to say on the question of X, on another card what writer B has to say about the same question, and so on.
>
> *Conclude your exploration with a tentative position for your own argument.* Which sources have contributed to your thinking? What arguments have you accepted and why?

Following Through

Read two or three arguments on a single issue. Then write a dialogue in which you have the writers set forth and challenge each other's ideas. You might also include yourself in the conversation, posing questions and listening to the alternating voices as they agree and disagree (see the questions for inquiry on pages 45–46). You need not take a side, but you do want to be a critical inquirer.

The Exploratory Essay

As a step toward composing an argument of your own, you may be assigned to write an essay that explores the various positions you have encountered in your reading. Such an essay does not begin with a thesis but rather with a description of the issue under debate and an overview of the conflicting positions. The purpose of the essay is to discover what you accept and reject among the arguments that make up public debate on the issue. Writing such an essay should help you find a position you can feel confident defending.

Whether your essay is an informal notebook entry or a piece revised for your classmates or instructor, it ought to take the following shape:

> *Introduction: defining and describing the issue.* The paragraphs in this section should introduce the topic and the issue. Include relevant factual information upon which everyone seems to agree. Also paraphrase the positions of the leading voices in the debate.
>
> *Inquiry: comparing points of disagreement.* The paragraphs in this section should compare the basic points of disagreement among the positions you have just described. Instead of devoting one or two paragraphs to each writer or position, try to organize your paragraphs around particular questions or points on which the writers differ: ("On the question of X, writer A and others who agree with her position argue. . . . Writer B, on the other hand, thinks. . . ."). Comment on the strengths and weaknesses of the contrasting views.
>
> *Conclusion: taking your own position.* Your exploratory essay should end with a statement of your own tentative position on the issue and an explanation of why you think it the best. You may support one of the arguments you have analyzed, modify one of those arguments, or offer a different argument of your own. The important thing is not to leave your readers hanging or yourself sitting on the fence. Make it clear what you think and why.

Three Opposing Positions

Following are three arguments on the topic of euthanasia. They all address the same issue: Should assisted suicide, what some call "active euthanasia," be made legal in the United States? You may already have read the first argument, which appears in Chapter 4; the others offer additional viewpoints on the issue. A sample exploratory essay comparing the three immediately follows the third argument.

WILLIAM F. MAY

Rising to the Occasion of Our Death

FOR MANY parents, a Volkswagen van is associated with putting chil- ¹
dren to sleep on a camping trip. Jack Kevorkian, a Detroit pathologist, has
now linked the van with the veterinarian's meaning of "putting to sleep."
Kevorkian conducted a dinner interview with Janet Elaine Adkins, a 54-year-
old Alzheimer's patient, and her husband and then agreed to help her commit
suicide in his VW van. Kevorkian pressed beyond the more generally accepted
practice of passive euthanasia (allowing a patient to die by withholding or
withdrawing treatment) to active euthanasia (killing for mercy).

Kevorkian, moreover, did not comply with the strict regulations that
govern active euthanasia in, for example, the Netherlands. Holland requires
that death be imminent (Adkins had beaten her son in tennis just a few days
earlier); it demands a more professional review of the medical evidence and
the patient's resolution than a dinner interview with a physician (who is a
stranger and who does not treat patients) permits; and it calls for the final,
endorsing signatures of two doctors.

So Kevorkian-bashing is easy. But the question remains: Should we develop a judicious, regulated social policy permitting voluntary euthanasia for
the terminally ill? Some moralists argue that the distinction between allowing
to die and killing for mercy is petty quibbling over technique. Since the patient
in any event dies—whether by acts of omission or commission—the route to
death doesn't really matter. The way modern procedures have made dying at
the hands of the experts and their machines such a prolonged and painful
business has further fueled the euthanasia movement, which asserts not simply
the right to die but the right to be killed.

But other moralists believe that there is an important moral distinction
between allowing to die and mercy killing. The euthanasia movement, these
critics contend, wants to engineer death rather than face dying. Euthanasia
would bypass dying to make one dead as quickly as possible. It aims to relieve
suffering by knocking out the interval between life and death. It solves the
problem of suffering by eliminating the sufferer.

The impulse behind the euthanasia movement is understandable in an ⁵
age when dying has become such an inhumanly endless business. But the
movement may fail to appreciate our human capacity to rise to the occasion
of our death. The best death is not always the sudden death. Those forewarned
of death and given time to prepare for it have time to engage in acts of
reconciliation. Also, advanced grieving by those about to be bereaved may ease
some of their pain. Psychiatrists have observed that those who lose a loved one
accidentally have a more difficult time recovering from the loss than those
who have suffered through an extended period of illness before the death.

Those who have lost a close relative by accident are more likely to experience what Geoffrey Gorer has called limitless grief. The community, moreover, may need its aged and dependent, its sick and its dying, and the virtues which they sometimes evince—the virtues of humility, courage, and patience—just as much as the community needs the virtues of justice and love manifest in the agents of care.

On the whole, our social policy should allow terminal patients to die but it should not regularize killing for mercy. Such a policy would recognize and respect that moment in illness when it no longer makes sense to bend every effort to cure or to prolong life and when one must allow patients to do their own dying. This policy seems most consonant with the obligations of the community to care and of the patient to finish his or her course.

Advocates of active euthanasia appeal to the principle of patient autonomy—as the use of the phrase "voluntary euthanasia" indicates. But emphasis on the patient's right to determine his or her destiny often harbors an extremely naïve view of the uncoerced nature of the decision. Patients who plead to be put to death hardly make unforced decisions if the terms and conditions under which they receive care already nudge them in the direction of the exit. If the elderly have stumbled around in their apartments, alone and frightened for years, or if they have spent years warehoused in geriatrics barracks, then the decision to be killed for mercy hardly reflects an uncoerced decision. The alternative may be so wretched as to push patients toward this escape. It is a huge irony and, in some cases, hypocrisy to talk suddenly about a compassionate killing when the aging and dying may have been starved for compassion for many years. To put it bluntly, a country has not earned the moral right to kill for mercy unless it has already sustained and supported life mercifully. Otherwise we kill for compassion only to reduce the demands on our compassion. This statement does not charge a given doctor or family member with impure motives. I am concerned here not with the individual case but with the cumulative impact of a social policy.

I can, to be sure, imagine rare circumstances in which I hope I would have the courage to kill for mercy—when the patient is utterly beyond human care, terminal, and in excruciating pain. A neurosurgeon once showed a group of physicians and an ethicist the picture of a Vietnam casualty who had lost all four limbs in a landmine explosion. The catastrophe had reduced the soldier to a trunk with his face transfixed in horror. On the battlefield I would hope that I would have the courage to kill the sufferer with mercy.

But hard cases do not always make good laws or wise social policies. Regularized mercy killings would too quickly relieve the community of its obligation to provide good care. Further, we should not always expect the law to provide us with full protection and coverage for what, in rare circumstances, we may morally need to do. Sometimes the moral life calls us out into a no-man's-land where we cannot expect total security and protection under the law. But no one said that the moral life is easy.

SIDNEY HOOK

In Defense of Voluntary Euthanasia

Sidney Hook (1902–1989) was a philosophy professor at New York University. This essay was originally printed in the New York Times *in 1987.*

A FEW short years ago, I lay at the point of death. A congestive heart failure was treated for diagnostic purposes by an angiogram that triggered a stroke. Violent and painful hiccups, uninterrupted for several days and nights, prevented the ingestion of food. My left side and one of my vocal cords became paralyzed. Some form of pleurisy set in, and I felt I was drowning in a sea of slime. At one point, my heart stopped beating; just as I lost consciousness, it was thumped back into action again. In one of my lucid intervals during those days of agony, I asked my physician to discontinue all life-supporting services or show me how to do it. He refused and predicted that someday I would appreciate the unwisdom of my request.

A month later, I was discharged from the hospital. In six months, I regained the use of my limbs, and although my voice still lacks its old resonance and carrying power I no longer croak like a frog. There remain some minor disabilities and I am restricted to a rigorous, low-sodium diet. I have resumed my writing and research.

My experience can be and has been cited as an argument against honoring requests of stricken patients to be gently eased out of their pain and life. I cannot agree. There are two main reasons. As an octogenarian, there is a reasonable likelihood that I may suffer another "cardiovascular accident" or worse. I may not even be in a position to ask for the surcease of pain. It seems to me that I have already paid my dues to death—indeed, although time has softened my memories they are vivid enough to justify my saying that I suffered enough to warrant dying several times over. Why run the risk of more?

Secondly, I dread imposing on my family and friends another grim round of misery similar to the one my first attack occasioned.

My wife and children endured enough for one lifetime. I know that for them the long days and nights of waiting, the disruption of their professional duties and their own familial responsibilities counted for nothing in their anxiety for me. In their joy at my recovery they have been forgotten. Nonetheless, to visit another prolonged spell of helpless suffering on them as my life ebbs away, or even worse, if I linger on into a comatose senility, seems altogether gratuitous.

But what, it may be asked, of the joy and satisfaction of living, of basking in the sunshine, listening to music, watching one's grandchildren growing into adolescence, following the news about the fate of freedom in a troubled world, playing with ideas, writing one's testament of wisdom and

1

5

folly for posterity? Is not all that one endured, together with the risk of its recurrence, an acceptable price for the multiple satisfactions that are still open even to a person of advanced years?

Apparently those who cling to life no matter what think so. I do not.

The zest and intensity of these experiences are no longer what they used to be. I am not vain enough to delude myself that I can in the few remaining years make an important discovery useful for mankind or can lead a social movement or do anything that will be historically eventful, no less event-making. My autobiography, which describes a record of intellectual and political experiences of some historical value, already much too long, could be posthumously published. I have had my fill of joys and sorrows and am not greedy for more life. I have always thought that a test of whether one had found happiness in one's life is whether one would be willing to relive it—whether, if it were possible, one would accept the opportunity to be born again.

Having lived a full and relatively happy life, I would cheerfully accept the chance to be reborn, but certainly not to be reborn again as an infirm octogenarian. To some extent, my views reflect what I have seen happen to the aged and stricken who have been so unfortunate as to survive crippling paralysis. They suffer, and impose suffering on others, unable even to make a request that their torment be ended.

I am mindful too of the burdens placed upon the community, with its rapidly diminishing resources, to provide the adequate and costly services necessary to sustain the lives of those whose days and nights are spent on mattress graves of pain. A better use could be made of these resources to increase the opportunities and qualities of life for the young. I am not denying the moral obligation the community has to look after its disabled and aged. There are times, however, when an individual may find it pointless to insist on the fulfillment of a legal and moral right.

10

What is required is no great revolution in morals but an enlargement of imagination and an intelligent evaluation of alternative uses of community resources.

Long ago, Seneca observed that "the wise man will live as long as he ought, not as long as he can."[1] One can envisage hypothetical circumstances in which one has a duty to prolong one's life despite its costs for the sake of others, but such circumstances are far removed from the ordinary prospects we are considering. If wisdom is rooted in knowledge of the alternatives of choice, it must be reliably informed of the state one is in and its likely outcome. Scientific medicine is not infallible, but it is the best we have. Should a rational person be willing to endure acute suffering merely on the chance that a miraculous cure might presently be at hand? Each one should be permitted to make his own choice—especially when no one else is harmed by it.

---

[1] Seneca (4 B.C.E.–65 C.E.) lived in Rome and taught a philosophy known as Stoicism, which advocated duty, self-discipline, and adherence to the natural order of things.

The responsibility for the decision, whether deemed wise or foolish, must be with the chooser.

MATTHEW E. CONOLLY

Euthanasia Is Not the Answer

Matthew E. Conolly, a professor of medicine at UCLA, delivered this speech before a 1985 conference sponsored by the Hemlock Society, an organization that advocates voluntary euthanasia.

FROM THE moment of our conception, each of us is engaged in a   1
personal battle that we must fight alone, a battle whose final outcome is never in any doubt, for, naked, and all too often alone, sooner or later we *all* must die.

We do not all make life's pilgrimage on equal terms. For some the path is strewn with roses, and after a long and healthy life, death comes swiftly and easily, for others it is not so. The bed of roses is supplanted by a bed of nails, with poverty, rejection, deformity, and humiliation the only lasting companions they ever know.

I know that many people here today carry this problem of pain in a personal way, or else it has been the lot of someone close to you. Otherwise you would not be here. So let me say right at the outset, that those of us who have not had to carry such a burden dare not criticize those who have, if they should plead with us for an early end to their dismal sojourn in this world.

HARD CASES MAKE BAD LAWS

Society in general, and the medical profession in particular, cannot just turn away. We must do *something;* the question is—what?

The "what" we are being asked to consider today, of course, is voluntary   5
euthanasia. So that there be no confusion, let me make it quite clear that to be opposed to the active taking of life, one does not have to be determined to keep the heart beating at all costs.

I believe I speak for all responsible physicians when I say that there clearly comes a time when death can no longer be held at bay, and when we must sue for peace on the enemy's terms. At such a time, attending to the patient's comfort in body, mind, and soul becomes paramount. There is no obligation, indeed no justification, for pressing on at such a time with so-called life-sustaining measures, be they respirators, intravenous fluids, CPR, or whatever. I believe that there is no obligation to continue a treatment once it has been started, if it becomes apparent that it is doing no good. Also, withholding useless treatment and letting nature take its course is *not* equivalent to active euthanasia. Some people have attempted to blur this distinction by creating the term "passive euthanasia." The least unkind thing that can be said about this term is that it is very confusing.

Today's discussion really boils down to the question—do hard and tragic cases warrant legalization of euthanasia? There can be no doubt that hard and tragic cases do occur. However, the very natural tendency to want to alleviate human tragedy by legislative change is fraught with hazard, and I firmly believe that every would-be lawmaker should have tattooed on his or her face, where it can be seen in the mirror each morning, the adage that HARD CASES MAKE BAD LAWS.

If we take the superficially humane step of tailoring the law to the supposed wishes of an Elizabeth Bouvia (who, incidentally, later changed her mind),[1] we will not only bring a hornet's nest of woes about our own ears, but, at a stroke, we will deny many relatives much good that we could have salvaged from a sad situation, while at the same time giving many *more* grief and guilt to contend with. Even worse, we will have denied our patients the best that could have been offered. Worst of all, that soaring of the human spirit to heights of inspiration and courage which only adversity makes possible will be denied, and we will all, from that, grow weaker, and less able to deal with the crisis of tomorrow.

UNLEASHING EUTHANASIA

Let's look at these problems one by one. The first problem is that once we unleash euthanasia, once we take to ourselves the right actively to terminate a human life, we will have no means of controlling it. Adolf Hitler showed with startling clarity that once the dam is breached, the principle somewhere compromised, death in the end comes to be administered equally to all—to the unwanted fetus, to the deformed, the mentally defective, the old and the unproductive, and thence to the politically inconvenient, and finally to the ethnically unacceptable. There is no logical place to stop.

The founders of Hemlock no doubt mean euthanasia only for those 10 who feel they can take no more, but if it is available for one it must be available for all. Then what about those precious people who even to the end put others before themselves? They will now have laid upon them the new and horrible thought that perhaps they ought to do away with themselves to spare their relatives more trouble or expense. What will they feel as they see their 210 days of Medicare hospice payments run out, and still they are alive. Not long ago, Governor Lamm of Colorado suggested that the old and incurable have a *duty* to get out of the way of the next generation. And can you not see where these pressures will be the greatest? It will be amongst the poor

[1]Elizabeth Bouvia, chronically ill with cerebral palsy and crippling arthritis, was well-known in the 1980s for her legal battles for the right to starve herself to death while she was hospitalized.

and dispossessed. Watts will have sunk in a sea of euthanasia long before the first ripple laps the shore of Brentwood. Is that what we mean to happen? Is that what we want? Is there nobility of purpose there?

It matters to me that my patients trust me. If they do so, it is because they believe that I will always act in their best interests. How could such trust survive if they could never be sure each time I approached the bed that I had not come to administer some *coup de grace* when they were not in a state to define their own wishes?

Those whose relatives have committed more conventional forms of suicide are often afterwards assailed by feelings of guilt and remorse. It would be unwise to think that euthanasia would bring any less in its wake.

A BETTER WAY

Speaking as a physician, I assert that unrelieved suffering need never occur, and I want to turn to this important area. Proponents of euthanasia make much of the pain and anguish so often linked in people's minds with cancer. I would not dare to pretend that the care we offer is not sometimes abysmal, whether because of the inappropriate use of aggressive technological medicine, the niggardly use of analgesics, some irrational fear of addiction in a dying patient, or a lack of compassion.

However, for many, the process of dying is more a case of gradually loosing life's moorings and slipping away. Oftentimes the anguish of dying is felt not by the patient but by the relatives: just as real, just as much in need of compassionate support, but hardly a reason for killing the patient!

But let us consider the patients who do have severe pain, turmoil, and   15 distress, who find their helplessness or incontinence humiliating, for it is these who most engage our sympathies. It is wrong to assert that they must make a stark choice between suicide or suffering.

There is another way.

Experience with hospice care in England and the United States has shown repeatedly that in *every* case, pain and suffering can be overwhelmingly reduced. In many cases it can be abolished altogether. This care, which may (and for financial reasons perhaps must) include home care, is not easy. It demands infinite love and compassion. It must include the latest scientific knowledge of analgesic drugs, nerve blocks, antinausea medication, and so on. But it can be done, it can be done, it can be done!

LIFE IS SPECIAL

Time and again our patients have shown us that life, even a deformed, curtailed, and, to us, who are whole, an unimaginable life, can be made noble and worth living. Look at Joni Earickson—paraplegic from the age of seventeen—now a most positive, vibrant and inspirational person who has become world famous for her triumph over adversity. Time and time again, once symptoms are relieved, patients and relatives share quality time together, when forgiveness can be sought and given—for many a time of great healing.

Man, made in the image of his Creator, is *different* from all other animals. For this reason, his life is special and may not be taken at will.

We do not know why suffering is allowed, but Old and New Testament *20* alike are full of reassurances that we have not been, and will not ever be, abandoned by our God. "Yea, though I walk through the valley of the shadow of death, I will fear no evil *for thou art with me.*"

CALL TO CHANGE DIRECTION

Our modern tragedy is that man has turned his back on God, who alone can help, and has set himself up as the measure of all things. Gone then is the absolute importance of man, gone the sanctity of his life, and the meaning of it. Gone too the motivation for loving care which is our responsible duty to the sick and dying. Goodbye love. Hello indifference.

With our finite minds, we cannot know fully the meaning of life, but though at times the storms of doubt may rage, I stake my life on the belief that to God we are special, that with Him, murder is unacceptable, and suicide (whatever you call it) becomes unnecessary.

Abandon God, and yes, you can have euthanasia. But a *good* death it can never be, and no subterfuge of law like that before us today can ever make it so.

My plea to the Hemlock Society is: Give up your goal of self-destruction. Instead, lend your energy, your anger, your indignation, your influence and creativity to work with us in the building of such a system of hospice care that death, however it come, need no longer be feared. Is not this a nobler cause? Is not this a better way?

A Sample Exploratory Essay

Exploring the Issue of Voluntary Euthanasia

THE QUESTION I am exploring is whether active euthanasia—assisted *1* suicide—should be legalized as it is in some foreign countries, such as the Netherlands. Debate on this issue has been stirred by the activities of a Michigan pathologist, Jack Kevorkian, who is under criminal indictment for helping several terminally or chronically ill Americans to take their own lives. The arguments that I read are devoted exclusively to the kind of euthanasia in which the patient is conscious and rational enough to make a decision about terminating his or her life.

I encountered two basic positions on this issue. Sidney Hook, a philosopher, represents the view that assisted suicide should be a legal option for the patient. After recovering from a life-threatening illness, Hook decided that each patient must "be permitted to make his own choice" and to ask that his or her suffering be ended (65). The other two writers take the opposing view that legalizing active euthanasia is bad social policy. However, their positions differ slightly. Matthew Conolly, a professor of medicine, argues that even the most extreme and tragic cases do not justify legalizing assisted suicide. His view is that proper medical and hospice care totally eliminates suicide as the only alternative to suffering. William May qualifies his opposition to active euthanasia by adding that in extreme cases it would be moral to break the law and to help someone die.

One question all three writers address is whether a patient's suffering justifies giving him or her the right to choose death. Hook argues that suffering can be too horrible to bear, and he supports this reason convincingly with evidence from his own experience with heart failure and stroke. The other writers counter by trying to see some inherent value in suffering. Both argue that it brings out distinctively human virtues, such as courage and patience. I find Hook more convincing on this question; an intelligent man, he did not "soar to heights of inspiration" as Conolly puts it (67), but rather felt he was "drowning in a sea of slime" as pleurisy filled his lungs (64). I agree that humans do have great capacity to carry on in spite of adversity, but that does not mean we should demand that they bear it. Their genuine feelings, from my own observations of dying relatives, are more likely fear and impatience, even self-pity.

The writers on both sides agree that the effects on loved ones of a patient's suffering are terrible. Hook offers this as the second of his two reasons for active euthanasia, claiming that his family's life during his illness was "a grim round of misery" (64). Conolly agrees that the family may feel more anguish than the patient (68). However, when he says that this grief does not justify "killing the patient," he overlooks that the patient would be the one making the choice. And the life the patient is sacrificing for the sake of loved ones is not one he or she finds worth living.

All three writers also touch upon the relationship between the larger community and those within it who are sick and dying. Conolly and May see these people in terms of how they benefit the community, while Hook sees them in terms of what they cost. Conolly and May argue that a civilized society must accept its duty to care for the sick and dying. In this sense, having the sick and dying around gives society a chance to practice a virtue that is in too short supply as it is. Legalizing assisted suicide would make it all too easy for our society to further ignore its duty; as May says, we would "kill for compassion only to reduce the demands on our compassion" (63). He is right that Americans do not have a good record on compassion for the elderly. Typically, ailing grandparents are institutionalized rather than cared for in the homes of family. And as Conolly points out, the poor suffer the most from our society's indifference (67). But to argue as May does that a society needs to have sick and dying members in order to bring forth the virtues of caring and compassion asks too much of the sick and dying. It is like saying that we

5

need to have the poor around in order to give the rich an opportunity to be charitable.

Hook agrees that the community has a "moral obligation" to "look after its disabled and aged" (65). But he sees these people more as a burden on community resources; caring for them can become costly, reducing the quality of life for the rest, especially the young. I admire the selflessness of this man, but his argument makes me ask, Is it right to let individuals choose to sacrifice themselves for the sake of the rest?

The answer to this question turns upon one other question that all three writers take up: How freely could one make the choice to die? Hook seems to assume that the choice for everyone would be as unpressured as he feels it would be in his case. But he wrote his argument as an old man with a highly successful life behind him—a man who had enjoyed so much he was in a position to be generous with his life. I tend to agree with Conolly that in poor families, guilt may replace generosity as the motive when insurance or Medicare funds run out (68). And May argues that elderly people who have lived alone or in institutions for years may choose death out of sheer despair (63). It is as if the whole society has coerced them into dying.

Hook, Conolly, and May touch on other points in common, but the preceding strike me as the questions most central to the debate. I approached this topic with an inclination to take a position in favor of legalizing assisted suicide. These readings made me see that this policy may bring with it certain dangers.

I agree with Conolly that the medical profession could do more to reduce the suffering of the terminally ill, and I agree with May that society needs to become more compassionate and responsible for quality of life among the aged and terminally ill. However, I do not see either of these desirable goals as alternatives to the option of active euthanasia. Extreme cases of suffering will continue, and they are not as rare as Conolly implies.

However, Conolly and May helped me to see that the apparent individual freedom of choice involved in assisted suicide may be an illusion, so I would want to qualify my position to include a process whereby the courts would be involved to protect the interests of the dying patient. This step may prolong the process of obtaining relief, but I think it ensures justice. Assisted suicide should be a choice, but it must involve more than simply patient, family, and doctor.

10

USING INQUIRY BY PEERS IN WRITING AN ARGUMENT

After some research into a topic you are preparing to write about, you will find that inquiry by your peers can help you reach a position you can defend. We will illustrate how inquiry works in class discussion with an ex-

ample of one student's presentation of her tentative position and her responses
to the questions raised by her classmates.

Dana's topic was harassment codes, which many colleges and universities
have recently enacted to restrict language or behavior that is offensive to minorities and other groups by making such behavior a punishable offense. For example, a code in effect at Southern Methodist University states that harassment
"directed towards one or more individuals because of race, ethnicity, religion,
sex, age, sexual orientation, or handicap is strictly prohibited. Harassment includes but is not limited to physical, psychological, oral, or written abuse."
Although such codes have been ruled unconstitutional at some public schools,
a number of private schools have been able to defend them successfully.

In preparation for writing an argument on this topic, students did some
assigned reading and outside research. Following is a transcript of how Dana
presented her initial position to the class in a brief statement.

Dana: I believe the antiharassment code is well-intentioned but dangerous because it threatens the atmosphere of free expression and inquiry that is
vital to a great university. The code is vague about what is prohibited, and
students will worry too much about expressing opinions that might be described as abusive.

[Next, to help Dana think through her argument, her classmates questioned
her position, even if they agreed with it, and Dana tried to answer their
objections.]

Q: Dana, I understand you to say that you are against the code, but you
admit it is well-intentioned. So you are saying that it would be a good thing
to curb harassment? [question about thesis]

A: I'm saying it is bad to harass, but it is also bad to have these codes
because it's hard to draw the line between what should be allowed and what
should not. Some opinions may hurt, but people should be allowed to say
them. For example, I found a case at one university where a gay student
complained because another student in the class said homosexuality was a
disease that was treatable. That's an opinion, and to prohibit its expression is a
blow against academic freedom.

Q: Are you assuming that our code actually does prohibit students from
expressing such opinions? [question about reasons and the assumptions behind
them]

A: Our code says psychological abuse is harassment. If a gay person was
offended by the opinion that homosexuality is an illness, he could claim to be
psychologically abused.

Q: So when you said "the spirit of free expression and inquiry" is vital
at a great university, you include the right to express offensive opinions? How
far would you take that? Would you include the opinions of the Ku Klux
Klan? Of Adolf Hitler? [question about definition and implications of the
argument]

A: Yes, it has to include offensive opinions—even those of the Klan and Hitler.

Q: Wouldn't these make some people very uncomfortable and even fearful? [question about implications]

A: Yes, but the academic environment requires that there be no restrictions on thought and its expression.

Q: So you are saying that it is more important to have academic freedom at a university than to have a climate where people are not made to feel abused? [question about values]

A: Yes, but to say so makes me sound insensitive. I'm not defending harassment; I just think it is essential that a university guarantees students the right to express opinions.

Q: If the line between offensive opinions and harassment could be drawn more clearly, do you think you could support the code? [question about thesis]

A: I don't think so. Anyway, I don't think it could be done.

Q: Would you say calling someone a "fag" was an opinion that should be protected? Can calling people names possibly be a part of the spirit of academic inquiry? [question about definition]

A: I agree that name-calling and epithets don't belong in an academic environment, but I have to think more about whether that kind of expression should be restricted and how a code might be worded to eliminate that sort of thing, but not free expression. I plan to look at the wording of some codes from other schools.

This dialogue, like all dialogues, could go on indefinitely. But from this brief exchange, you can see that if Dana is to be confident that she has arrived at the best position on the issue, she has to think more about her definition of "free inquiry" and her priorities regarding free expression versus protection from harassment. She also will have to consider the meaning of "harassment"; if she can think of examples of expressions and behavior that would constitute clear harassment, she will have to admit that a different wording of the code might be more defensible.

Following Through

If your class has been exploring topics for argument, write a statement of fifty to one hundred words on the position you are planning to take. As Dana did in the preceding example, include in your statement your main claim, or thesis, and explain why you feel the way you do. Then present your statement to a classmate or small group and together construct a written "conversation" about your position. Or present your statement to the whole class for inquiry.

CHAPTER SIX

Making Your Case: Arguing to Convince

The last chapter ended where inquiry ends—with the attempt to formulate a position, an opinion that we can assert with some confidence. Once our aim shifts from inquiry to convincing, everything changes.

The most significant change is in audience. In inquiry our audience consists of our fellow inquirers, generally friends, classmates, and teachers we can talk with face-to-face; we seek assurance that our position is at least plausible and defensible, a claim to truth that can be respected whether or not the audience agrees with it. In convincing, our audience now consists of readers whose positions differ from our own or who have no positions at all on the issue. The audience shifts from a small, inside group that helps us develop our argument to a larger, public audience that will either accept or reject it.

As the audience changes, so does the situation or need for argument. Inquiry is a cooperative use of argument. It cannot take place unless people are willing to work together. Convincing, conversely, is competitive. We pit our case against the case(s) of others in an effort to win the assent of readers who will compare the various arguments and ask, Who makes the best case? With whom should I agree?

Because of the change in audience and situation our thinking also changes, becoming more strategic and calculated to influence the readers. In inquiry, we try to make a case we can believe in; in convincing, we must make a case that readers can believe in. What we find compelling in inquiry will sometimes also convince our readers, but we will always have to adapt our reasoning to appeal to their beliefs, values, and self-interest. We will also likely offer reasons that did not occur to us at all in inquiry but that come as we attempt to imagine the people we hope to convince. This shift to convincing does not, however, mean abandoning the work of inquiry. Our version of the truth, our convictions, must first be earned through inquiry before we can seek to convince others in the public arena.

In this chapter we will first look at the structure and strategy of complete essays that aim to convince. Then we will provide a step-by-step analysis of the kind of thinking necessary to produce a successful essay that argues to convince.

THE NATURE OF CONVINCING: STRUCTURE AND STRATEGY

In Chapter 1 we defined argument as an assertion supported by a reason. To convince an audience, writers need to expand on this basic plan; they usually have to offer more than one reason, and they must support all reasons with evidence. In this chapter we use the term "case structure" to describe a flexible plan for making any argument to any audience that expects good reasoning. We use the term "case strategy" to describe the moves writers make to shape a particular argument directed toward a specific audience. Strategic moves include selecting reasons, ordering the reasons, developing evidence, and linking the sections of the argument so that it will have the maximum impact on an audience.

Case Structure

All cases have at least three levels of assertion. The first level is the thesis, or central claim, which everything else in the case must support. The second level provides the reason or reasons the arguer advances for holding that thesis. The third level is the evidence offered to support each reason, generally drawn from some authoritative source.

In the abstract, then, cases look like this:

Our illustration shows three reasons, but because case structure is flexible, a good case could be built with just one reason or with many more than three. We refer to this plan as a "structure" because the parts are built upon each other: the reasons support the thesis and the evidence supports each reason.

Case Strategy

In Chapter 3 we explained that you can read an argument with greater comprehension if you begin with a sense of the rhetorical context in which the writer worked. Likewise, in preparing to write an argument, you should consider the following rhetorical issues:

Who is your intended audience? What preconceptions and biases might they hold about your topic?

What is your aim for writing?

What claim do you want your readers to accept? How strong a claim can you realistically expect them to accept?

What reasons are likely to appeal to this audience?

How should you arrange the reasons to make the greatest impression on your readers?

How should you lead into the argument? How should you conclude it?

What can you do to present yourself as a person the audience can trust and respect?

By working out answers to these questions in your writer's notebook, you will create a rhetorical prospectus that will help you envision a context within which to write and a tentative plan to follow.

To demonstrate case strategy we will look at an argument by Anne Marie O'Keefe, a psychologist and lawyer, that deals with drug testing in the workplace; it was published originally in *Psychology Today* in 1987. As a lawyer, O'Keefe is clearly concerned about employees' rights to privacy; as a psychologist she is sensitive to what drug testing does to human relationships. After careful inquiry, including library research, she has reached the position that despite the dangers of drugs, the practice of testing people for drug use in the workplace should be prohibited.

Thinking about Audience

In order to make an effective case for her position, O'Keefe keeps in mind an audience that may favor workplace drug screening, and her strategy is to use reasons and evidence to convince readers who initially disagree with her. To do so, she had to consider the likely responses of such readers. Developing a strategy for her argument, then, O'Keefe had to begin with these questions:

Who will my readers be?

How will they be predisposed to view drug testing?

What will they have on their minds as soon as they see that my argument is against testing?

Based on these questions, O'Keefe made the following assumptions about her audience's views:

Most people feel that drugs are a serious problem in the United States, there is widespread sentiment that something must be done about the problem, and drug testing is a form of specific action. But given Americans' suspicion of authority and high regard for individual rights, support for drug testing cannot run very deep. People may feel that it is necessary under the circumstances but regard it as an invasion of privacy.

Strategy, then, must begin with some thought about the audience, its values and preconceptions. Next we will examine how O'Keefe shapes the elements of case structure—thesis, reasons, and evidence—to appeal to her readers.

Formulating the Thesis

Assuming that her audience shares her esteem for constitutional rights, O'Keefe refines her position to a more specific thesis. While it may not appear word for word in the text of the argument, a thesis forecasts how a case will be made. Because you need a clear sense of what you are claiming in order to build the rest of your case, you should always write out a thesis as the first level of your argument's structure. O'Keefe's thesis does not appear explicitly in the text of her argument, but it can be summarized easily: Drug testing in the workplace is an unjustifiable intrusion on the privacy of workers.

Choosing Reasons

O'Keefe's thesis indicates that she will show drug testing to be an invasion of privacy and, as such, a wrong that cannot be justified. She builds her case on three reasons, aimed strategically at appealing to her audience and undermining their support for drug testing in the workplace.

Thesis: Drug testing in the workplace is an unjustifiable intrusion on the privacy of workers.

Reason 1: Drug abuse is actually declining, and the push for drug testing in the workplace is motivated solely by politics and profit making. (Strategy: O'Keefe wants her readers to question the need for testing and the motives of those who advocate testing.)

Reason 2: Drug tests are highly unreliable. (Strategy: O'Keefe wants to undermine any confidence her readers may have in the technology of drug testing.)

Reason 3: Drug testing violates our constitutional right to privacy and destroys employee morale. (Strategy: O'Keefe wants to appeal to American values and the self-interest of employers.)

While O'Keefe does mention the high cost to employers of drug testing, you'll notice that she has not chosen this as a main reason, as she might have had she been writing primarily for the business leaders she criticizes. Rather, she builds her case on values.

As you read O'Keefe's argument, notice how she has arranged her three reasons. We will have more to say later about her strategies for introducing each reason and supporting it with evidence.

ANNE MARIE O'KEEFE

The Case against Drug Testing

DURING 1986, the nation's concern over illegal drug use reached   *1*
almost hysterical proportions. The U.S. House of Representatives passed legislation that, had the Senate agreed, would have suspended certain constitutional protections and required the death penalty for some drug offenses. The
President issued an executive order calling for the mass drug testing of federal
employees in "sensitive" positions. Federal courts have deemed such testing to
be illegal for some classes of federal workers; however, these decisions are still
being appealed, and the administration is determined to forge ahead with its
drug-testing program. And private employers have turned increasingly to
chemical laboratories to determine who is fit for hiring, promotion, and con-
tinuing employment. Between 1982 and 1985, the estimated proportion of
Fortune 500 companies conducting routine urinalysis rose from 3 to nearly 30
percent—a figure expected to reach 50 percent by this year or next year.

While there are issues of legitimate concern about drug use and public
safety, the speed and enthusiasm with which many of our elected representatives and business leaders have embraced drug testing as a panacea has left
many questions unanswered. Why did our national drug problem so rapidly
become the focus of political and business decisions? Did this change reflect a
sudden, serious worsening of the problem? Why did mass drug testing suddenly gain favor? Was it shown to be particularly effective in detecting and
deterring illegal drug use? And finally, what are the costs of making employees
and job applicants take urine tests?

Our country has a serious drug problem. The National Institute on
Drug Abuse (NIDA) estimates that nearly two-thirds of those now entering
the work force have used illegal drugs—44 percent within the past year. But
ironically, the drug-testing craze has come just when most types of drug use
are beginning to wane. NIDA reports that for all drugs except cocaine, current
rates are below those of 1979, our peak year of drug use.

Why the furor now? The drug-testing fad might be viewed as the product of both election-year posturing and well-timed and well-financed market-
ing efforts by test manufacturers. During the 1970s, the relatively low-cost
chemical assay (called EMIT) that promised to detect drugs in urine was first
manufactured. In the beginning, these tests were used only by crime laboratories, drug-treatment programs and the military. By the early 1980s, a handful
of private employers were also using them. But more recently, sales of drug
tests have gotten a big boost from the attitudes and edicts of the Reagan
administration. On March 3, 1986, the President's Commission on Organized
Crime recommended that all employees of private companies contracting with
the federal government be regularly subjected to urine testing for drugs as a
condition of employment. Then came the President's executive order on September 15, requiring the head of each executive agency to "establish a program

to test for the use of illegal drugs by employees in sensitive positions." It remains unclear how many millions of federal workers will be subject to such testing if the President gets his way.

Strangely, drug testing is becoming widespread despite general agreement that the results of mass tests are often highly inaccurate. Error rates reflect both inherent deficiencies in the technology and mistakes in handling and interpreting test results. In a series of studies conducted by the federal Centers for Disease Control (CDC) and NIDA, urine samples spiked with drugs were sent periodically to laboratories across the country serving methadone treatment centers. Tests on these samples, which the labs knew had come from CDC, revealed drug-detection error rates averaging below 10 percent. However, when identical samples subsequently were sent to the same laboratories, but not identified as coming from CDC, error rates increased to an average of 31 percent, with a high of 100 percent. These errors were "false negatives," cases in which "dirty" urine samples were identified as "clean."

Independent studies of laboratory accuracy have also confirmed high error rates. One group of researchers reported a 66.5 percent rate of "false positives" among 160 urine samples from participants in a methadone treatment center. False-positive mistakes, identifying a "clean" urine sample as containing an illegal drug, are far more serious in the context of worker screening than are false-negative mistakes. This is because false positives can result in innocent people losing their jobs. Ironically, since the error rates inherent in the drug tests are higher than the actual rate of illegal drug use in the general working population, as reported by NIDA, the tests are more likely to label innocent people as illegal drug users than to identify real users.

Many of the false-positive results stem from a phenomenon known as "cross-reactivity." This refers to the fact that both over-the-counter and prescription drugs, and even some foods, can produce false-positive results on the tests. For example, Contac, Sudafed, certain diet pills, decongestants, and heart and asthma medications can register as amphetamines on the tests. Cough syrups containing dextromethorphan can cross-react as opiates, and some antibiotics show up as cocaine. Anti-inflammatory drugs and common painkillers, including Datril, Advil, and Nuprin, mimic marijuana. Even poppy seeds, which actually contain traces of morphine, and some herbal teas containing traces of cocaine can cause positive test results for these drugs.

Commercial testing companies almost always claim very high accuracy and reliability. But because these laboratories are not uniformly regulated, employers who buy their services may find it hard to confirm these claims or even to conduct informed comparative shopping. Companies that mass-market field-testing kits such as EMITs (which cost an estimated $15 to $25 per test) usually recommend that positive test results be confirmed with other laboratory procedures, which can run from $100 to $200 per test. But relatively few employers seem to be using the expensive back-up procedures before firing employees who test positive. Even when employers do verify positive results, employees who turn out to be drug-free upon retesting will already be stigmatized.

The tests have other critical failings, particularly their limited sensitivity to certain drugs, a shortcoming the drug-test manufacturers readily admit. Consider cocaine, for example. Despite great concern in the 1980s over the use of cocaine, the only illicit drug whose use is on the rise, this is the drug to which the tests are least sensitive since its chemical traces dissipate in a few days. Alcohol, which is legal but potentially detrimental to job performance, is also hard to detect, since traces disappear from within 12 to 24 hours. By contrast, urine testing is, if anything, overly sensitive to marijuana; it can detect the drug's chemical byproducts (not its active ingredient) for weeks after its use and can even pick up the residue of passive inhalation. Drug testing does not indicate the recency of use, nor does it distinguish between chronic and one-time use. Most important, though urinalysis can reveal a lot about off-the-job activities, it tells nothing about job performance.

Mass drug testing is expensive, but its greatest costs are not financial and   *10* cannot be neatly quantified. The greatest costs involve violations of workers' rights and the poor employee morale and fractured trust that result when workers must prove their innocence against the presumption of guilt.

The most important cost of drug testing, however, may be the invasion of workers' privacy. Urinalysis may be highly inaccurate in detecting the use of illegal drugs, but it can reveal who is pregnant, who has asthma, and who is being treated for heart disease, manic-depression, epilepsy, diabetes, and a host of other physical and mental conditions.

In colonial times, King George III justified having his soldiers break into homes and search many innocent people indiscriminately on the grounds that the procedure might reveal the few who were guilty of crimes against the Crown. But the founders of our nation chose to balance things quite differently. An important purpose and accomplishment of the Constitution is to protect us from government intrusion. The Fourth Amendment is clear that "the right of the people to be secure in their persons . . . against unreasonable searches and seizures, shall not be violated. . . ." Searches are permitted only "upon probable cause, supported by Oath or affirmation, and particularly describing the place to be searched, and the persons or things to be seized."

The U.S. Supreme Court has ruled that extracting bodily fluids constitutes a search within the meaning of this Amendment. Therefore, except under extraordinary circumstances, when the government seeks to test an employee's urine, it must comply with due process and must first provide plausible evidence of illegal activity. People accused of heinous crimes are assured of this minimum protection from government intrusion. Because employees in our government work force deserve no less, most courts reviewing proposals to conduct mass tests on such employees have found these programs to be illegal.

Unfortunately, workers in the private sector are not as well protected. The Constitution protects citizens only from intrusions by government (county, state, and federal); it does not restrict nongovernmental employers from invading workers' privacy, although employers in the private sector are subject to some limitations. The constitutions of nine states have provisions specifically protecting citizens' rights to privacy and prohibiting unreasonable searches and seizures. Several private lawsuits against employers are now testing the applicability of these shields. Local governments, can, if they wish, pass legislation to protect private employees from unwarranted drug tests; in fact, San Francisco has done so. In addition, union contracts and grievance procedures may give some workers protection from mass drug testing, and civil-rights laws could block the disproportionate testing of minorities. Nonetheless, private employees have relatively little legal protection against mandatory drug testing and arbitrary dismissal.

Civil libertarians claim that as long as employees do their work well, *15* inquiries into their off-duty drug use are no more legitimate than inquiries into their sex lives. Then why has drug testing become so popular? Perhaps because it is simple and "objective"—a litmus test. It is not easily challenged because, like the use of lie detectors, it relies on technology that few understand. It is quicker and cheaper than serious and sustained efforts to reduce illegal drug use, such as the mass educational efforts that have successfully reduced cigarette smoking. And finally, while drug testing may do little to address the real problem of drug use in our society, it reinforces the employer's illusion of doing something.

Apparently some employers would rather test their employees for drugs than build a relationship with them based on confidence and loyalty. Fortunately, there are employers, such as the Drexelbrook Engineering Company in Pennsylvania, who have decided against drug testing because of its human costs. As Drexelbrook's vice president put it, a relationship "doesn't just come from a paycheck. When you say to an employee, 'you're doing a great job; just the same, I want you to pee in this jar and I'm sending someone to watch you,' you've undermined that trust."

Arranging Reasons

Throughout her argument, O'Keefe's strategy is to deal with the likely preconceptions of her readers. After two introductory paragraphs, paragraphs 3 and 4 counter the justification for drug testing based on the belief that the problem of drug abuse is so great that extraordinary measures are required to cope with it. Yes, we have a substance-abuse problem, O'Keefe says, but illegal drug use as a whole is declining and has been declining without drug testing. Having weakened this underlying rationale, she goes on to expose what she sees as the genuine motives behind drug testing—hysteria, political advantage, and money. Her strategy here—to discredit the politicians and business leaders who advocate drug testing—plays to the prejudices of many Americans who view the Washington political establishment and big business as being generally motivated by self-interest.

O'Keefe next seeks to destroy her readers' confidence in the technology of drug testing. She devotes much space (paragraphs 5–9) to this reason, probably because she assumes her readers share the American faith in technology to provide clean, efficient, and relatively simple solutions for complex social problems. Undermining this faith, O'Keefe explicitly points out the "inherent deficiencies" in drug testing technology.

O'Keefe's third and final reason (paragraphs 10–16) achieves its full force based on reasons one and two. If (1) there is no compelling need for drug testing and the people pushing it are acting out of self-interest and (2) the technology is by nature faulty, then (3) we have to take more seriously the violation of constitutional rights and the undermining of trust between employee and employer that are inherent in drug testing.

Using Evidence

How well has O'Keefe used the third level of case structure, the supporting evidence for each reason? For her first reason she briefly cites NIDA reports that the rate of drug use in 1987 was lower than that in 1979, a "peak year." She acknowledges that cocaine is an exception, but the authority of the source and the overall direction of the statistics would sway most readers. She then alleges that businesses and politicians are benefitting from the testing fad; this she supports with a chronological presentation of facts about the advocacy of these tests by the Reagan administration up to 1986, an election year. The strategy here is simply to make the political connection.

O'Keefe offers a wealth of evidence to support her second reason: that drug tests are unreliable (paragraphs 5–9). Her strategy in presenting this evidence is fairly simple but nonetheless effective. She divides her evidence in two parts and begins with the less serious charge: that drug tests can result in false negatives, or failures to detect the presence of illegal drugs. After calling our attention to the failures of drug testing in achieving its primary purpose, to identify users, she goes on to describe the more serious problem of false positives, which can cause innocent people to lose their jobs or be stigmatized in the workplace. She further contrasts error rates in labs that know they are being monitored with error rates in labs that don't, encouraging readers to conclude that the labs are careless and therefore untrustworthy.

In paragraph 8 O'Keefe recognizes a contradictory piece of evidence that defenders of drug testing would be likely to point out: that relatively reliable, more expensive tests exist. In granting the existence of such tests, O'Keefe defends her own case by suggesting that rather than go to the expense of double-checking, most employers will choose simply to fire employees based on the less expensive, less reliable test.

In backing up her third reason, an abstract argument about the right to privacy, O'Keefe appeals strongly and concretely to her readers' fears and their values. Urinalysis reveals "who is pregnant, who has asthma, and who is being treated for heart disease," and so on (paragraph 11), information that has nothing to do with illegal drugs and which most people feel is nobody's business but one's own and one's doctor's. Finally, O'Keefe refers to the authority of history and the Fourth Amendment's protection from unwarranted government intrusion, a basic American value associated with the founders of our nation.

Introducing and Concluding the Argument

We have analyzed O'Keefe's strategic use of the three levels of case structure—thesis, reasons, evidence—to build an argument that will convince her audience not to support drug testing. Arguing to convince also requires that a writer think strategically of ways to open and close his or her presentation of the case.

The Introduction   O'Keefe's opening strategy is to cast her argument in terms of reasoned reaction as opposed to emotional overreaction. Note the careful choice of words in her opening sentence: "During 1986, the nation's concern over illegal drug use reached almost hysterical proportions." She goes on in the rest of the paragraph to "prove" her point with sentences that amount to a list: The U.S. House of Representatives did this . . . the president did that . . . private employers have done this. In other words, each of her points after her opening assertion is designed to strengthen our acceptance of "almost hysterical" as an accurate and plausible description of the reaction during 1986 to illegal drug use.

In paragraph 2, O'Keefe poses questions having to do with her three areas of discussion that advocates of drug testing have not answered: Why are the tests being done? How well do they work? What effects do they have? This opening strategy accomplishes two purposes. First, it provokes the reader to think, to share in her skepticism. Second, it predicts the rest of O'Keefe's essay, which goes on to answer these questions.

The Conclusion   O'Keefe's strategy in concluding her complex argument is fairly simple: she attempts to present a fair and rational evaluation of drug testing as a solution to the drug problem. First, in paragraph 15 she again questions why these tests have become so popular. This time her tone is less accusatory, and she seems to be trying to understand her well-intentioned but ill-informed opposition. In the final paragraph she effectively presents a flat alternative: Either we can test employees for drugs, or we can build employer-employee relationships based on mutual respect. She then closes with an image that cannot fail to stick: the undignified position of urinating in a jar while someone watches to make sure the sample is not tampered with. The lack of trust and the cold impersonality of corporate drug testing comes through in a conclusion of real power, made all the more effective because she actually quotes a corporate executive critical of drug testing.

Following Through

A successful essay has smooth transitions between its opening and its first reason and between its last reason and its conclusion, as well as between each of the reasons in the body of the essay. In your writer's notebook, describe how O'Keefe (1) announces that she is moving on from her introduction to her first reason, from her first reason to her second, and so on and (2) at the same time links each section with what has come before.

THE PROCESS OF CONVINCING

Few people draft an essay sequentially, beginning with the first sentence of the first paragraph and ending with the last sentence of the last paragraph. But the final version of any essay must read as if it had been written sequentially, with the writer fully in control throughout the process.

A well-written essay is like a series of moves in a chess game, each made to achieve some end or ends, to gain a strategic advantage, as part of an overall plan to win. In the case of convincing, the overall plan is to win the agreement of the reader.

While readers may not be fully aware of the moves that make up a convincing argument, the writer probably created most of them through conscious design, or strategy. As the first half of this chapter has shown, we can learn much about how to convince by studying finished essays—polished arguments that convince. However, it is one thing to understand how something works but quite another to produce it ourselves. In part, the difficulty is that we cannot see from the final product everything that went into making it work so well. Just as the audience for a movie typically cannot imagine all the rehearsals and the many takes and the process of editing that make a scene so powerful, so it is hard for us to imagine all the research and thinking, the many drafts, and the process of editing and proofreading that O'Keefe must have gone through to make "The Case against Drug Testing" worth printing. And yet it is precisely this process you must understand and immerse yourself in if you are to go beyond appreciating the structure and strategies of someone else's writing and actually produce convincing arguments of your own.

The following discussion of the composing process assumes that the work of inquiry (Chapter 5) and research (Appendix A) has already been done; as such, it does not recapitulate these phases of preparing to write. It also assumes that you have worked out a rhetorical prospectus to guide you in combining structure with strategy.

Preparing a Brief

Before you begin to draft, it is a good idea to prepare a brief. Recall that we defined case structure as an abstract form making up the elements of any case. In a brief, you customize and fill in that structure to make a particular argument. The brief shows the thesis and reasons that you plan to use, as well as some indication of how you will support each reason with evidence. The brief ought to indicate a tentative plan for arranging the reasons, but that plan may change as you draft and revise. In the following section, we will take you through the process of creating a brief.

Working toward a Position

First, we need to distinguish a *position* from a *thesis.* A position (or a stance or opinion) amounts to an overall, summarizing attitude or judgment about some issue. "Universities often exploit student athletes" is an example of a position. A thesis is not only more specific and precise but also more strategic, designed to appeal to readers and to be consistent with available evidence. For example, "Student athletes in revenue-generating sports ought to be paid for their services" would be one thesis representing the preceding position, perhaps for an audience of college students. Since a case is nothing more than the reasons and evidence that support a thesis, we cannot construct a case without a thesis. But without a position we do not know where we stand in general on an issue and so cannot experiment with various thesis formulations. Clearly, then, we must have a position before we can have a thesis.

The goal of inquiry is to earn an opinion, to find a stance that holds up in dialogue with other inquirers. What often happens in inquiry, however, is that we begin with a strong opinion, usually unearned, find it failing under scrutiny, discover positions advanced by others that do not fully satisfy us, and so emerge from inquiry uncertain about what we do think. Another common path in inquiry is to start out with no opinion at all, find ourselves attracted to several conflicting positions, and so wind up in much the same condition as the person whose strong initial position collapses under scrutiny—unsure, often even confused and vexed, because we can't decide what we think.

In such situations, resolve first to be patient with yourself. Certainty is often cheap and easy; the best, most mature positions typically come to us only after a struggle. Second, take out your writer's notebook and start making lists. Look over your research materials, especially the notecards on which you have recorded positions and evidence from your sources. Make lists in response to these questions:

> What positions have you encountered in research and class discussion?
> What seems strongest and weakest in each stance? What modifications might be made to eliminate or minimize the weak points? Are there other possible positions? What are their strong and weak points?
> What pieces of evidence impressed you? What does each of these imply or suggest? What connections can you draw among the pieces of evidence given in various sources? If there is conflict in the implications of the evidence, state for yourself what the conflict is.

While all this list-making may seem at times to be only doodling, you can often begin to see convergences as your mind begins to sort things out.

Bear in mind that emotional commitment to ideas and values is important to a healthy life but is often an impediment to clear thought and effective convincing. Sometimes we find our stance by relinquishing a strongly held opinion that proves hard to make a case for—perhaps for lack of compelling reasons or evidence that can appeal to readers outside the group that already agrees with us. The more emotional the issue—abortion, pornography, affirmative action, among others—the more likely we are to cling to a position that is difficult to defend. When we sense deep conflict, when we want to argue a position even in the face of strong contradictory evidence and counter-arguments we cannot respond to, it is time to reconsider our emotional commitments, perhaps even to change our minds.

Finally, if you find yourself holding out for the "perfect" position, the one that is all strength and no weakness, the best advice is to give up. Controversial issues are controversial precisely because no one stance convinces everyone, because there is always room for counterargument and for other positions that have their own power to convince.

Student Sample: Working toward a Position   Justin Spidel's class began by reading many arguments about attitudes in our country toward homosexuals and discussing issues related to gay rights. Of these, Justin decided to investigate whether same-sex marriage should be legal. His initial perspective on the issue was that same-sex marriage ought to be legal because he thought that gays and lesbians should be treated as equals and that no harm would result. As he researched, he learned that a large majority of Americans strongly oppose same-sex marriage, mainly because they believe its legalization would change a long-standing definition of marriage and alter its sacred bond. Justin read articles opposing gay marriage by such well-known public figures as William Bennett, but he also read many in favor. He found especially convincing the arguments by gays and lesbians who were deeply in love with their partners in long-standing, monogamous relationships but who were barred from marrying them. Justin's initial round of research led him to the position "Gays and lesbians should be able to marry."

During the inquiry stage, Justin discussed his position with his classmates and instructor. Since knowing that gays and lesbians do now get married in churches, Justin's classmates asked him to clarify the phrase "able to marry." Justin explained that his position advocated the legal recognition of same-sex marriages by individual state governments and, therefore, all states, since marriage in any one state is recognized by all the rest. When asked if other countries recognize same-sex marriage, Justin admitted that only Denmark does. He decided to argue for his position anyway on the grounds that the United States should take the lead in valuing equality and individual rights. He was asked about the implications of his position: Would granting legal status to same-sex marriage devalue the institution of marriage? Justin responded that the people who are fighting for legalization have the deepest respect for marriage and that marriage is more about love and commitment than people's sex lives.

Following Through

Formulate a tentative position on a topic that you have researched and inquired into. Write it up with some brief explanation of why you support this stand. Be prepared to defend your position in class or with a peer in a one-on-one exchange of position statements.

Analyzing the Audience

Before you decide on a thesis, give some thought to the rhetorical context of your argument. Who needs to hear it? What are their values? What common ground might you share with them? How might you have to qualify your position to influence their opinions?

In order to provoke thought, people occasionally make cases for theses that they know have little chance of winning significant assent. One example is the argument for legalizing all drug use; although reasonably good cases have been made for this position, because it is so radical, most Americans find even the best argument for legalizing all drug use unconvincing. If you want to convince rather than to provoke thought or play devil's advocate, you will need to formulate a thesis that both represents your position and creates as little resistance in your readers as possible. Instead of arguing for legalizing drugs, for example, you might argue that much of the staggering amount of money spent on drug enforcement, prosecution, and imprisonment be diverted to finance rehabilitation centers and to address the social problems connected with drug abuse. Because most positions allow for many possible theses, writers need to analyze their audience before settling on one.

Student Sample: Analyzing the Audience   Justin, whose position on gay and lesbian marriage we looked at earlier, knew that many people would view same-sex marriage as a very radical idea. Some possible audiences, such as conservative Christians, would never assent to it. So Justin targeted an audience he had some chance of convincing—people who opposed same-sex marriage but were not intolerant of homosexuals. Justin sketched the following audience profile.

> My audience would be heterosexual adults who accept that some people are homosexual or lesbian; they may know people who are. They would be among the nearly forty-seven percent of Americans who do not have objections to same-sex relationships between consenting adults. They may be fairly well-educated and could be any age from college students to their grandparents. They are not likely to have strong religious objections, so my argument will not have to go deeply into the debate about whether homosexuality is a sin. However, these readers oppose legalizing marriage between gays and

lesbians because they think it would threaten the traditional role of marriage as the basis of family life. They think that marriage has come into enough trouble lately, because of divorce, and they want to preserve its meaning as much as possible. Their open-minded position would be that if same-sex couples want to live together and act like they're married, there is nothing to stop them, so they are really not being hurt by leaving things as they are. They believe in the value of heterosexual marriage for the individual and society, so I can appeal to that. They also hold to basic American principles of equal rights and the right to the "pursuit of happiness." But mainly I want to show my readers that gays and lesbians are missing out on some basic civil rights, and that letting them marry would have benefits for everyone.

Following Through

Write a profile of the audience you hope to reach through an argument you are currently planning. Try to be as specific as possible, including any information—age, gender, economic status, and so forth—that may contribute to your audience's outlook and attitudes. What interests, beliefs, and values may be influencing them? How might you have to alter your position or phrase your thesis to give your argument a chance of succeeding? What reasons might they be willing to consider? What would you have to rule out?

Developing a Thesis

A good thesis grows out of a combination of things: your position, your research into that position, an exploration of reasons you could use to support your position, and an understanding of your audience, including what they will be willing to accept. Later on, during the process of drafting, you may refine the thesis by phrasing it more precisely, but for now you should concentrate only on making a thesis that states your position as one main point in clear and direct language.

We would advise you against trying to make your thesis do more than simply present the claim. Naturally, your mind runs to reasons in support, but hold off on these. It makes more sense to save the reasons until you can present them thoroughly as the body of the paper unfolds.

Student Sample: Developing a Thesis   Justin's original statement, "Gays and lesbians should be able to marry," expresses a position, but it could be more precise and more directed toward the readers Justin defined in his audience profile. He already had some reasons to support his argument, and he wanted the thesis to represent his current position accurately, without locking him into some rigid plan. He refined his position to the following:

A couple's right to marry should not be restricted based on sexual preference.

This version emphasized that marriage is a right everyone should enjoy, but it did not go far enough in suggesting why the readers should care or recognize it as a right. Justin tried again:

Every couple who wishes to commit to each other in marriage should have the right to do so, regardless of sexual preference.

Justin was fairly satisfied with this version because it appealed to a basic family value—commitment.

He then started thinking about how committed relationships benefit the whole society, an argument that would appeal to his readers. He wondered if he could point the thesis not just in the direction of rights for homosexuals and lesbians but also in the direction of benefits for everyone, which would broaden his appeal. It would also allow him to develop his essay more by using some good arguments he had encountered in his reading. He tried one more time and settled on the following thesis.

Everyone, gay and straight, will benefit from extending the basic human right of marriage to all couples, regardless of sexual preference.

Following Through

1. Write at least three versions of a tentative thesis for the essay you are currently working on. For each version, write an evaluation of its strengths and weaknesses. Why is the best version the best?
2. As we saw in analyzing William May's case against assisted suicide (Chapter 4), sometimes a thesis needs to be qualified and exceptions to the thesis need to be stated and clarified. Now is a good time to think about qualifications and exceptions.

   Basically, you can handle qualifications and exceptions in two ways. First, you can add a phrase to your thesis that puts some limitations on it, as William May did in his argument on assisted suicide: "*On the whole,* our social policy . . . should not regularize killing for mercy." May admits that a few extreme cases of suffering justify helping someone die. The other method would be to word the thesis in such a way that exceptions or qualifications are implied rather than spelled out. As an example consider the following thesis: "Life sentences with no parole are justifiable for all sane people found guilty of first-degree murder." Here, the exceptions would be "those who are found insane" and "those tried on lesser charges."

   Using your best thesis statement from the previous exercise, decide whether qualifications and exceptions are needed. If they are, determine how best to handle them.

Analyzing the Thesis

Once you have a thesis, your next task is to unpack it to determine, given that thesis, what you must argue. To do this, put yourself in the place of your readers, those who oppose your position. In order to be won over to that position, what are they going to have to find in your argument? Answering that question requires looking very closely at what the thesis actually says as well as what it implies. It also requires thinking about the position and attitudes of your readers, as you described them earlier in your audience profile.

As an example, consider Anne Marie O'Keefe's thesis, "Drug testing in the workplace is an unjustifiable intrusion on individuals' privacy." Since there is no qualifier, the reader is going to expect an argument opposing *all* drug testing in the workplace. The argument will have to give good reasons why the intrusion on privacy is not justified. But O'Keefe realized that her readers might not believe that privacy is necessary in the workplace, so establishing workers' rights to privacy was another area of development required by this thesis.

Many thesis sentences appear simple, but analysis shows that they are quite complex. Let's consider a thesis on the issue of whether Mark Twain's *Huckleberry Finn* should be taught in the public schools. One side has argued that Twain's classic novel should be taken off required reading lists because a number of readers, especially African American readers, find its subject matter and language offensive; in some schools the novel is not assigned at all, while at others it may be assigned but students have the option of choosing to study another novel of the same period instead. In our example thesis, the writer supports the teaching of the novel: "Mark Twain's *Huckleberry Finn* should be required reading for all high school students in the United States."

Unpacking this thesis, we see that the writer must first argue for *Huckleberry Finn* as required reading—not just as a good book but one that is indispensable to an education in American literature. The writer must also argue that the book be required reading at the high school level, rather than in middle school or in college. Finally, knowing that the audience for this argument finds some of the passages racially offensive, the author must defend the novel from charges of racism, even though the thesis does not explicitly state, "*Huckleberry Finn* is not a racist book." Otherwise, these charges stand by default; to ignore them is to ignore the context of the issue.

Student Sample: Analyzing the Thesis   By analyzing his thesis—"Everyone, gay and straight, will benefit from extending the basic human right of marriage to all couples, regardless of sexual preference"—Justin realized that his main task was to explain specific benefits that would follow from allowing gays to marry. He knew he would have to cite ways in which the whole society will be better off as well as those in same-sex relationships who want to marry. He knew that his readers would agree that marriage is a "basic human right" for heterosexual adults, but he could not assume that they would see it that way for homosexual couples. Therefore, he had to make them see that same-sex couples have the same needs as other couples. He also wanted to make certain that his readers understood that he was arguing only that the law of the land recognize such marriages, not that all churches and denominations sanctify them.

Following Through

Unpack a tentative thesis of your own or one that your instructor gives you to see what key words and phrases an argument based on that thesis must address. Also consider what an audience would expect you to argue, given a general knowledge about the topic and the current context of the dispute.

Finding Reasons

For the most part no special effort goes into finding reasons to support a thesis. They come to us as we attempt to justify our opinions, as we listen to the arguments of our classmates, as we encounter written arguments in research, and as we think about how to reach the readers we hope to convince. Given good writing preparation, we seldom formulate a thesis without already having some idea of the reasons we will use to defend it. Our problem, rather, is usually selection, picking out the best reasons and shaping and stating those reasons in a way that appeals to our readers. When we do find ourselves searching for reasons, however, it helps to be aware of the basic sources of reasons.

The Audience's Belief System   Ask yourself, What notions of the real, the good, and the possible will my readers entertain? Readers will find any reason unconvincing if it is not consistent with their understanding of reality. For example, people will accept or reject arguments about how to treat illness based on their particular culture's notions about disease. Likewise, people have differing notions of what is good. Some people think it is good to exploit natural resources so that we can live with more conveniences; those who place less value on conveniences see more good in conserving the environment. Finally, people disagree about what is possible. Those who believe it is not possible to change human nature will not accept arguments that certain types of criminals can be rehabilitated.

Special Rules or Principles   Good reasons can also be found in a community's accepted rules and principles. For example, in the United States citizens accept the principle that a person is innocent until proven guilty. The Fifth Amendment states that no one may be "deprived of life, liberty, or property, without due process of law." We apply this principle in all sorts of nonlegal situations whenever we argue that someone should be given the benefit of the doubt.

The law is only one source of special rules or principles. We also find them in politics ("one person, one vote"), in business (the principle of seniority, which gives preference to employees who have been on a job longest), and even in the home, where each family formulates its own house rules. In other words, all human settings and activities have their own norms, and we must ask ourselves in any search for reasons what norms may apply to our particular topic or thesis.

Expert Opinion and Hard Evidence   Probably the next most common source of reasons is expert opinion, which we must rely on when we lack direct experience with a particular subject. Most readers respect the opinion of a trained professional with advanced degrees and prestige in his or her field. And when you can show that experts are in agreement, you have an even better reason.

Hard evidence can also provide good reasons. Readers generally respect the scientific method of gathering objective data upon which conclusions can be drawn. Research shows, for example, that wearing a bicycle helmet significantly reduces the incidence of head injuries from accidents. Therefore, we can support the thesis "Laws should require bicycle riders to wear helmets" with the reason "because statistics show that fewer serious head injuries occurred in bicycle accidents when the riders were wearing helmets than when no helmets were worn."

When you argue about any topic, you will be at a disadvantage if you don't have detailed, current information about it in the form of expert opinion and hard evidence.

Tradition   We can sometimes strengthen a position by citing or alluding to well-known sources that are part of our audience's cultural tradition: for example, the Bible, the Constitution, and the sayings or writings of people our readers recognize and respect. Although reasons drawn from tradition may lose their force if many audience members identify with different cultures or are suspicious of tradition itself, they will almost always be effective when readers revere the source.

Comparison   A reason based on similarity argues that what is true in one instance should be true in another. For example, we could make a case for legalizing marijuana by showing that it is similar in effect to alcohol, which is legal—and also a drug. The argument might look like this:

> *Thesis:* Marijuana use should be decriminalized.
>
> *Reason:* Marijuana is no more harmful than alcohol.

Many comparison arguments attempt to show that present situations are similar to past ones. For example, many who argue for the civil rights of gay men and lesbians say that discrimination based on sexual preference should not be tolerated today just as discrimination based on race, common thirty years ago, is no longer tolerated.

A special kind of argument based on similarity is an analogy, which attempts to explain one thing, usually abstract, in terms of something else, usually more concrete. For example, in an argument opposing sharing the world's limited resources, philosopher Garrett Hardin reasons that requiring the wealthy nations of the world to feed the starving nations is analogous to requiring the occupants of a lifeboat filled to a safe capacity to take on board those still in the water, until the lifeboat sinks and everyone perishes.

Arguments of comparison can also point to difference, showing how two things are not the same, or not analogous. For example, many Americans supported engagement in the 1992 Persian Gulf War by arguing that unlike the disastrous conflict in Vietnam, this war was winnable. The argument went as follows:

> *Thesis:* America can defeat Iraq's military.
>
> > *Reason:* Warfare in the deserts of Kuwait and Iraq is very different from warfare in the jungles of Vietnam.

The Probable or Likely   Of course, all reasoning about controversial issues relies on making a viewpoint seem probable or likely, but specific reasons drawn from the probable or likely may often come into play when we want to defend one account of events over another or when we want to attack or support a proposed policy. For example, defenders of Supreme Court nominee Clarence Thomas attempted to discredit Anita Hill's accusations of sexual harassment in a number of ways, all related to probability: Is it likely, they asked, that she would remember so clearly and in such detail events that happened as long as ten years ago? Is it probable that a woman who had been harassed would follow Thomas from one job to another, as Hill did?

Because a proposed policy may have no specific precedent, particularly if it is designed to deal with a new situation, speculating about its probable success or failure is sometimes all a writer arguing for or against the new policy can do. For example, the collapse of communism in eastern Europe and the former Soviet Union has left the United States in the unusual position of having no serious military threat to its own or its allies' security. What, then, should we do—disband NATO? drastically reduce our armed forces, especially the nuclear arsenal? redirect part of what we once spent on defense into dealing with pressing domestic problems? Any proposal for confronting this new situation is defended and attacked based on what we are likely to face in the foreseeable future.

Cause and Effect   People generally agree that most circumstances result from some cause or causes, and they also agree that most changes in circumstances will result in some new effects. This human tendency to believe in cause-and-effect relationships can provide reasons for certain arguments. For example, environmentalists have successfully argued for reductions in the world's output of hydrofluorocarbons by showing that the chemicals damage the earth's ozone layer.

Cause-and-effect arguments are difficult to prove; witness the fact that cigarette manufacturers have argued for years that the connection between smoking and lung disease cannot be demonstrated. Responsible arguments from cause and effect depend on credible and adequate hard evidence and expert opinion. And they must always acknowledge the possible existence of hidden factors; smoking and lung disease, for example, may be influenced by genetic predisposition.

Definition   All arguments require definitions for clarification. However, a definition can often provide a reason in support of the thesis, as well. If we define a term by placing it in a category, we are saying that whatever is true for the category is true for the term we are defining. For example, Elizabeth Cady Stanton's landmark 1892 argument for women's rights ("The Solitude of Self") was based on the definition "women are individuals":

> *Thesis:* Women must have suffrage, access to higher education, and sovereignty over their own minds and bodies.
>
> *Reason:* Women are individuals.

If Stanton's audience, American congressmen, accepted that all individuals are endowed with certain inalienable rights, Stanton's definition reminded them that women fit into the category of "individual" just as much as men do and so deserve the same rights.

Almost all good reasons come from one or some combination of these eight sources. However, simply knowing the sources will not automatically provide you with good reasons for your argument. Nothing can substitute for thoughtful research and determined inquiry. Approach each of these sources as an angle from which to think about your thesis statement and the results of your research and inquiry. They can help you generate reasons initially or find better reasons when the ones you have seem inadequate.

Finally, do not feel that quantity is crucial in finding good reasons. While it is good to brainstorm for as many as you can find, you will want to focus on those that you think will appeal most to your audience and that you can develop thoroughly. A good argument is often based on just one or two good reasons.

Student Sample: Finding Reasons   Justin used the eight sources listed in the preceding section to help find some of his reasons. He also considered his audience and the beliefs they would likely hold. Below are the possible reasons he found. Note that each reason is stated as a complete sentence.

> *From the audience's belief system:*
>
> Marriage is primarily about love and commitment, not sex.
> Marriage is a stabilizing influence in society.
>
> *From rules or principles the audience would likely subscribe to:*
>
> Everyone has an equal right to life, liberty, and the pursuit of happiness.
>
> *From expert opinion (in this case, a lawyer and some noted authors on gay rights):*

Denying gays and lesbians the right to marry is an incredible act of discrimination.

Allowing gays and lesbians to marry will promote family values such as monogamy and the two-parent family.

From comparison or analogy:

Just as we once thought marriage between blacks and whites should be illegal, we now think same-sex marriage should be illegal.

Gay and lesbian couples can love each other just as devotedly as heterosexual couples.

From cause and effect:

Marriage is a way for people to take care of each other rather than being a burden on society should they become ill or unemployed.

Clearly, Justin now had far more ideas for his case than he needed. He now had to evaluate his list to check the fit between the reasons he thought were best and his thesis sentence.

Following Through

Here is one way of brainstorming for reasons. First, list the eight sources for finding reasons (pages 91–94) in your writer's notebook, perhaps on the inside front cover or on the first or last page—someplace where you can easily find them. Practice using these sources by writing your current thesis at the top of another page and then going through the list, writing down reasons as they occur to you.

Exchange notebooks with other class members. See if you can help each other generate additional reasons.

Selecting and Ordering Reasons

Selecting reasons from a number of possibilities depends primarily on two considerations: your thesis and your readers. Any thesis demands a certain line of reasoning. For example, the writer contending that *Huckleberry Finn* should be required reading in high school must offer a compelling reason for accepting no substitute—not even another novel by Mark Twain. Such a reason might be, "Since many critics and novelists see *Huckleberry Finn* as the inspiration for much subsequent American fiction, we cannot understand the American novel if we are not familiar with *Huckleberry Finn*." A reason of this kind—one that focuses on the essential influence of the book—is likely to appeal to teachers or school administrators.

It is often difficult to see how to order reasons prior to drafting. Since we can easily reorder reasons as we write and rewrite, in developing our case we need only attempt to discover an order that seems right and satisfies us as an overall sequence. The writer advocating *Huckleberry Finn,* for example, should probably first defend the novel from the charge that it is racist. Readers unaware of the controversy will want to know why the book needs defending, and well-informed readers will expect an immediate response to the book's critics since it is the effort to remove the book from classrooms that has created the controversy. Once the charge of racism has been disposed of, readers will be prepared to hear the reasons for keeping it on required reading lists.

The readers' needs and expectations must take precedence in all decisions about sequencing reasons. We should also consider relationships among the reasons themselves, how one may lead to another. For instance, Anne Marie O'Keefe's case against drug testing first establishes the unreliability of the tests and then focuses on the damage such tests inflict on innocent employees and the violation of civil rights they represent. This sequence is effective because each reason prepares the reader for the next one. If drug tests are often inaccurate, then innocent people will be falsely accused; if innocent people are falsely accused, the unwarranted invasion of privacy seems much worse—indeed, indefensible.

Besides thinking about what your readers need and expect and how one reason may gain force by following another one, you should also keep in mind a simple fact about memory: We recall best what we read last and next best what we read first. A good rule of thumb, therefore, is to begin and end your defense of a thesis with your strongest reasons, the ones you want to emphasize. A strong beginning also helps keep the reader reading, while a strong conclusion avoids a sense of anticlimax.

Student Sample: Selecting and Ordering Reasons Justin generated eight possible reasons to support his position on gay and lesbian marriage. To help decide which ones to use, he looked again at his audience profile. What had he said about the concerns of people who oppose same-sex marriage? Which of his potential reasons would best address these concerns?

Since his audience did not believe that the ban on same-sex marriage was a great loss to gays and lesbians, Justin decided to use the lawyer's point about how the ban is discriminatory. The audience's other main concern was about how gay marriage would affect the rest of society, particularly traditional marriage and family. Therefore, Justin decided to use the reasons about the benefits of same-sex marriage to society: how family values would be reinforced and how marriage keeps people from burdening society if they become unable to support themselves.

Justin noticed that some of his reasons overlapped each other: for example, the point about marriage being a stabilizing influence was just a general statement that was better expressed in combination with his more specific reasons about economic benefits and family values. And his reason that mentioned discrimination overlapped his point that it is wrong to deny "life, liberty, and the pursuit of happiness." Overlapping is common, since there are many ways of saying the same idea.

What would be the best strategy for arranging these reasons? At first Justin wanted to begin with the point about discrimination, but then he decided to soften up the audience and appeal to their interests by listing the advantages first. Saving the argument about discrimination until the second half of his essay would let him end with an appeal to the readers' sympathy and sense of fairness, a stronger ending.

Then Justin rechecked his thesis to confirm that the reasons really supported it. He decided that his readers might not buy that marriage is a "basic human right" for those of the same sex, so he decided to add one more reason in support of the similarities between heterosexuals and homosexuals.

Justin wrote up the following brief version of his argument:

> *Thesis:* Everyone, gay and straight, will benefit from extending the basic human right of marriage to all couples, regardless of sexual preference.
>
> > *Reason:* It would reinforce family values such as monogamy and the two-parent family.
> >
> > *Reason:* It would provide a means of keeping people from burdening society.
> >
> > *Reason:* Denying them the right to marry is discrimination.
> >
> > *Reason:* The love homosexuals have for each other is not different from love between heterosexuals.

Following Through

We call the case structure a flexible plan because as long as you maintain the three-level structure of thesis, reasons, and evidence, you can change everything else at will: throwing out one thesis for another or altering its wording, adding or taking away reasons or evidence or reordering both to achieve the desired impact. So when writing your brief, don't feel that the order in which you have found your reasons and evidence should determine their order in your essay. Rather, make your decisions based on the following questions:

What will my audience need or expect to read first?
Will one reason help set up another?
Which of my reasons are strongest? Can I begin and conclude my argument with the strongest reasons I have?

To a thesis you have already refined, now add the second level of your brief, the reason or reasons. Be ready to explain your decisions about selection and arrangement. Final decisions about ordering will often be made quite late in the drafting process—in a second or third writing. Spending a little time now, however, to think through possible orderings can save time later and make composing less difficult.

Using Evidence

The skillful use of evidence involves many complex judgments. Let's begin with some basic questions.

What Counts as Evidence?   Because science and technology rely on the hard data of quantified evidence—especially statistics—some people assume that hard data is the only really good source of evidence. Such a view, however, is far too narrow for our purposes. Besides hard data, evidence includes:

> Quotation from authorities: expert opinion, statements from people with special knowledge about an issue, and traditional or institutional authorities such as respected political leaders, philosophers, well-known authors, and people who hold positions of power and influence. Besides books and other printed sources, you can gather both data and quotations from interviews with experts or leaders on campus and in the local community.
>
> Constitutions, statutes, court rulings, organizational bylaws, company policy statements, and the like.
>
> Examples and case histories (that is, extended narratives about an individual's or an organization's experience).
>
> The results of questionnaires, which you devise and administer.
>
> Personal experience.

In short, evidence includes anything that confirms a good reason or anything that might increase your readers' acceptance of a reason advanced to justify your thesis.

What Kind of Evidence Is Best?   What evidence is best depends on what particular reasons call for. To argue for bicycle-helmet legislation, we need to cite facts and figures—hard data—to back up our claim that wearing helmets will reduce the number of serious head injuries caused by bicycling accidents. To defend *Huckleberry Finn* by saying that it is an indictment of racism will require evidence of a different kind: quoted passages from the novel itself, statements from respected interpreters, and so forth.

When you have many pieces of evidence to choose from, what is best depends on the quality of the evidence itself and its likely impact on readers. In general—especially for hard data—the best evidence is the most recent. Also, the more trusted and prestigious the source, the more authority it will have for readers. Arguments about the AIDS epidemic in the United States, for example, often draw on data from the Centers for Disease Control in Atlanta, a respected research facility that specializes in the study of epidemics. And since the nature of the AIDS crisis changes relatively quickly, the most recent information would be more authoritative than that of a year ago.

Finally, always look for evidence that will give you an edge in winning reader assent. For example, given the charge that *Huckleberry Finn* is offensive to blacks, its vigorous defense by an African-American literary scholar would ordinarily carry more weight than its defense by a white scholar.

How Much Evidence Do I Need?   The amount of evidence required depends on two judgments: (1) the more crucial a reason is to your case and (2) the more resistant readers are likely to be to a reason. Most cases have at least one pivotal reason, one point upon which the whole case is built and upon which, therefore, the whole case stands or falls. Anne Marie O'Keefe's case against drug testing in the workplace turns on our accepting the inherent inaccuracy of the tests themselves. Such a pivotal reason needs to be supported at length, regardless of the degree of reader resistance to it; about one third of O'Keefe's essay supports her contention that drug tests are unreliable. Compare this with the relatively small amount of space she devotes to showing that drug use is on the decline.

Of course, a pivotal reason may also be the reason to which readers will be most resistant. For instance, many arguments supporting women's right to choose abortion turn on the reason that a fetus cannot be considered a human being until a certain point in its development and, therefore, does not qualify for protection under the law. This reason is obviously both pivotal and likely to be contested by many readers, so devoting much space to evidence for the reason would be a justified strategy.

Student Sample: Using Evidence   Justin took the brief showing his case so far and on a large table laid out all of his notecards and the material he had photocopied and marked up during his research. He needed to find the expert opinions, quotations, statistics, dates, and any other hard evidence that would support the reasons he intended to use. Doing this before starting to draft is a good idea because it reveals where evidence is lacking or thin and what further research is necessary. If you have a lot of sources, it may help to use different-colored markers to indicate which passages will work with which of your reasons. Justin was now able to add the third level—evidence—to his case structure, including the sources from which he took it. When an article was longer than one page, he included page numbers to turn to as he drafted his paper.

> *Thesis:* Everyone, gay and straight, will benefit from extending the basic human right of marriage to all couples, regardless of sexual preference.
>
>> *Reason:* It would reinforce family values such as monogamy and the two-parent family.
>>> *Evidence:* Marriage stabilizes relationships. (Sources: Rauch 23; Dean 114)
>>> *Evidence:* Children of gays and lesbians should not be denied having two parents. (Sources: Dean 114; Sullivan; Salholz)
>>> *Evidence:* If gays can have and adopt children, they should be able to marry. (Source: Salholz)
>
>> *Reason:* It would provide a means of keeping people from burdening society.

Evidence: Spouses take care of each other. (Source: Rauch)

Reason: Denying gays and lesbians the right to marry is
discriminatory.

> *Evidence:* Marriage includes rights to legal benefits. (Source:
> Dean 112)
>
> *Evidence:* Domestic partnerships fail to provide these rights.
> (Sources: Dean 112; Salholz)
>
> *Evidence:* Barring these marriages violates many democratic
> principles. (Sources: "Declaration"; Dean 113; Salholz)

Reason: The love homosexuals have for each other is not different
from love between heterosexuals.

> *Evidence:* Many gays and lesbians are in monogamous
> relationships. (Source: Ayers 5)
>
> *Evidence:* They have the same need to make a public, legal
> commitment. (Source: Sullivan)

Following Through

Prepare a complete brief for an argument. Include both reasons and some
indication of the evidence you will use to support each one, along with a note
about sources. Remember that a brief is a flexible plan, not an outline en-
graved in stone. The plan can change as you begin drafting.

From Brief to Draft

Turning a rough outline, or brief, of your argument into a piece of prose
is never easy. Even if you know what points to bring up and in what order,
you will have to (1) determine how much space to devote to each reason,
(2) work in your evidence from sources, and (3) smoothly incorporate and
correctly cite all quotations, summaries, and paraphrases. Furthermore, you
will have to create parts of the essay that are not represented in the brief, such
as an introduction that appeals to your audience and a conclusion that does
not simply rehash all that you have said before. As you draft, you may also see
a need for paragraphs that provide background on your topic, clarify or define
an important term, or present and rebut an opposing argument. Following are
some suggestions and examples that you may find helpful as you begin to draft.

The Introduction

Some writers must work through a draft from start to finish, beginning
every piece of writing with the introductory paragraph. They ask, How can
you possibly write the middle unless you know what the beginning is like?
Other writers feel they can't write the introduction until they have written
the body of the argument. They ask, How can you introduce something until

you know what it is you are introducing? Either approach will eventually get the job done, as long as the writer takes the rhetorical context and strategy into account when drafting the introduction and goes back to revise it when the draft is completed.

Introductions are among the hardest things to write well. Remember that an introduction need not be one paragraph; it is often two or even three short ones. A good introduction (1) meets the needs of the audience by setting up the topic with just enough background information, and (2) goes right to the heart of the issue as it relates to the audience's concerns.

Should the introduction end with the thesis statement? This strategy works well in offering the easiest transition from brief to draft; it immediately sets the stage for the reasons. However, the thesis need not be the last sentence in the introduction, and it may not appear explicitly until much later in the draft—or even not at all, providing that the reader can tell what it is from the title or from reading the essay.

Student Sample: The Introduction   Our student writer Justin had to consider whether he needed to provide his readers with a detailed history of the institution of marriage and even whether people feel strongly about the value of marriage. Because they oppose same-sex marriage, he assumed that his readers were familiar with the traditions underpinning the institution. What would these readers need to be told in the introduction? Essentially that the gay and lesbian rights movement calls for extending to same-sex couples the legal right to marry and that Justin's argument supported its position.

For example, if Justin had opened with, "Americans' intolerant attitudes toward homosexuality are preventing a whole class of our citizens from exercising the right to marry," he would have been assuming that there are no valid reasons for denying same-sex marriage. Such a statement would offend his target audience members, who are not homophobic and might resent the implication that their arguments are based only in prejudice. Rather than confronting his readers, Justin's introduction attempts to establish some common ground with them:

> When two people fall deeply in love, they want to share every part of their lives with each other. For some, that could mean making a commitment, living together, and maybe having children together. But most people in love want more than that; they want to make their commitment public and legal through the ceremony of marriage, a tradition thousands of years old that has been part of almost every culture.
>
> But not everyone has the right to make that commitment. In this country, and in most others, gays and lesbians are denied the right to marry. According to many Americans, allowing them to marry would destroy the institution and threaten traditional family values. Nevertheless, "advances in gay and lesbian civil rights [are] bringing awareness and newfound determination to many," and hundreds of

same-sex couples are celebrating their commitment to each other in religious ceremonies (Ayers 6). These couples would like to make their unions legal, and we should not prohibit them. Everyone, gay and straight, will benefit from extending the basic human right of marriage to all couples, regardless of sexual preference.

Justin's first paragraph builds common ground by offering an overview of marriage that his readers are likely to share. In the second paragraph he goes on to introduce the conflict, showing his own awareness of the main objections offered by thoughtful critics of same-sex marriage. Notice the even tone with which he presents these views; this sort of care is what we defined in Chapter 1 as paying attention to ethos—in other words, presenting your own character as fair and responsible. Finally, Justin builds common ground by showing the gay and lesbian community in a very positive light, as people who love and commit to each other just as heterosexuals do.

A good introduction attracts the reader's interest. To do this, writers use a number of techniques, some more dramatic than others. They may open with the story of a particular person whose experience illustrates some aspect of the topic. Or they may attempt to startle the reader with a surprising fact or opinion, as Jonathan Rauch, one of Justin's sources did when he began his essay this way: "Whatever else marriage may or may not be, it is certainly falling apart." Generally, dictionary definitions are dull openers, but a *Newsweek* writer used one effectively to start her article on gay marriage: "Marry. 1 a) to join as husband and wife; unite in wedlock, b) to join (a man) to a woman as her husband, or (a woman) to a man as his wife." The technique works partly because the writer chose not to use the definition in an opening sentence but rather as an epigraph—words set off at the beginning of a piece of writing to introduce its theme. Pithy quotations work especially well as epigraphs. All of the above are fairly dramatic techniques, but the best and most common bit of advice about openings is that specifics work better than generalizations at catching a reader's notice; this same *Newsweek* article had as its first sentence, "Say marriage and the mind turns to three-tiered cakes, bridal gowns, baby carriages."

How you choose to open will depend on your audience. Popular periodicals like *Newsweek* are a more appropriate setting for high drama than are academic journals and college term papers, but every reader appreciates a writer's efforts to spark his or her attention.

Presenting Reasons and Evidence

We now turn to drafting the body paragraphs of the argument. While it is possible in a short argument for one paragraph to fully develop one reason, avoid thinking in terms of writing only one paragraph per reason. Multiple paragraphs are generally required to develop and support a reason.

The key thing to remember about paragraphs is that each one is a unit that performs some function in presenting the case. You ought to be able to say what the function of a given paragraph is—and your reader ought to be able to sense it. Does it introduce a reason? Does it define a term? Does it support a reason by setting up an analogy? Does another paragraph support the same reason by offering examples or some hard data or an illustrative case?

Not all paragraphs need topic sentences to announce their main point. Worry instead about opening each paragraph with some hints that allow readers to recognize the function of the paragraph. For example, some transitional word or phrase could announce to readers that you are turning from one reason to a new one. When you introduce a new reason, be sure that readers can see how it relates to the thesis. Repeating a key word or offering a synonym for one of the words in the thesis is a good idea.

Student Sample: Presenting Reasons and Evidence   As an example let's look at how Justin developed the first reason in his case. Recall that he decided to put the two reasons about benefits to society ahead of his reasons about discrimination. Of the two benefits he planned to cite, the one about strengthening family values seemed the stronger reason, so he decided to lead off with that one. Notice how Justin uses a transitional phrase to connect his first reason with the introductory material (printed earlier), which had mentioned opposing views. Also observe how Justin develops his reason over a number of paragraphs and by drawing upon multiple sources, using both paraphrase and direct quotation. (See Appendix A for guidelines on quoting and citing sources.)

> In contrast to many critics' arguments, allowing gays and lesbians to marry actually promotes family values because it encourages monogamy and gives children a two-parent home. As Jonathan Rauch, a gay writer, explains, marriage stabilizes relationships:
>
> > One of the main benefits of publicly recognized marriage is that it binds couples together not only in their own eyes but also in the eyes of society at large. Around the partners is woven a web of expectations that they will spend nights together, go to parties together, take out mortgages together, buy furniture at Ikea together, and so on—all of which helps tie them together and keep them off the streets and at home. (23)
>
> Some people would say that gays and lesbians can have these things without marriage simply by living together, but if you argue that marriage is not necessary for commitment, you are saying marriage is not necessary for heterosexuals either. Many people think it is immoral to live together and not have the legal bond of marriage. If gays and lesbians could marry, they would be "morally correct" according to this viewpoint. Craig Dean, a Washington, D.C. lawyer and activist for gay marriage, says that it is "paradoxical that mainstream America stereotypes Gays and Lesbians as unable to maintain long-term relationships, while at the same time denying them the very institutions to stabilize such relationships" (114).

Furthermore, many homosexual couples have children from previous marriages or by adoption. According to a study by the American Bar Association, gay and lesbian families with children make up six percent of the population in the United States (Dean 114). A secure environment is very important for raising children, and allowing same-sex couples to marry would promote these children having two parents, not just one. It would also send these children the positive message that marriage is the foundation for family life. As Andrew Sullivan, a senior editor of *The New Republic* asks, why should gays be denied the very same family values that many politicians are arguing everyone else should have? Why should their children be denied these values? *Newsweek* writer Eloise Salholz describes a paradox: If "more and more homosexual pairs are becoming parents . . . but cannot marry, what kind of bastardized definition of family is society imposing on their offspring?"

At this point Justin is ready to take up his next reason: Marriage provides a system by which people take care of each other, lessening the burden on society. Justin's entire essay appears on pages 109–112. You may wish to look it over carefully before you begin to draft your own paper. Note which paragraphs bring in the remaining reasons and which paragraphs smoothly present and rebut some opposing views.

The Conclusion

Once you have presented your case, what else is there to say? You probably do not need to sum up your case; going over your reasons one more time is not generally a good strategy and will likely bore your readers. And yet you know that the conclusion is no place to introduce new issues.

Strategically, you want to end by saying, "Case made!" Here are some suggestions for doing so:

Look back at your introduction. Perhaps some idea that you used there to attract your readers' attention could come into play again to frame the argument. A question you posed has an answer, a problem you raised has a solution.

Think about the larger context your argument fits into. For example, an argument about why *Huckleberry Finn* should be taught in public high schools, even if some students are offended by its language, could end by pointing out that education becomes diluted and artificial when teachers and administrators design a curriculum that avoids all controversy.

Ending with a well-worded quotation discovered in your research is sometimes effective, but try to follow it up with some words of your own, as you normally would whenever you quote.

Too many conclusions run on after their natural endings. If you are dissatisfied with your conclusion, try lopping off the last one, two, or three sentences. You may uncover the real ending.

Pay attention to style, especially in the last sentence. An awkwardly worded sentence will not have a sound of finality, but one with some rhythmic punch or consciously repeated sounds can wrap up an essay neatly.

Student Sample: The Conclusion   Following is Justin's conclusion to his argument on same-sex marriage.

> It's only natural for people in love to want to commit to each other; this desire is the same for homosexuals and lesbians as it is for heterosexuals. One recent survey showed that "over half of all lesbians and almost 40% of gay men" live in committed relationships and share a house together (Ayers 5). As Sullivan, who is gay, explains, "At some point in our lives, some of us are lucky enough to meet the person we truly love. And we want to commit to that person in front of family and country for the rest of our lives. It's the most simple, the most natural, the most human instinct in the world. How could anyone seek to oppose that?" And what does anyone gain when that right is denied? That's a question that everyone needs to ask themselves.

Justin's conclusion is unusual because although reasons usually appear in the body paragraphs of a written argument, Justin offers his fourth reason in the last paragraph: Gay and lesbian couples can love each other with the same devotion and commitment as can heterosexual couples. This reason and its development as a paragraph make an effective conclusion because they enable Justin to place the topic of same-sex marriage into the larger context of what marriage means and why anyone wishes to enter into it. Also, Justin was able to find a particularly moving quotation to convince his audience that this meaning is the same for homosexuals. The quotation could have ended the essay, but Justin wanted to conclude with words of his own that would make the readers think about their own positions.

Following Through

Using your brief as a guide, write a draft version of your argument to convince. In addition to the advice in this chapter, refer to Appendix A, which covers paraphrasing, summarizing, quoting, and incorporating and documenting source material.

Revising the Draft

Too often revising is confused with editing. Revising, however, implies making large changes in content and organization, not simply sentence-level corrections or even stylistic changes, which fall into the category of editing.

To get a sense of what is involved in revising, you should know that the brief of Justin Spidel's essay on pages 99–100 is actually a revised version.

Justin had originally written a draft with his reasons presented in a different order and without three of the sources that now appear in his paper. When Justin exchanged drafts with another classmate who was writing on the same topic, he discovered that some of her sources would also help him develop his own case more solidly. The paragraph printed below was the original third paragraph of Justin's draft, immediately following the thesis. Read this draft version, and then note how in the revised essay, printed on pages 109–112, Justin improved this part of his argument by developing the point more thoroughly in two paragraphs and by placing them toward the end of the paper.

> Not to allow same-sex marriage is clearly discriminatory. The Human Rights Act of 1977 in the District of Columbia "prohibits discrimination based on sexual orientation. According to the Act, 'every individual shall have an equal opportunity to participate in the economic, cultural, and intellectual life of the District and have an *equal opportunity to participate in all aspects of life*'" (Dean 112). If politicians are going to make such laws, they need to recognize all their implications, and follow them. Not allowing homosexuals to marry is denying the right to "participate" in an aspect of life that is important to every couple that has found love in each other. Also, the Constitution guarantees equality to every man and woman; that means nondiscrimination, something that is not happening for gays and lesbians in the present.

Read Your Own Writing Critically

As we explained in Chapter 3, being a critical reader of arguments means being an analytical reader. In that chapter we made suggestions for reading any argument; here we show what to look for in reading your own writing critically.

Read with an Eye toward Structure Remember, different parts of an argument perform different jobs. Read to see if you can divide your draft easily into its strategic parts, and be sure you can identify what role each group of paragraphs plays in the overall picture. The draft should reflect your brief, or you should be able to create a new brief from what you have written. If you have trouble identifying the working parts and how they fit together, you need to see where points are overlapping, where you are repeating yourself, or what distant parts actually belong together. This may be the time for scissors and paste, or electronic cutting and pasting if you are working at a computer.

Read with an Eye toward Rhetorical Context You may need to revise to make the rhetorical context clearer: why are you writing, with what aim, and to whom. You establish this reader awareness in the introduction, and so you need to think about your readers' values and beliefs, as well as any obvious personal data that might help explain their position on the issue—age, gender, race, occupation, economic status, and so on. You may need to revise your introduction now, finding a way to interest your readers in what you have to say. The more specific you can make your opening, the more likely your success.

Inquire into Your Own Writing   Have a dialogue with yourself about your own writing. Some of the questions that we listed on pages 44–45 will be useful here:

> Ask what you mean by the words that are central to the argument. Have you provided definitions when they are needed?
>
> Find the reasons, and note their relation to the thesis. Be able to state the connection, ideally, with the word "because": *Thesis* because *Reason.*
>
> Be able to state what assumptions lie behind your thesis and any of your reasons. Ask yourself, What else would someone have to believe to accept this as valid? If your audience is unlikely to share the assumption, then you must add an argument for it—or change your thesis.
>
> Look at your comparisons and analogies. Are they persuasive?
>
> Look at your evidence. Have you offered facts, expert opinion, illustrations, and so on? Have you presented these in a way that would not raise doubts but eliminate them?
>
> Consider your own bias. What do you stand to gain from advocating the position you take? Is your argument self-serving or truth-serving?

Get Feedback from Other Readers

Because it is hard to be objective about your own work, getting a reading from a friend, classmate, teacher, or family member is a good way to see where revision would help. An unfocused reading, however, usually isn't critical enough; casual readers may applaud the draft too readily if they agree with the thesis and condemn it if they disagree. Therefore, have your readers use a revision checklist, such as the one outlined in the box "Reader's Checklist for Revision."

Following Through

1. After you have written a draft of your own argument, revise it using the preceding suggestions. Then exchange your revised draft with a classmate's and use the "Reader's Checklist for Revision" to guide you in making suggestions for each other's drafts.

2. Read the final version of Justin Spidel's argument on pages 109–112. Then apply the questions for inquiry listed on pages 44–45 to inquire into the case presented in his argument.

3. You may or may not agree with Justin Spidel's views on same-sex marriage; however, if you were assigned to give him suggestions on how to improve his written argument, what would you advise him to do? Reread his audience profile, and use the "Reader's Checklist for Revision" to help you decide how his presentation could be improved.

READER'S CHECKLIST FOR REVISION

1. First be sure you understand the writer's intended audience, by either discussing this with the writer or reading any notes the writer has provided. Then read through the entire draft. It is helpful to number all the paragraphs so you can later refer to them by number.

2. If you can find an explicit statement of the author's thesis, underline or highlight it. If you cannot find one, do you think it is necessary that the thesis be stated explicitly, or would any reader be able to infer it easily? If the thesis is easily inferred, put it in your own words at the top of the draft.

3. How could the thesis be improved? Is it offensive, vague, or too general? Does it have a single focus? Is it clearly stated? Suggest more concrete diction, if possible.

4. Circle the key terms of the thesis—that is, the words most central to the point. Could there be disagreement about the meaning of any of these terms? If so, has the author clarified what he or she means by these terms?

5. Look for the structure and strategy of the argument. Underline or highlight the sentences that most clearly present the reasons, and write Reason 1, Reason 2, and so forth in the margin. If identifying the reasons is not easy, indicate this problem to the author. Think also about whether the author has arranged the reasons in the best order. Make suggestions for improvement.

6. Which is the author's best reason? Why would it appeal to the audience? Has the author strategically placed it in the best position for making his or her case?

7. Look for any weak parts in the argument. What reasons need more or better support? Next to any weakly supported reasons, write questions to let the author know what factual information seems lacking, what sources don't seem solid or credible, what statements sound too general, or what reasoning—such as analogies—seems shaky. Are there any reasons for which more research is in order?

8. Does the author show an awareness of opposing arguments? Where? If not, should this be added? Even if you agree with this argument, take the viewpoint of a member of the opposition: What are the best challenges you can make to anything the author has said?

9. Evaluate the introduction and conclusion.

Editing and Proofreading

The final steps of writing any argument are editing and proofreading, which we take up in Appendix B.

Student Sample: An Essay to Convince

JUSTIN SPIDEL
Who Should Have the Right to Marry?

WHEN TWO people fall deeply in love, they want to share every part   *1*
of their lives with each other. For some, that could mean making a commitment, living together, and maybe having children together. But most people
in love want more than that; they want to make their commitment public and
legal through the ceremony of marriage, a tradition thousands of years old that
has been part of almost every culture.

But not everyone has the right to make that commitment. In this country, and in most others, gays and lesbians are denied the right to marry. According to many citizens and politicians, allowing them the right to marry
would destroy the institution and threaten traditional family values. Nevertheless, "advances in gay and lesbian civil rights [are] bringing awareness and
newfound determination to many," and hundreds of same-sex couples are
celebrating their commitment to each other in religious ceremonies (Ayers 6).
These couples would like to make their unions legal, and we should not
prohibit them. Everyone, gay and straight, will benefit from extending the
basic human right of marriage to all couples, regardless of sexual preference.

In contrast to many critics' arguments, allowing gays and lesbians to
marry actually promotes family values because it encourages monogamy and
gives children a two-parent home. As Jonathan Rauch, a gay writer, explains,
marriage stabilizes relationships:

> One of the main benefits of publicly recognized marriage is that it
> binds couples together not only in their own eyes but also in the eyes
> of society at large. Around the partners is woven a web of expectations
> that they will spend nights together, go to parties together, take out
> mortgages together, buy furniture at Ikea together, and so on—all of
> which helps tie them together and keep them off the streets and at
> home. (23)

Some people would say that gays and lesbians can have these things without
marriage simply by living together, but if you argue that marriage is not necessary for commitment, you are saying marriage is not necessary for heterosexuals
either. Many people think it is immoral to live together and not have the legal
bond of marriage. If gays and lesbians could marry, they would be "morally
correct" according to this viewpoint. Craig Dean, a Washington, D.C., lawyer
and activist for gay marriage, says that it is "paradoxical that mainstream America stereotypes Gays and Lesbians as unable to maintain long-term relationships, while at the same time denying them the very institutions to stabilize
such relationships" (114).

Furthermore, many homosexual couples have children from previous marriages or by adoption. According to a study by the American Bar Association, gay and lesbian families with children make up six percent of the population in the United States (Dean 114). A secure environment is very important for raising children, and allowing same-sex couples to marry would promote these children having two parents, not just one. It would also send these children the positive message that marriage is the foundation for family life. As Andrew Sullivan, a senior editor of *The New Republic,* asks, why should gays be denied the very same family values that many politicians are arguing everyone else should have? Why should their children be denied these values? *Newsweek* writer Eloise Salholz describes a paradox: If "more and more homosexual pairs are becoming parents . . . but cannot marry, what kind of bastardized definition of family is society imposing on their offspring?"

Also, binding people together in marriage benefits society because marriage provides a system for people to take care of each other. Marriage means that individuals are not a complete burden on society when they become sick, injured, old, or unemployed. Jonathan Rauch argues, "If marriage has any meaning at all, it is that when you collapse from a stroke, there will be at least one other person whose 'job' it is to drop everything and come to your aid" (22). Rauch's point is that this benefit of marriage would result from gay marriages as well as straight, and in fact, may be even more important for homosexuals and lesbians because their relationships with parents and other relatives may be strained, and they are also less likely than heterosexuals to have children to take care of them in their old age. Same-sex couples already show such devotion to each other; it's just that the public recognition of legal marriage helps to keep all spouses together through hard times.

In spite of these benefits, many people say that same-sex marriage should not be allowed because it would upset our society's conventional definition of marriage as a bond between people of opposite sexes. As William Bennett has written, letting people of the same sex marry "would obscure marriage's enormously consequential function—procreation and childrearing." Procreation may be a consequence of marriage, but it is not the main reason anymore that people get married. Today "even for heterosexuals, marriage is becoming an emotional union and commitment rather than an arrangement to produce and protect children" ("Marriage" 770). And what about heterosexual couples who are sterile? No one would say that they should not be allowed to marry. If the right to marry is based on the possibility of having children, "then a post-menopausal woman who applies for a marriage license should be turned away at the courthouse door" (Rauch 22). No one would seriously expect every couple who gets married to prove that they are capable of having children and intend to do so. That would be a clear violation of their individual rights.

In the same way, to outlaw same-sex marriage is clearly discriminatory. According to Craig Dean, "Marriage is an important civil right because it gives societal recognition and legal protection to a relationship and confers numerous benefits to spouses" (112). Denying same-sex marriage means that gays and lesbians cannot enjoy material benefits such as health insurance through a spouse's employer, life insurance benefits, tax preferences, leaves for bereavement, and inheritance. In some states, laws about domestic partnership give same-sex couples some of these rights, but they are never guaranteed as they would be if the couple were legally next-of-kin. Thomas Stoddard, a lawyer, says that domestic partnership is the equivalent of "second-class citizenship" (qtd. in Salholz).

Aside from these concrete types of discrimination, denying same-sex marriage keeps gay and lesbian citizens from enjoying the basic human right to "life, liberty, and the pursuit of happiness." The Human Rights Act of 1977 in the District of Columbia makes one of the strongest stands against discrimination based on sexual orientation. According to the Act, "every individual shall have an equal opportunity to participate in the economic, cultural, and intellectual life of the District and have an equal opportunity to participate in all aspects of life" (qtd. in Dean 113). Not allowing homosexuals to marry does deny them the right to "participate" in an aspect of life that is important to most every couple that has found love in each other. The Hawaii Supreme Court ruled in 1993 that the ban on gay marriage is probably in violation of the Constitution (Salholz).

Of course, many churches will never agree to perform these marriages because they believe that homosexuality is a sin. It is possible to debate the interpretations of the Bible passages that these people cite as evidence, and many religious leaders do. The separation of church and state allows all churches to follow their own doctrines, and many things that are legal in this country are disapproved of by some churches. My point is that the government should not deny the *legal* right to marry in relationships where couples want to express their love towards each other.

It's only natural for people in love to want to commit to each other; this *10* desire is the same for homosexuals and lesbians as it is for heterosexuals. One recent survey showed that "over half of all lesbians and almost 40% of gay men" live in committed relationships and share a house together (Ayers 5). As Sullivan, who is gay, explains, "At some point in our lives, some of us are lucky enough to meet the person we truly love. And we want to commit to that person in front of family and country for the rest of our lives. It's the most simple, the most natural, the most human instinct in the world. How could anyone seek to oppose that?" And what does anyone gain when that right is denied? That's a question that everyone needs to ask themselves.

WORKS CITED

Ayers, Tess, and Paul Brown. *The Essential Guide to Lesbian and Gay Weddings.* San Francisco: Harper San Francisco, 1994.

Bennett, William, "Leave Marriage Alone." *Newsweek* June 3, 1996: 27.

Dean, Craig R. "Gay Marriage: A Civil Right." *The Journal of Homosexuality* 27.3/4 (1994): 111–15.

"Marriage." *The Encyclopedia of Homosexuality.* Ed. Wayne R. Dynes. New York: Garland Publishing, 1990.

Rauch, Jonathan. "For Better or Worse?" *The New Republic* May 6, 1996: 18–23.

Salholz, Eloise. "For Better or For Worse." *Newsweek* May 24, 1993: 69.

Sullivan, Andrew. "Let Gays Marry." *Newsweek* June 3, 1996: 26.

CHAPTER SEVEN

Appealing to the Whole Person: Arguing to Persuade

In Chapter 1 we defined persuasion as "convincing *plus*" to suggest the three forms of appeal in addition to reason that are required for persuasion: the appeals to the writer's character; to the emotions of the audience; and to style, the artful use of language itself. Building on what you learned about making cases in Chapter 6, this chapter's goal is to help you understand and control this wider range of appeals. But why? Shouldn't reason be enough?

Perhaps it would be if human beings were like *Star Trek*'s Mr. Spock, truly rational creatures. But human beings are only sometimes rational—and even then imperfectly. We often agree with an argument but lack the courage or motivation to translate our assent into action.

Persuasion, then, aims to close the gap between assent and action. Because persuasion seeks a deeper and stronger commitment from readers, it appeals to the whole person, to our full humanity, not just to the mind. It offers reasons, of course, because people respond to good reasons. But it also encourages the reader to identify with the writer, because people respond not just to the quality of an argument but also to the quality of the arguer. In addition, the persuader wants to stir the reader's emotions, because strong feelings reinforce the will to act; persuasion works on the heart as much as the mind. Finally, choices about style matter in persuasion, because human beings are language-using animals whose response to what is said depends on how well it is said.

A MATTER OF EMPHASIS: WHEN TO CONVINCE AND WHEN TO PERSUADE

When should you aim to persuade rather than to convince? Always notice what an academic assignment calls for, because the full range of persuasive appeal is not always appropriate for written arguments in college. In general, the more academic the audience or the more purely intellectual the issue, the less appropriate it is to appeal to the whole person. A philosophy or science paper might often require you to convince but rarely to persuade. In such cases you should confine yourself primarily to thesis, reasons, and evidence.

But when you are working with public issues, with matters of policy or questions of right and wrong, persuasion's fuller range of appeal is usually appropriate because such topics address a broader readership and involve a more inclusive community. Arguments in these areas affect not just how we think but how we act, and the heightened urgency of persuasion goes further in sparking action or fundamental change.

While convincing primarily requires that we control case-making, persuasion asks us to make conscious decisions about three other appeals as well. One, we must gain our readers' confidence and respect through the deliberate projection of our good character. Two, we must touch our readers' emotions. And, three, we must focus on language itself as a means of affecting people's thoughts and behavior. The writer who aims to persuade integrates these other forms of appeal with a well-made case, deliberately crafting the essay so that they all work together.

As with convincing, writing a persuasive argument begins with inquiry and research—a patient search for the truth as preparation for earning a claim to truth. However, before you can move from a general idea of your own position to a specific thesis, you must think about the audience you seek to persuade.

ANALYZING YOUR READERS

Persuasion begins with difference and, when it works, ends with identity. That is, we expect that before reading our argument, our readers will differ from us not only in beliefs but also in attitudes and desires. A successful persuasive argument brings readers and writer together; it creates a sense of connection between parties that were previously separate in viewpoint. But what means can we use to overcome difference and create a sense of identity? First, we need to focus on our readers and attempt to understand their frame of mind using the following questions.

Who Is the Audience, and How Do They View the Topic?

Who are my readers? How do I define them in terms of age, economic and social class, gender, education, and so forth?

What typical attitudes or stances toward my topic do they have?

What in their background or daily experiences helps explain their point of view?

What are they likely to know about my topic?

How might they be uninformed or misinformed about it?

How would they like to see the problem, question, or issue resolved, answered, or handled? Why? That is, what personal stake do they have in the topic?

In what larger framework—religious, ethical, political, economic—do they place my topic? That is, what general beliefs and values are involved?

As you answer these questions, you should begin to see possible appeals to your readership. But keep in mind that good persuaders are able to empathize and sympathize with other people, building bridges of commonality and solidarity.

What Are Our Differences?

Audience analysis is not complete until you can specify exactly what divides you from your readers. Sometimes specifying difference is difficult to do before formulating a detailed case; understanding exactly what divides you from your readers comes later, at the point of the first draft. But as soon as you can, you must clarify differences; knowing exactly what separates you from your readers tells you what to emphasize in making your case and in choosing other strategies of appeal. These questions can help:

Is the difference a matter of assumptions? If so, how can I shake my readers' confidence in their assumptions and offer another set of assumptions favorable to my position?

Is the difference a matter of principle, the application of general rules to specific cases? If so, should I dispute the principle itself and offer a competing one the audience will also value? Or should I show why the principle should not apply in some specific instance relevant to my case?

Is the difference a matter of a hierarchy of values—that is, do we value the same things but to different degrees? If so, how might I restructure my readers' values?

Is the difference a matter of ends or of means? If of ends, how can I show that my vision of what ought to be is better or that realizing my ends will also secure the ends my readers value? If a difference of means, how can I show that my methods are justified and effective, more likely to bear fruit than others?

Is the difference a matter of interpretation? If so, how can I shake my readers' confidence in the traditional or common interpretation of something and show them that my interpretation is better, that it accounts for the facts more adequately?

Is the difference a matter of implications or consequences? If so, how can I convince my readers that what they fear may happen will not happen, that it will not be as bad as they think, or that other implications or consequences outweigh any negatives?

What Do We Have in Common?

In seeking to define the common ground you and your readers share, the key point to remember is that no matter how sharp the disagreements that divide you from those you hope to persuade, resources for identification always exist and may be discovered through these sorts of questions:

Do we have a shared local identity—as members of the same organization, for example, or students at the same university?

Do we share a more abstract, collective identity—as citizens of the same region or nation, as worshippers in the same religion, and so forth?

Do we share a common cause—such as promoting the good of the community, preventing child abuse, or overcoming racial prejudice?

Is there a shared experience or human activity—raising children, caring for aging parents, helping a friend in distress, struggling to make ends meet?

Can we connect through a well-known event or cultural happening—a popular movie, a best-selling book, something in the news that would interest both you and your readers?

Is there a historical event, person, or document that we both respect?

READING A PERSUASIVE ESSAY

To illustrate the importance of audience analysis, we will turn to a classic essay of the twentieth century, Martin Luther King's "Letter from Birmingham Jail," a brilliant example of the art of persuasion. As we will see, King masterfully analyzed his audience and used the full range of appeals to suit that particular readership.

Background

To appreciate King's persuasive powers, we must first understand the events that led up to the "Letter" and also the actions King wanted to move his readers to take. As president of the Southern Christian Leadership Conference, a civil rights organization dedicated to nonviolent social change, King had been organizing and participating in demonstrations in Birmingham, Alabama, in 1963. He was arrested, and while he was in jail, eight white Alabama clergymen of various denominations issued a public statement reacting to his activities. Published in a local newspaper, the statement deplored the illegal demonstrations of King and his organization as "unwise and untimely":

We the undersigned clergymen are among those who, in January, issued "An Appeal for Law and Order and Common Sense," in dealing with racial problems in Alabama. We expressed understanding that honest convictions in racial matters could properly be pursued in the courts, but urged that decisions of those courts should in the meantime be peacefully obeyed.

Since that time there had been some evidence of increased forbearance and a willingness to face facts. Responsible citizens have undertaken to work on various problems which cause racial friction and unrest. In Birmingham, recent public events have given indication that we all have opportunity for a new constructive and realistic approach to racial problems.

However, we are now confronted by a series of demonstrations by some of our Negro citizens, directed and led in part by outsiders. We recognize the natural impatience of people who feel that their hopes are slow in being realized. But we are convinced that these demonstrations are unwise and untimely.

We agree rather with certain local Negro leadership which has called for honest and open negotiation of racial issues in our area. And we believe this kind of facing of issues can best be accomplished by citizens of our own metropolitan area, white and Negro, meeting with their knowledge and experience of the local situation. All of us need to face that responsibility and find proper channels for its accomplishment.

Just as we formerly pointed out that "hatred and violence have no sanction in our religious and political traditions," we also point out that such actions as incite to hatred and violence, however technically peaceful those actions may be, have not contributed to the resolution of our local problems. We do not believe that these days of new hope are days when extreme measures are justified in Birmingham.

We commend the community as a whole, and the local news media and law enforcement officials in particular, on the calm manner in which these demonstrations have been handled. We urge the public to continue to show restraint should the demonstrations continue, and the law enforcement officials to remain calm and continue to protect our city from violence.

We further strongly urge our own Negro community to withdraw support from these demonstrations, and to unite locally in working peacefully for a better Birmingham. When rights are consistently denied, a cause should be pressed in the courts and in negotiations among local leaders, and not in the streets. We appeal to both our white and Negro citizenry to observe the principles of law and order and common sense.

Signed by:
C. C. J. Carpenter, D.D., LL.D., *Bishop of Alabama*
Joseph A. Durick, D.D., *Auxiliary Bishop, Diocese of Mobile,*
    Birmingham
Rabbi Milton L. Grafman, *Temple Emanu-El, Birmingham, Alabama*
Bishop Paul Hardin, *Bishop of the Alabama-West Florida Conference*
    of the Methodist Church

> *Bishop* Nolan B. Harmon, *Bishop of the North Alabama Conference*
> *of the Methodist Church*
> George M. Murray, D.D., LL.D., *Bishop Coadjutor, Episcopal Diocese*
> *of Alabama*
> Edward V. Ramage, *Moderator, Synod of the Alabama Presbyterian*
> *Church in the United States*
> Earl Stallings, *Pastor, First Baptist Church, Birmingham, Alabama*

In his cell, King began his letter on the margins of that newspaper page, addressing it specifically to the eight clergymen in the hope that he could move them from disapproval to support, from inaction to a recognition of the necessity of the demonstrations. As a public figure, King knew that his letter would reach a larger audience, including the demonstrators themselves, who were galvanized by its message when 50,000 copies were later distributed by his supporters. In the years since, King's letter has often been published, reaching an audience around the world with its argument for civil disobedience in the service of a higher, moral law.

The Basic Message

King's letter is long; he even apologizes to his readers for having written so much. Its length is not due to its basic message, however, but to its persuasive appeals—to the way the main points are made. Before turning to King's "Letter from Birmingham Jail," read the following summary, which differs as greatly from King's prose as a nursery song differs from a Beethoven symphony.

> Because I am the leader of an organization that fights injustice, it is most appropriate for me to be in Birmingham, where human rights are being violated. Our campaign of nonviolent civil disobedience was not rash and unpremeditated but the result of a history of failed negotiations and broken promises. We aim to increase tensions here until the city leaders realize that dialogue must occur. Our actions are not untimely but long overdue, given that blacks have been denied their civil rights in this country for over 340 years.
>
> While we advocate breaking some laws, we distinguish between moral laws and immoral laws that degrade the human personality. The former must be obeyed, the latter disobeyed openly and lovingly. We may be extremists, but people who accomplish great things are often so labeled, and our nonviolent protests are preferable to inaction.
>
> In failing to support us, white Southern religious leaders such as yourselves fail to meet the challenges of social injustice. You should not praise the police for their work at breaking up the demonstrations, but rather praise the demonstrators for standing up for their human dignity.

MARTIN LUTHER KING, JR.
Letter from Birmingham Jail

April 16, 1963

My Dear Fellow Clergymen:

WHILE CONFINED here in the Birmingham city jail, I came across your   *1*
recent statement calling my present activities "unwise and untimely." Seldom do
I pause to answer criticism of my work and ideas. If I sought to answer all the
criticisms that cross my desk, my secretaries would have little time for anything
other than such correspondence in the course of the day, and I would have no
time for constructive work. But since I feel that you are men of genuine good
will and that your criticisms are sincerely set forth, I want to try to answer your
statement in what I hope will be patient and reasonable terms.

I think I should indicate why I am here in Birmingham, since you have
been influenced by the view which argues against "outsiders coming in." I have
the honor of serving as president of the Southern Christian Leadership Conference, an organization operating in every southern state, with headquarters in
Atlanta, Georgia. We have some eighty-five affiliated organizations across the
South, and one of them is the Alabama Christian Movement for Human Rights.
Frequently we share staff, educational, and financial resources with our affiliates.
Several months ago the affiliate here in Birmingham asked us to be on call to
engage in a nonviolent direct-action program if such were deemed necessary. We
readily consented, and when the hour came we lived up to our promise. So I,
along with several members of my staff, am here because I was invited here. I am
here because I have organizational ties here.

But more basically, I am in Birmingham because injustice is here. Just as the
prophets of the eighth century B.C. left their villages and carried their "thus saith
the Lord" far beyond the boundaries of their home towns, and just as the Apostle
Paul left his village of Tarsus and carried the gospel of Jesus Christ to the far
corners of the Greco-Roman world, so am I compelled to carry the gospel of
freedom beyond my own home town. Like Paul, I must constantly respond to
the Macedonian call for aid.

Moreover, I am cognizant of the interrelatedness of all communities and
states. I cannot sit idly by in Atlanta and not be concerned about what happens in
Birmingham. Injustice anywhere is a threat to justice everywhere. We are caught
in an inescapable network of mutuality, tied in a single garment of destiny. Whatever affects one directly, affects all indirectly. Never again can we afford to live
with the narrow, provincial "outside agitator" idea. Anyone who lives inside the
United States can never be considered an outsider anywhere within its bounds.

You deplore the demonstrations taking place in Birmingham. But your   *5*
statement, I am sorry to say, fails to express a similar concern for the conditions
that brought about the demonstrations. I am sure that none of you would want
to rest content with the superficial kind of social analysis that deals merely
with effects and does not grapple with underlying causes. It is unfortunate that

demonstrations are taking place in Birmingham, but it is even more unfortunate that the city's white power structure left the Negro community with no alternative.

In any nonviolent campaign there are four basic steps: collection of the facts to determine whether injustices exist; negotiation; self-purification; and direct action. We have gone through all these steps in Birmingham. There can be no gainsaying the fact that racial injustice engulfs this community. Birmingham is probably the most thoroughly segregated city in the United States. Its ugly record of brutality is widely known. Negroes have experienced grossly unjust treatment in the courts. There have been more unsolved bombings of Negro homes and churches in Birmingham than in any other city in the nation. These are the hard, brutal facts of the case. On the basis of these conditions, Negro leaders sought to negotiate with the city fathers. But the latter consistently refused to engage in good-faith negotiation.

Then, last September, came the opportunity to talk with leaders of Birmingham's economic community. In the course of the negotiations, certain promises were made by the merchants—for example, to remove the stores' humiliating racial signs. On the basis of these promises, the Reverend Fred Shuttlesworth and the leaders of the Alabama Christian Movement for Human Rights agreed to a moratorium on all demonstrations. As the weeks and months went by, we realized that we were the victims of a broken promise. A few signs, briefly removed, returned; the others remained.

As in so many past experiences, our hopes had been blasted, and the shadow of deep disappointment settled upon us. We had no alternative except to prepare for direct action, whereby we would present our very bodies as a means of laying our case before the conscience of the local and the national community. Mindful of the difficulties involved, we decided to undertake a process of self-purification. We began a series of workshops on nonviolence, and we repeatedly asked ourselves: "Are you able to accept blows without retaliating?" "Are you able to endure the ordeal of jail?" We decided to schedule our direct-action program for the Easter season, realizing that except for Christmas, this is the main shopping period of the year. Knowing that a strong economic-withdrawal program would be the by-product of direct action, we felt that this would be the best time to bring pressure to bear on the merchants for the needed change.

Then it occurred to us that Birmingham's mayoral election was coming up in March, and we speedily decided to postpone action until after election day. When we discovered that the Commissioner of Public Safety, Eugene "Bull" Connor, had piled up enough votes to be in the run-off, we decided again to postpone action until the day after the run-off so that the demonstrations could not be used to cloud the issues. Like many others, we waited to see Mr. Connor defeated, and to this end we endured postponement after postponement. Having aided in this community need, we felt that our direct-action program could be delayed no longer.

You may well ask: "Why direct action? Why sit-ins, marches and so forth? Isn't negotiation a better path?" You are quite right in calling for ne-   *10* gotiation. Indeed, this is the very purpose of direct action. Nonviolent direct action seeks to create such a crisis and foster such a tension that a community which has constantly refused to negotiate is forced to confront the issue. It seeks so to dramatize the issue that it can no longer be ignored. My citing the creation of tension as part of the work of the nonviolent-resister may sound rather shocking. But I must confess that I am not afraid of the word "tension." I have earnestly opposed violent tension, but there is a type of constructive, nonviolent tension which is necessary for growth. Just as Socrates felt that it was necessary to create a tension in the mind so that individuals could rise from the bondage of myths and half-truths to the unfettered realm of creative analysis and objective appraisal, so must we see the need for nonviolent gadflies to create the kind of tension in society that will help men rise from the dark depths of prejudice and racism to the majestic heights of understanding and brotherhood.

The purpose of our direct-action program is to create a situation so crisis-packed that it will inevitably open the door to negotiation. I therefore concur with you in your call for negotiation. Too long has our beloved South-land been bogged down in a tragic effort to live in monologue rather than dialogue.

One of the basic points in your statement is that the action that I and my associates have taken in Birmingham is untimely. Some have asked: "Why didn't you give the new city administration time to act?" The only answer that I can give to this query is that the new Birmingham administration must be prodded about as much as the outgoing one, before it will act. We are sadly mistaken if we feel that the election of Albert Boutwell as mayor will bring the millennium to Birmingham. While Mr. Boutwell is a much more gentle person than Mr. Connor, they are both segregationists, dedicated to mainte-nance of the status quo. I have hope that Mr. Boutwell will be reasonable enough to see the futility of massive resistance to desegregation. But he will not see this without pressure from devotees of civil rights. My friends, I must say to you that we have not made a single gain in civil rights without deter-mined legal and nonviolent pressure. Lamentably, it is an historical fact that privileged groups seldom give up their privileges voluntarily. Individuals may see the moral light and voluntarily give up their unjust posture; but, as Rein-hold Niebuhr has reminded us, groups tend to be more immoral than individuals.

We know through painful experience that freedom is never voluntarily given by the oppressor; it must be demanded by the oppressed. Frankly, I have yet to engage in a direct-action campaign that was "well timed" in the view of those who have not suffered unduly from the disease of segregation. For years now I have heard the word "Wait!" It rings in the ear of every Negro with piercing familiarity. This "Wait" has almost always meant "Never." We must come to see, with one of our distinguished jurists, that "justice too long delayed is justice denied."

We have waited for more than 340 years for our constitutional God-given rights. The nations of Asia and Africa are moving with jetlike speed toward gaining political independence, but we still creep at horse-and-buggy pace toward gaining a cup of coffee at a lunch counter. Perhaps it is easy for those who have never felt the stinging darts of segregation to say, "Wait." But when you have seen vicious mobs lynch your mothers and fathers at will and drown your sisters and brothers at whim; when you have seen hate-filled policemen curse, kick, and even kill your black brothers and sisters; when you see the vast majority of your twenty million Negro brothers smothering in an airtight cage of poverty in the midst of an affluent society; when you suddenly find your tongue twisted and your speech stammering as you seek to explain to your six-year-old daughter why she can't go to the public amusement park that has just been advertised on television, and see tears welling up in her eyes when she is told that Funtown is closed to colored children, and see ominous clouds of inferiority beginning to form in her little mental sky, and see her beginning to distort her personality by developing an unconscious bitterness toward white people; when you have to concoct an answer for a five-year-old son who is asking: "Daddy, why do white people treat colored people so mean?"; when you take a cross-country drive and find it necessary to sleep night after night in the uncomfortable corners of your automobile because no motel will accept you; when you are humiliated day in and day out by nagging signs reading "white" and "colored"; when your first name becomes "nigger," your middle name becomes "boy" (however old you are), and your last name becomes "John," and your wife and mother are never given the respected title "Mrs."; when you are harried by day and haunted by night by the fact that you are a Negro, living constantly at tiptoe stance, never quite knowing what to expect next, and are plagued with inner fears and outer resentments; when you are forever fighting a degenerating sense of "nobodiness"—then you will understand why we find it difficult to wait. There comes a time when the cup of endurance runs over, and men are no longer willing to be plunged into the abyss of despair. I hope, sirs, you can understand our legitimate and unavoidable impatience.

You express a great deal of anxiety over our willingness to break laws.   15
This is certainly a legitimate concern. Since we so diligently urge people to obey the Supreme Court's decision of 1954 outlawing segregation in the public schools, at first glance it may seem rather paradoxical for us consciously to break laws. One may well ask: "How can you advocate breaking some laws and obeying others?" The answer lies in the fact that there are two types of laws: just and unjust. I would be the first to advocate obeying just laws. One has not only a legal but a moral responsibility to obey just laws. Conversely, one has a moral responsibility to disobey unjust laws. I would agree with St. Augustine that "an unjust law is no law at all."

Now, what is the difference between the two? How does one determine whether a law is just or unjust? A just law is a man-made code that squares with the moral law or the law of God. An unjust law is a code that is out of harmony with the moral law. To put it in the terms of St. Thomas Aquinas: An unjust law is a human law that is not rooted in eternal law and natural law.

Any law that uplifts human personality is just. Any law that degrades human personality is unjust. All segregation statutes are unjust because segregation distorts the soul and damages the personality. It gives the segregator a false sense of superiority and the segregated a false sense of inferiority. Segregation, to use the terminology of the Jewish philosopher Martin Buber, substitutes an "I–it" relationship for an "I–thou" relationship and ends up relegating persons to the status of things. Hence, segregation is not only politically, economically, and sociologically unsound, it is morally wrong and sinful. Paul Tillich has said that sin is separation. Is not segregation an existential expression of man's tragic separation, his awful estrangement, his terrible sinfulness? Thus it is that I can urge men to obey the 1954 decision of the Supreme Court, for it is morally right; and I can urge them to disobey segregation ordinances, for they are morally wrong.

Let us consider a more concrete example of just and unjust laws. An unjust law is a code that a numerical or power majority group compels a minority group to obey but does not make binding on itself. This is *difference* made legal. By the same token, a just law is a code that a majority compels a minority to follow and that it is willing to follow itself. This is *sameness* made legal.

Let me give another explanation. A law is unjust if it is inflicted on a minority that, as a result of being denied the right to vote, had no part in enacting or devising the law. Who can say that the legislature of Alabama which set up that state's segregation laws was democratically elected? Throughout Alabama all sorts of devious methods are used to prevent Negroes from becoming registered voters, and there are some counties in which, even though Negroes constitute a majority of the population, not a single Negro is registered. Can any law enacted under such circumstances be considered democratically structured?

Sometimes a law is just on its face and unjust in its application. For instance, I have been arrested on a charge of parading without a permit. Now, there is nothing wrong in having an ordinance which requires a permit for a parade. But such an ordinance becomes unjust when it is used to maintain segregation and to deny citizens the First-Amendment privilege of peaceful assembly and protest.

I hope you are able to see the distinction I am trying to point out. In no sense do I advocate evading or defying the law, as would the rabid segregationist. That would lead to anarchy. One who breaks an unjust law must do so openly, lovingly, and with a willingness to accept the penalty. I submit that an individual who breaks a law that conscience tells him is unjust, and who willingly accepts the penalty of imprisonment in order to arouse the conscience of the community over its injustice, is in reality expressing the highest respect for law.

Of course, there is nothing new about this kind of civil disobedience. It was evidenced sublimely in the refusal of Shadrach, Meshach, and Abednego to obey the laws of Nebuchadnezzar, on the ground that a higher moral law was at stake. It was practiced superbly by the early Christians, who were

20

willing to face hungry lions and the excruciating pain of chopping blocks rather than submit to certain unjust laws of the Roman Empire. To a degree, academic freedom is a reality today because Socrates practiced civil disobedience. In our own nation, the Boston Tea Party represented a massive act of civil disobedience.

We should never forget that everything Adolf Hitler did in Germany was "legal" and everything the Hungarian freedom fighters did in Hungary was "illegal." It was "illegal" to aid and comfort a Jew in Hitler's Germany. Even so, I am sure that, had I lived in Germany at the time, I would have aided and comforted my Jewish brothers. If today I lived in a Communist country where certain principles dear to the Christian faith are suppressed, I would openly advocate disobeying that country's antireligious laws.

I must make two honest confessions to you, my Christian and Jewish brothers. First, I must confess that over the past few years I have been gravely disappointed with the white moderate. I have almost reached the regrettable conclusion that the Negro's great stumbling block in his stride toward freedom is not the White Citizen's Counciler or the Ku Klux Klanner, but the white moderate, who is more devoted to "order" than to justice; who prefers a negative peace which is the presence of tension to a positive peace which is the presence of justice; who constantly says: "I agree with you in the goal you seek, but I cannot agree with your methods of direct action"; who paternalistically believes he can set the timetable for another man's freedom; who lives by a mythical concept of time and who constantly advises the Negro to wait for a "more convenient season." Shallow understanding from people of good will is more frustrating than absolute misunderstanding from people of ill will. Lukewarm acceptance is much more bewildering than outright rejection.

I had hoped that the white moderate would understand that law and order exist for the purpose of establishing justice and that when they fail in this purpose they become the dangerously structured dams that block the flow of social progress. I had hoped that the white moderate would understand that the present tension in the South is a necessary phase of the transition from an obnoxious negative peace, in which the Negro passively accepted his unjust plight, to a substantive and positive peace, in which all men will respect the dignity and worth of human personality. Actually, we who engage in nonviolent direct action are not the creators of tension. We merely bring to the surface the hidden tension that is already alive. We bring it out in the open, where it can be seen and dealt with. Like a boil that can never be cured so long as it is covered up but must be opened with all its ugliness to the natural medicines of air and light, injustice must be exposed, with all the tension its exposure creates, to the light of human conscience and the air of national opinion before it can be cured.

In your statement you assert that our actions, even though peaceful, must *25* be condemned because they precipitate violence. But is this a logical assertion?

Isn't this like condemning a robbed man because his possession of money precipitated the evil act of robbery? Isn't this like condemning Socrates because his unswerving commitment to truth and his philosophical inquiries precipitated the act by the misguided populace in which they made him drink hemlock? Isn't this like condemning Jesus because his unique God-consciousness and never-ceasing devotion to God's will precipitated the evil act of crucifixion? We must come to see that, as the federal courts have consistently affirmed, it is wrong to urge an individual to cease his efforts to gain his basic constitutional rights because the quest may precipitate violence. Society must protect the robbed and punish the robber.

I had also hoped that the white moderate would reject the myth concerning time in relation to the struggle for freedom. I have just received a letter from a white brother in Texas. He writes: "All Christians know that the colored people will receive equal rights eventually, but it is possible that you are in too great a religious hurry. It has taken Christianity almost two thousand years to accomplish what it has. The teachings of Christ take time to come to earth." Such an attitude stems from a tragic misconception of time, from the strangely irrational notion that there is something in the very flow of time that will inevitably cure all ills. Actually, time itself is neutral; it can be used either destructively or constructively. More and more I feel that the people of ill will have used time much more effectively than have the people of good will. We will have to repent in this generation not merely for the hateful words and actions of the bad people but for the appalling silence of the good people. Human progress never rolls in on wheels of inevitability; it comes through the tireless efforts of men willing to be co-workers with God, and without this hard work, time itself becomes an ally of the forces of social stagnation. We must use time creatively, in the knowledge that the time is always ripe to do right. Now is the time to make real the promise of democracy and transform our pending national elegy into a creative psalm of brotherhood. Now is the time to lift our national policy from the quicksand of racial injustice to the solid rock of human dignity.

You speak of our activity in Birmingham as extreme. At first I was rather disappointed that fellow clergymen would see my nonviolent efforts as those of an extremist. I began thinking about the fact that I stand in the middle of two opposing forces in the Negro community. One is a force of complacency, made up in part of Negroes who, as a result of long years of oppression, are so drained of self-respect and a sense of "somebodiness" that they have adjusted to segregation; and in part of a few middle-class Negroes who, because of a degree of academic and economic security and because in some ways they profit by segregation, have become insensitive to the problems of the masses. The other force is one of bitterness and hatred, and it comes perilously close to advocating violence. It is expressed in the various black nationalists groups that are springing up across the nation, the largest and best-known being Elijah Muhammad's Muslim movement. Nourished by the Negro's frustration over the continued existence of racial discrimination, this movement is made up of people who have lost faith in America, who have absolutely repudiated Christianity, and who have concluded that the white man is an incorrigible "devil."

I have tried to stand between these two forces, saying that we need emulate neither the "do-nothingism" of the complacent nor the hatred and despair of the black nationalist. For there is the more excellent way of love and nonviolent protest. I am grateful to God that, through the influence of the Negro church, the way of nonviolence became an integral part of our struggle.

If this philosophy had not emerged, by now many streets of the South would, I am convinced, be flowing with blood. And I am further convinced that if our white brothers dismiss as "rabble-rousers" and "outside agitators" those of us who employ nonviolent direct action, and if they refuse to support our nonviolent efforts, millions of the Negroes will, out of frustration and despair, seek solace and security in black-nationalist ideologies—a development that would inevitably lead to a frightening racial nightmare.

Oppressed people cannot remain oppressed forever. The yearning for *30* freedom eventually manifests itself, and that is what has happened to the American Negro. Something within has reminded him of his birthright of freedom, and something without has reminded him that it can be gained. Consciously or unconsciously, he has been caught up by the *Zeitgeist,* and with his black brothers of Africa and his brown and yellow brothers of Asia, South America, and the Caribbean, the United States Negro is moving with a sense of great urgency toward the promised land of racial justice. If one recognizes this vital urge that has engulfed the Negro community, one should readily understand why public demonstrations are taking place. The Negro has many pent-up resentments and latent frustrations, and he must release them. So let him march; let him make prayer pilgrimages to the city hall; let him go on freedom rides—and try to understand why he must do so. If his repressed emotions are not released in nonviolent ways, they will seek expression through violence; this is not a threat but a fact of history. So I have not said to my people: "Get rid of your discontent." Rather, I have tried to say that this normal and healthy discontent can be channeled into the creative outlet of nonviolent direct action. And now this approach is being termed extremist.

But though I was initially disappointed at being categorized as an extremist, as I continued to think about the matter I gradually gained a measure of satisfaction from the label. Was not Jesus an extremist for love: "Love your enemies, bless them that curse you, do good to them that hate you, and pray for them which despitefully use you, and persecute you." Was not Amos an extremist for justice: "Let justice roll down like waters and righteousness like an ever-flowing stream." Was not Paul an extremist for the Christian gospel: "I bear in my body the marks of the Lord Jesus." Was not Martin Luther an extremist: "Here I stand; I cannot do otherwise, so help me God." And John Bunyan: "I will stay in jail to the end of my days before I make a butchery of my conscience." And Abraham Lincoln: "This nation cannot survive half slave and half free." And Thomas Jefferson: "We hold these truths to be self-evident, that all men are created equal. . . ." So the question is not whether we will be extremists, but what kind of extremists we will be. Will we be extremists for hate or for love? Will we be extremists for the preservation of injustice or for the extension of justice? In that dramatic scene on Calvary's hill three men were crucified. We must never forget that all three were crucified for the same crime—the crime of extremism. Two were extremists for immorality, and thus fell below their environment. The other, Jesus Christ, was an extremist for love, truth and goodness, and thereby rose above his environment. Perhaps the South, the nation and the world are in dire need of creative extremists.

I had hoped that the white moderate would see this need. Perhaps I was too optimistic; perhaps I expected too much. I suppose I should have realized that few members of the oppressor race can understand the deep groans and passionate yearnings of the oppressed race, and still fewer have the vision to see that injustice must be rooted out by strong, persistent, and determined action. I am thankful, however, that some of our white brothers in the South have grasped the meaning of this social revolution and committed themselves to it. They are still all too few in quantity, but they are big in quality. Some—such as Ralph McGill, Lillian Smith, Harry Golden, James McBride Dabbs, Ann Braden, and Sarah Patton Boyle—have written about our struggle in eloquent and prophetic terms. Others have marched with us down nameless streets of the South. They have languished in filthy, roach-infested jails, suffering the abuse and brutality of policemen who view them as "dirty nigger-lovers." Unlike so many of their moderate brothers and sisters, they have recognized the urgency of the moment and sensed the need for powerful "action" antidotes to combat the disease of segregation.

Let me take note of my other major disappointment. I have been so greatly disappointed with the white church and its leadership. Of course, there are some notable exceptions. I am not unmindful of the fact that each of you has taken some significant stands on this issue. I commend you, Reverend Stallings, for your Christian stand on this past Sunday, in welcoming Negroes to your worship service on a nonsegregated basis. I commend the Catholic leaders of this state for integrating Spring Hill College several years ago.

But despite these notable exceptions, I must honestly reiterate that I have been disappointed with the church. I do not say this as one of those negative critics who can always find something wrong with the church. I say this as a minister of the gospel, who loves the church; who was nurtured in its bosom; who has been sustained by its spiritual blessings and who will remain true to it as long as the cord of life shall lengthen.

When I was suddenly catapulted into the leadership of the bus protest in Montgomery, Alabama, a few years ago, I felt we would be supported by the white church. I felt that the white ministers, priests, and rabbis of the South would be among our strongest allies. Instead, some have been outright opponents, refusing to understand the freedom movement and misrepresenting its leaders; all too many others have been more cautious than courageous and have remained silent behind the anesthetizing security of stained-glass windows.

In spite of my shattered dreams, I came to Birmingham with the hope that the white religious leadership of this community would see the justice of our cause and, with deep moral concern, would serve as the channel through which our just grievances could reach the power structure. I had hoped that each of you would understand. But again I have been disappointed.

I have heard numerous southern religious leaders admonish their worshipers to comply with a desegregation decision because it is the law, but I have longed to hear white ministers declare: "Follow this decree because integration is morally right and because the Negro is your brother." In the midst of blatant injustices inflicted upon the Negro, I have watched white churchmen stand on the sideline and mouth pious irrelevancies and sanctimonious trivialities. In the midst of a mighty struggle to rid our nation of racial and economic injustice, I have heard many ministers say: "Those are social issues, with which the gospel has no real concern." And I have watched many churches commit themselves to a completely otherworldly religion which makes a strange, un-Biblical distinction between body and soul, between the sacred and the secular.

I have traveled the length and breadth of Alabama, Mississippi, and all the other southern states. On sweltering summer days and crisp autumn mornings I have looked at the South's beautiful churches with their lofty spires pointing heavenward. I have beheld the impressive outlines of her massive religious-education buildings. Over and over I have found myself asking: "What kind of people worship here? Who is their God? Where were their voices when the lips of Governor Barnett dripped with words of interposition and nullification? Where were they when Governor Wallace gave a clarion call for defiance and hatred? Where were their voices of support when bruised and weary Negro men and women decided to rise from the dark dungeons of complacency to the bright hills of creative protest?"

Yes, these questions are still in my mind. In deep disappointment I have wept over the laxity of the church. But be assured that my tears have been tears of love. There can be no deep disappointment where there is not deep love. Yes, I love the church. How could I do otherwise? I am in the rather unique position of being the son, the grandson, and the great-grandson of preachers. Yes, I see the church as the body of Christ. But, oh! How we have blemished and scarred that body through social neglect and through fear of being nonconformists.

There was a time when the church was very powerful—in the time *40* when the early Christians rejoiced at being deemed worthy to suffer for what they believed. In those days the church was not merely a thermometer that recorded the ideas and principles of popular opinion; it was a thermostat that transformed the mores of society. Whenever the early Christians entered a town, the people in power became disturbed and immediately sought to convict the Christians for being "disturbers of the peace" and "outside agitators." But the Christians pressed on, in the conviction that they were "a colony of heaven," called to obey God rather than man. Small in number, they were big in commitment. They were too God-intoxicated to be "astronomically intimidated." By their effort and example they brought an end to such ancient evils as infanticide and gladiatorial contests.

Things are different now. So often the contemporary church is a weak, ineffectual voice with an uncertain sound. So often it is an archdefender of the status quo. Far from being disturbed by the presence of the church, the power structure of the average community is consoled by the church's silent—and often even vocal—sanction of things as they are.

But the judgment of God is upon the church as never before. If today's church does not recapture the sacrificial spirit of the early church, it will lose its authenticity, forfeit the loyalty of millions, and be dismissed as an irrelevant social club with no meaning for the twentieth century. Every day I meet young people whose disappointment with the church has turned into outright disgust.

Perhaps I have once again been too optimistic. Is organized religion too inextricably bound to the status quo to save our nation and the world? Perhaps I must turn my faith to the inner spiritual church, the church within the church, as the true *ekklesia* and the hope of the world. But again I am thankful to God that some noble souls from the ranks of organized religion have broken loose from the paralyzing chains of conformity and joined us as active partners in the struggle for freedom. They have left their secure congregations and walked the streets of Albany, Georgia, with us. They have gone down the highways of the South on tortuous rides for freedom. Yes, they have gone to jail with us. Some have been dismissed from their churches, have lost the support of their bishops and fellow ministers. But they have acted in the faith that right defeated is stronger than evil triumphant. Their witness has been the spiritual salt that has preserved the true meaning of the gospel in these troubled times. They have carved a tunnel of hope through the dark mountain of disappointment.

I hope the church as a whole will meet the challenge of this decisive hour. But even if the church does not come to the aid of justice, I have no despair about the future. I have no fear about the outcome of our struggle in Birmingham, even if our motives are at present misunderstood. We will reach the goal of freedom in Birmingham and all over the nation, because the goal of America is freedom. Abused and scorned though we may be, our destiny is tied up with America's destiny. Before the pilgrims landed at Plymouth, we were here. Before the pen of Jefferson etched the majestic words of the Declaration of Independence across the pages of history, we were here. For more than two centuries our forebears labored in this country without wages; they made cotton king; they built the homes of their masters while suffering gross injustice and shameful humiliation—and yet out of a bottomless vitality they continued to thrive and develop. If the inexpressible cruelties of slavery could not stop us, the opposition we now face will surely fail. We will win our freedom because the sacred heritage of our nation and the eternal will of God are embodied in our echoing demands.

Before closing I feel impelled to mention one other point in your state- ment that has troubled me profoundly. You warmly commended the Birming- ham police force for keeping "order" and "preventing violence." I doubt that you would have so warmly commended the police force if you had seen its dogs sinking their teeth into unarmed, nonviolent Negroes. I doubt that you would so quickly commend the policemen if you were to observe their ugly and inhumane treatment of Negroes here in the city jail; if you were to watch them push and curse old Negro women and young Negro girls; if you were to see them slap and kick old Negro men and young boys; if you were to observe them, as they did on two occasions, refuse to give us food because we wanted to sing our grace together. I cannot join you in your praise of the Birmingham police department.

It is true that police have exercised a degree of discipline in handling the demonstrators. In this sense they have conducted themselves rather "nonvio- lently" in public. But for what purpose? To preserve the evil system of segre- gation. Over the past few years I have consistently preached that nonviolence demands that the means we use must be as pure as the ends we seek. I have tried to make clear that it is wrong to use immoral means to attain moral ends. But now I must affirm that it is just as wrong, or perhaps even more so, to use moral means to preserve immoral ends. Perhaps Mr. Connor and his police- men have been rather nonviolent in public, as was Chief Pritchett in Albany, Georgia, but they have used the moral means of nonviolence to maintain the immoral end of racial injustice. As T. S. Eliot has said: "The last temptation is the greatest treason: To do the right deed for the wrong reason."

I wish you had commended the Negro sit-inners and demonstrators of Birmingham for their sublime courage, their willingness to suffer and their amazing discipline in the midst of great provocation. One day the South will recognize its real heroes. They will be the James Merediths, with the noble sense of purpose that enables them to face jeering and hostile mobs, and with the agonizing loneliness that characterizes the life of the pioneer. They will be old, oppressed, battered Negro women, symbolized in a seventy-two-year-old woman in Montgomery, Alabama, who rose up with a sense of dignity and with her people decided not to ride segregated buses, and who responded with ungrammatical profundity to one who inquired about her weariness: "My feets is tired, but my soul is at rest." They will be the young high school and college students, the young ministers of the gospel and a host of their elders, courageously and nonviolently sitting in at lunch counters and willingly going to jail for conscience' sake. One day the South will know that when these disinherited children of God sat down at lunch counters, they were in reality standing up for what is best in the American dream and for the most sacred values in our Judaeo-Christian heritage, thereby bringing our nation back to those great wells of democracy which were dug deep by the founding fathers in their formulation of the Constitution and the Declaration of Independence.

45

Never before have I written so long a letter. I'm afraid it is much too long to take your precious time. I can assure you that it would have been much shorter if I had been writing from a comfortable desk, but what else can one do when he is alone in a narrow jail cell, other than write long letters, think long thoughts, and pray long prayers?

If I have said anything in this letter that overstates the truth and indicates an unreasonable impatience, I beg you to forgive me. If I have said anything that understates the truth and indicates my having a patience that allows me to settle for anything less than brotherhood, I beg God to forgive me.

I hope this letter finds you strong in faith. I also hope that circumstances *50* will soon make it possible for me to meet each of you, not as an integrationist or a civil-rights leader but as a fellow clergyman and a Christian brother. Let us all hope that the dark clouds of racial prejudice will soon pass away and the deep fog of misunderstanding will be lifted from our fear-drenched communities, and in some not too distant tomorrow the radiant stars of love and brotherhood will shine over our great nation with all their scintillating beauty.

Yours for the cause of Peace and Brotherhood

MARTIN LUTHER KING, JR.

King's Analysis of His Audience: Identification and Overcoming Difference

King's letter is worth studying for his use of the resources of identification alone. For example, he appeals in his salutation to "My Dear Fellow Clergymen," which emphasizes at the outset that he and his readers share a similar role. Elsewhere he calls them "my friends" (paragraph 12) and "my Christian and Jewish brothers" (paragraph 23). In many other places, King alludes to the Bible and to other religious figures; these references would put him on common ground with his readers.

King's letter also successfully deals with various kinds of difference between his readers and himself.

Assumptions

King's readers assumed that if black people waited long enough, their situation would naturally grow better. Therefore, they argued for patience. King, in paragraph 26, questions "the strangely irrational notion that . . . the very flow of time . . . will inevitably cure all ills." Against this common assumption that "time heals," King offers the view that "time itself is neutral," something "that can be used either destructively or constructively."

Principles

King's readers believed in the principle of always obeying the law, a principle blind to both intent and application. King substitutes another principle: Obey just laws, but disobey, openly and lovingly, unjust laws (paragraphs 15–20).

Hierarchy of Values

King's readers elevated the value of reducing racial tension over the value of securing racial justice. In paragraph 10, King's strategy is to talk about "constructive, nonviolent tension," clearly an effort to get his readers to see tension as not necessarily a bad thing but a condition for achieving social progress.

Ends and Means

King's audience seems not to disagree with him about the ends for which he was working, but rather over means. King, therefore, focuses not on justifying civil rights but on justifying civil disobedience.

Interpretation

King's audience interpreted extremism as always negative, never justifiable. King counters by showing, first, that he is actually a moderate, neither a "do-nothing" nor a militant (paragraph 28). But then he redefines their interpretation of extremism, arguing that extremism for good causes is justified and citing examples from history to support his point (paragraph 31).

Implications or Consequences

King's readers doubtless feared the consequences of supporting the struggle for civil rights too strongly—losing the support of more conservative members of their congregations. But as King warns, "If today's church does not recapture the sacrificial spirit of the early church, it will . . . be dismissed as an irrelevant social club" (paragraph 42). King's strategy is to turn his readers' attention away from short-term consequences and toward long-term consequences—the loss of the vitality and relevance of the church itself.

Following Through

As a class look closely at one of the essays from an earlier chapter, and consider it in terms of audience analysis. What audience did the writer attempt to reach? How did the writer connect or fail to connect with the audience's experience, knowledge, and concerns? What exactly divides the author from his or her audience, and how did the writer attempt to overcome the division? How effective were the writer's strategies for achieving identification? What can you suggest that might have worked better?

USING THE FORMS OF APPEAL

We turn now to the forms of appeal in persuasion, noting how Martin Luther King, Jr., used them in his letter.

The Appeal to Reason

Persuasion, we have said, uses the same appeal to reason that we find in convincing; that is, the foundation of a persuasive argument is the case structure of thesis, reasons, and evidence. King, however, seems to have realized that an argument organized like a case would seem too formal and public for his purposes, so he chose instead to respond to the clergymen's statement with a personal letter, organized around their criticisms of him. In fact, most of King's letter amounts to self-defense and belongs to the rhetorical form known as *apologia,* from which our word "apology" derives. An *apologia* is an effort to explain and justify what one has done, or chosen not to do, in the face of condemnation or at least of widespread disapproval or misunderstanding.

While his overall organization does not present a case, King still relies heavily on reason. He uses a series of short arguments, occupying from one to as many as eight paragraphs, in responding to his readers' criticisms. These are the more important ones, in order of appearance:

> Refutation of "outside agitator" concept (paragraphs 2–4)
> Defense of nonviolent civil disobedience (paragraphs 5–11)
> Definitions of "just" versus "unjust" laws (paragraphs 15–22)
> Refutation and defense of the label "extremist" (paragraphs 27–31)
> Rejection of the ministers' praise for the conduct of the police during the Birmingham demonstration (paragraphs 45–47)

In addition to defending himself and his cause, King pursues an offensive strategy, advancing his own criticisms, most notably of the "white moderate" (paragraphs 23–26) and the "white church and its leadership" (paragraphs 33–44). This concentration on rational appeal is both effective and appropriate: it confirms King's character as a man of reason, and it appeals to an audience of well-educated professionals.

King also cites evidence that his readers must respect. In paragraphs 15 and 16, for example, he enlists the words of St. Thomas Aquinas, Martin Buber, and Paul Tillich—who represent, respectively, the Catholic, Jewish, and Protestant traditions—to defend his position on the nature of just and unjust laws. He has chosen these authorities carefully, so that each of his eight accusers has someone from his own tradition with whom to identify. The implication, of course, is that King's distinction between just and unjust laws and the course of action that follows from this distinction is consistent with Judeo-Christian thought as a whole.

Following Through

1. Look at paragraphs 2, 3, and 4 of King's letter. What reasons does King give to justify his presence in Birmingham? How well does he support each reason? How do his reasons and evidence reflect a strategy aimed at his clergy audience?

2. King's argument for civil disobedience (paragraphs 15–22) is based on one main reason. What is it, and how does he support it?

3. What are the two reasons King gives to refute his audience's charge that he is an extremist (paragraphs 27–31)?

4. Think about a time in your life when you did (or did not do) something for which you were unfairly criticized. Choose one or two of the criticisms that were made, and attempt to defend yourself in a short case of your own. Remember that your argument must be persuasive to your accusers, not just to you. Ask yourself, as King did, how can I appeal to my readers? What will they find reasonable?

The Appeal to Character

In Chapter 6 our concern was how to make a good case. We did not discuss self-presentation explicitly there, but in fact when you formulate a clear and plausible thesis and defend it with good reasons and sufficient evidence, you are at the same time creating a positive impression of your own character. A good argument will always reveal the writer's values, his or her intelligence, knowledge of the subject, grasp of the reader's needs and concerns, and so on. We tend to respect and trust a person who reasons well, even when we do not assent to his or her particular case.

In terms of the appeal to character, the difference between convincing and persuading is a matter of degree. In convincing this appeal is implicit, indirect, and diffused throughout the argument; in persuading the appeal to character is often quite explicit, direct, and concentrated in a specific section of the essay. The effect on readers is consequently rather different: in convincing we are seldom consciously aware of the writer's character as such; in persuasion the writer's character assumes a major role in determining how we respond to the argument.

The perception of his character was a special problem for King when he wrote his letter. He was not a national hero in 1963 but rather a very controversial civil rights leader whom many viewed as a troublemaker. Furthermore, of course, he wrote this now celebrated document while in jail—hardly a condition that inspires respect and trust in readers. Self-presentation, then, was very significant for King, something he concentrated on throughout his letter and especially at the beginning and end.

In his opening paragraph, King acknowledges the worst smirch on his character—that he is currently in jail. But he goes on to establish himself as a professional person like his readers, with secretaries, correspondence, and important work to do.

Just prior to his conclusion (paragraphs 48–50), King offers a strongly worded critique of the white moderate and the mainstream white church, taking the offensive in a way that his readers are certain to perceive as an attack. In paragraph 48, however, he suddenly becomes self-deprecating and almost apologetic: "Never before have I written so long a letter." As unexpected as it is, this sudden shift of tone disarms the reader. Then, with gentle irony (the letter, he says, would have been shorter "if I had been writing from a comfortable desk"), King explains the length of his letter as the result of his having no other outlet for action. What can one do in jail but "write long letters, think long thoughts, and pray long prayers?" King paradoxically turns the negative of being in jail into a positive, an opportunity rather than a limitation on his freedom.

His next move is equally surprising, especially after the confident tone of his critique of the church. He begs forgiveness—from his readers if he has overstated his case and from God if he has understated his case or shown too much patience with injustice. This daring, dramatic penultimate paragraph is just the right touch, the perfect gesture of reconciliation. Since he asks so humbly, his readers must forgive him. What else can they do? The further subordination of his own will to God's is the stance of the sufferer and martyr in both the Jewish and Christian tradition.

Finally, King sets aside that which divides him from his readers—the issue of integration and his role as a civil rights leader—in favor of that which unifies him with his audience: all are men of God and brothers in faith. Like an Old Testament prophet, he envisions a time when the current conflicts are over, when "the radiant stars of love and brotherhood will shine over our great nation." In other words, King holds out the possibility for transcendence, for rising above racial prejudice to a new age, a new America. In the end, his readers are encouraged to soar with him, to hope for the future.

Here King enlists the power of identification to overcome the differences separating writer and reader, invoking his status as a "fellow clergyman and a Christian brother" as a symbol of commonality. The key to identification is to reach beyond the individual self, associating one's character with something larger—the Christian community, the history of the struggle for freedom, national values, "spaceship Earth," or any appropriate cause or movement in which readers can also participate.

Following Through

We have already seen how King associates himself with the Christian community in the essay's final paragraph. Look at the list of questions for creating audience identification on page 116. Find some examples in King's letter where he employs some of these resources of identification. Which parts of the letter are most effective in creating a positive impression of character? Why? What methods does King use that any persuader might use?

The Appeal to Emotion

Educated people aware of the techniques of persuasion are often deeply suspicious of emotional appeal. Among college professors—those who will be reading and grading your work—this prejudice can be especially strong, since all fields of academic study claim to value reason, dispassionate inquiry, and the critical analysis of data and conclusions. Many think of emotional appeal as an impediment to sound thinking and associate it with politicians who prey on our fears, with dictators and demagogues who exploit our prejudices, and with advertisers and television evangelists who claim they will satisfy our dreams and prayers.

Of course, we can all cite examples of the destructive power of emotional appeal. But to condemn it wholesale, without qualification, is to exhibit a lack of self-awareness. Most scientists will concede, for instance, that they are passionately committed to the methods of their field, and mathematicians will confess that they are moved by the elegance of certain formulas and proofs. In fact, all human activity has some emotional dimension, strongly felt adherence to a common set of values.

Moreover, we ought to have strong feelings about certain things: revulsion at the horrors of the Holocaust, pity and anger over the abuse of children, happiness when a war is concluded or when those kidnapped by terrorists are released, and so on. We cease to be human if we are not responsive to emotional appeal.

Clearly we must distinguish between legitimate and illegitimate emotional appeals, condemning the latter and learning to use the former when appropriate. While distinguishing the two is not always easy, there are certain questions that can help us do so:

Do the emotional appeals substitute for knowledge and reason?
Do they work with stereotypes and pit one group against another?
Do they offer a simple, unthinking reaction to a complex situation?

Whenever the answer is yes, our suspicions should be aroused.

Perhaps an even better test is to ask yourself, "If I act on the basis of how I feel, who will benefit, and who will suffer?" You may be saddened, for example, to see animals used in medical experiments, but an appeal showing only these animals and ignoring the benefits of experimentation for human life is pandering to the emotions.

On the other hand, legitimate emotional appeal supplements argument rather than substituting for it, drawing on knowledge and often first-hand experience. At its best, it can bring alienated groups together and create empathy or sympathy where these are lacking. Many examples could be cited from Martin Luther King's letter, but the most effective passage is surely paragraph 14:

We have waited for more than 340 years for our constitutional God-given rights. The nations of Asia and Africa are moving with jetlike speed toward gaining political independence, but we still creep at horse-and-buggy pace toward gaining a cup of coffee at a lunch counter. Perhaps it is easy for those who have never felt the stinging darts of segregation to say, "Wait." But when you have seen vicious mobs lynch your mothers and fathers at will and drown your sisters and brothers at whim; when you have seen hate-filled policemen curse, kick, and even kill your black brothers and sisters; when you see the vast majority of your twenty million Negro brothers smothering in an airtight cage of poverty in the midst of an affluent society; when you suddenly find your tongue twisted and your speech stammering as you seek to explain to your six-year-old daughter why she can't go to the public amusement park that has just been advertised on television, and see tears welling up in her eyes when she is told that Funtown is closed to colored children, and see ominous clouds of inferiority beginning to form in her little mental sky, and see her beginning to distort her personality by developing an unconscious bitterness toward white people; when you have to concoct an answer for a five-year-old son who is asking: "Daddy, why do white people treat colored people so mean?"; when you take a cross-country drive and find it necessary to sleep night after night in the uncomfortable corners of your automobile because no motel will accept you; when you are humiliated day in and day out by nagging signs reading "white" and "colored"; when your first name becomes "nigger," your middle name becomes "boy" (however old you are), and your last name becomes "John," and your wife and mother are never given the respected title "Mrs."; when you are harried by day and haunted by night by the fact that you are a Negro, living constantly at tiptoe stance, never quite knowing what to expect next, and are plagued with inner fears and outer resentments; when you are forever fighting a degenerating sense of "nobodiness"—then you will understand why we find it difficult to wait. There comes a time when the cup of endurance runs over, and men are no longer willing to be plunged into the abyss of despair. I hope, sirs, you can understand our legitimate and unavoidable impatience.

Just prior to this paragraph King has concluded an argument justifying the use of direct action to dramatize social inequities and to demand rights and justice denied to oppressed people. Direct-action programs are necessary, he says, because "freedom is never voluntarily given by the oppressor; it must be demanded by the oppressed." It is easy for those not oppressed to urge an underclass to wait. But "[t]his 'Wait' has almost always meant 'Never.'"

At this point King deliberately sets out to create in his readers a feeling of outrage. Having ended paragraph 13 by equating "wait" with "never," King next refers to a tragic historical fact: For 340 years, since the beginning of slavery in the American colonies, black people have been waiting for their freedom. He sharply contrasts the "jetlike speed" with which Africa is overcoming colonialism with the "horse-and-buggy pace" of integration in the United States. In African homelands black people are gaining their political independence; but here, in the land of the free, they are denied even "a cup of coffee at a lunch counter." Clearly this is legitimate emotional appeal, based on fact and reinforcing reason.

In the long and rhythmical sentence that takes up most of the rest of the paragraph, King unleashes the full force of emotional appeal in a series of concrete images designed to make his white, privileged readers feel the anger, frustration, and humiliation of the oppressed. In rapid succession King alludes to mob violence, police brutality, and economic discrimination—the more public evils of racial discrimination—then moves to the personal, everyday experience of segregation, concentrating especially on what it does to the self-respect of innocent children. For any reader with even the least imaginative capacity for sympathy, these images must strike home, creating identification with the suffering of the oppressed and angry impatience toward the evil system that perpetuates this suffering. In short, through the use of telling detail drawn from his own experience, King succeeds in getting his audience to feel what he feels—feelings, in fact, that they ought to share, that are wholly appropriate to the problem of racial prejudice.

What have we learned from King about the available means of emotional appeal? Instead of telling his audience they should feel a particular emotion, he has brought forth that emotion using five specific rhetorical techniques:

Concrete examples
Personal experiences
Metaphors and similes
Sharp contrasts and comparisons
Sentence rhythm, particularly the use of intentional repetition

We will now consider how style contributes to a persuasive argument.

Following Through

1. We have said that emotional appeals need to be both legitimate and appropriate—that is, honest and suitable for the subject matter, the audience, and the kind of discourse being written. Find examples of arguments from various publications—books, newspapers, magazines, and professional journals—and discuss the use or avoidance of emotional appeal in each. On the basis of this study, try to generalize about what kinds of subjects, audiences, and discourse allow direct emotional appeal and what kinds do not.

2. Write an essay analyzing the tactics of emotional appeal in the editorial columns of your campus or local newspaper. Compare the strategies with those used by King. Then evaluate the appeals. How effective are they in moving your emotions? How well do they reinforce the reasoning offered? Be sure to discuss both how the appeals work and their legitimacy and appropriateness.

The Appeal through Style

By "style" we mean the choices a writer makes at the level of words, phrases, and sentences. It would be a mistake to think of style as a final touch, put on to dress up an argument. Style actually involves all of a writer's choices about what words to use and how to arrange them. Ideas and arguments do not develop apart from style, and all of the appeals discussed so far involve stylistic choices. For example, you are concerned with style when you consider what words will state a thesis most precisely or make yourself sound knowledgeable or provide your reader with a compelling image. The appeal of style works hand-in-hand with the appeals of reason, character, and emotion.

Further, style makes what we say memorable. George Bush may wish he had never said it, but his statement "Read my lips: no new taxes" was a message that generated high enthusiasm and, to the former president's dismay, remained in people's minds long after he had compromised himself on that stand. Since the persuasive effect we have on readers depends largely on what they remember, the appeal to style matters as much as the appeal to reason, character, and emotion.

Writers with effective style make conscious choices on many levels. One choice involves the degree of formality or familiarity they want to convey. You will notice that King strikes a fairly formal and professional tone throughout most of his letter, choosing words like "cognizant" (paragraph 4) rather than the more common "aware." Writers also consider the connotation of words (what a word implies or what we associate it with) as much as their denotation (a word's literal meaning). For example, King opens his letter with the phrase "While confined here in the Birmingham city jail." The word "confined" denotes the same condition as being "incarcerated" but has less unfavorable connotations, since people can also be "confined" in ways that evoke our sympathy.

Memorable writing often appeals to the senses of sight and sound. Concrete words can paint a picture; in paragraph 45, for example, King shows us "dogs sinking their teeth" into the nonviolent demonstrators. Writers may also evoke images through implied and explicit comparisons (respectively, metaphor and simile). King's "the stinging darts of segregation" (paragraph 14) is an example of metaphor. In this same paragraph, King refers to the "airtight cage of poverty," the "clouds of inferiority" forming in his young daughter's "mental sky," and the "cup of endurance" that has run over for his people— each a metaphor with a powerful emotional effect.

Even when read silently, language has sound. Therefore, style includes the variation of sentence length and the use of rhythmic patterns as well. For example, a writer may emphasize a short, simple sentence by placing it at the end of a series of long sentences or a single long sentence, as King does in paragraph 14. One common rhythmic pattern is the repetition of certain phrases to emphasize a point or to play up a similarity or contrast; in the fourth sentence of paragraph 14, King repeats the words "when you" a number of times, piling up examples of racial discrimination and creating a powerful rhythm that carries readers through this unusually long sentence. Another common rhythmic pattern is parallelism. Note the following phrases, again from the fourth sentence of paragraph 14:

> lynch your mothers and fathers at will
>
> drown your sisters and brothers at whim

Here, King uses similar words in the same places, even paralleling the number of syllables in each phrase. The parallelism here is further emphasized by King's choice of another stylistic device known as *alliteration,* the repetition of consonant sounds. In another passage from paragraph 14, King achieves a sound pattern that suggests violence when he describes the actions of police who "curse, kick, and even kill" black citizens. The repetition of the hard "k" sound, especially in words of one syllable, suggests the violence of the acts themselves.

Beyond the level of words, phrases, and sentences, the overall arrangement of an essay's main points or topics can also be considered a matter of style, for such arrangement determines how one point contrasts with another, how the tone changes, how the force of the argument builds. When we discuss style we usually look at smaller units of an essay, but actually all the choices a writer makes contribute in some way to the essay's style.

Following Through

1. Analyze King's style in paragraphs 6, 8, 23, 24, 31, and 47. Compare what King does in these paragraphs with paragraph 14. How are they similar? How are they different? Why?
2. To some extent style is a gift or talent that some people have more of than others. But it is also learned, acquired by imitating authors we admire. Use your writer's notebook to increase your stylistic options; whenever you hear or read something stated effectively, copy it down and analyze why it is effective. Try to make up a sentence of your own using the same choices but with a different subject matter. In this way you can begin to use analogy, metaphor, repetition, alliteration, parallelism, and other stylistic devices. Begin by imitating six or so sentences or phrases that you especially liked in King's letter.
3. Write an essay analyzing your own style in a previous essay. What would you do differently now? Why?

DRAFTING A PERSUASIVE ESSAY

Outside of the classroom, persuasion begins, as Martin Luther King's letter did, with a real need to move people to action. In a writing course, you may have to create the circumstances for your argument. You should begin by thinking of an issue that calls for persuasion. Your argument must go beyond merely convincing your readers to believe as you do; now you must decide what action you want them to take and move them to do it.

Conceiving a Readership

Assuming that the task you have chosen or been assigned calls for persuasion, finding and analyzing your readership is your first concern. Because instructors evaluate the writing of their students, it is probably unavoidable that college writers, to some extent, tend to write for their instructors. However, real persuasion has a genuine readership, some definite group of people with a stake in the question or issue being addressed. Whatever you say must be adapted for this audience, for moving the reader is the whole point of persuasion.

How can you go about conceiving a readership? First, you should throw out the whole notion of writing to the "general public." Such a "group" is a nearly meaningless abstraction, not defined enough to give you much guidance. If, for example, you are arguing that sex education in public schools must include a moral dimension as well as the clinical facts of reproduction and venereal disease, you need to decide if you are addressing students, who may not want the moral lectures; school administrators, who may not want the added responsibility and curriculum changes; or parents, who may not want the schools to take over what they see as the responsibility of family or church.

Second, given the issue and the position you will probably take, you should ask who you would want to persuade. On the one hand you do not need to persuade those who already agree with you; on the other hand it would be futile to try to persuade those so committed to an opposing position that nothing you could say would make any difference. An argument against logging in old growth forests, for example, would probably be aimed neither at staunch environmentalists nor at workers employed in the timber industry but rather at some readership between these extremes—say, people concerned in general about the environment but not focused specifically on the threat to mature forests.

Third, when you have a degree of choice among possible readerships, you should select your target audience based on two primary criteria. Since persuasion is directly concerned with making decisions and taking action, seek above all to influence those readers best able to influence events. When this group includes a range of readers (and it often will), also consider which of these readers you know the most about and can therefore appeal to best.

Because all appeals in persuasion are addressed to an audience, try to identify your reader early in the process. You can, of course, change your mind later on, but doing so will require considerable rethinking and rewriting. Devoting time at the outset to thinking carefully about your intended audience can save much time and effort in the long run.

Following Through

For a persuasive argument you are about to write, determine your audience; that is, decide who can make a difference with respect to this issue and what they can do to make a difference. Be sure that you go beyond the requirements of convincing when you make these decisions. For example, you may be able to make a good case that just as heterosexuals do not "choose" their attraction to the opposite sex, so homosexuality is also not voluntary. Based on this point you could argue to a local readership of moderate-to-liberal voters that they should press state legislators to support a bill extending full citizens' rights to homosexuals. But with such a desire for action in mind, you would have to think even more about your audience, why they might resist such a measure or not care enough to support it strongly.

In your writer's notebook, respond to the questions "Who is my audience?" and "What are our differences?" (refer to the lists of questions on pages 114 and 115 to help formulate answers). Use your responses to write an audience profile that is more detailed than the one you wrote for an argument to convince.

Discovering the Resources of Appeal

With an audience firmly in mind, you are ready to begin thinking about how to appeal to them. Before and during the drafting stage, you will be making choices about

how to formulate a case and support it with research, as needed;

how to present yourself;

how to move your readers' emotions; and

how to make the style of your writing contribute to the argument's effectiveness.

All of these decisions will be influenced by your understanding of your readers' needs and interests.

Appealing through Reason

In both convincing and persuading, rational appeal amounts to making a case or cases—advancing a thesis or theses and providing supporting reasons and evidence. What you learned in Chapter 6 about case-making applies here as well, so you may want to review that chapter as you work on rational appeal for a persuasive paper. Of course, inquiry into the truth (Chapter 5) and research (Appendix B) are as relevant to persuasion as they are to convincing.

One difference between convincing and persuading, however, is that in persuasion you will devote much of your argument to defending a course of action. The steps here are basically a matter of common sense:

You must show that there is a need for action.

If your audience, like that for Martin Luther King's letter, is inclined to inactivity, you must show urgency as well as need—we must act and act now.

Finally, you must satisfy the need, showing that your proposal for action meets the need or will solve the problem; one way to do this is to compare your course of action with other proposals or solutions, indicating why yours is better than the others.

Sometimes your goal will be to persuade your audience *not* to act because what they want to do is wrong or inappropriate or because the time is not right. Need is still the main issue, the difference being, obviously, the goal of showing that no need exists or that it is better to await other developments before a proposed action will be appropriate or effective.

Following Through

Prepare a brief of your argument (see Chapter 5). Be ready to present an overview of your audience and to defend your brief, either before the class or in small groups. Pay special attention to how well the argument establishes a need or motivation to act (or shows that there is no need for action) for your defined audience. If some action is called for, assess the solution in the context of other, common proposals: Will the proposed action meet the need? Is it realistic—that is, can it be done?

Appealing through Character

A reader who finishes your essay should have the following impressions:

The author is well-informed about the topic.

The author is confident about his or her own position and sincere in advocating it.

The author has been fair and balanced in dealing with other positions.

The author understands my concerns and objections and has dealt with them.

The author is honest.

The author values what I value; his or her heart is in the right place.

What can you do to communicate these impressions? Basically, you must earn these impressions just as you must earn a conviction and a good argument. There are no shortcuts, and educated readers can seldom be fooled.

To seem well informed, you must be well informed. This requires that you dig into the topic, thinking about it carefully, researching it thoroughly and taking notes, discussing the topic and your research with other students, consulting campus experts, and so on. This work will provide you with the following hallmarks of being well informed:

> The ability to make references in passing to relevant events and people connected with the issue now or recently,
>
> The ability to create a context or provide background information, which may include comments on the history of the question or issue,
>
> The ability to produce sufficient, high-quality evidence to back up contentions.

Just as digging in will make you well informed, so inquiry (struggling to find the truth) and convincing (making a case for your conviction about the truth) will lend your argument sincerity and confidence. Draw upon personal experience when it has played a role in determining your position, and don't be reluctant to reveal your own stake in the issue. Make your case boldly, qualifying it as little as possible. If you have prepared yourself with good research, genuine inquiry, and careful case-making, you have earned authority; what remains is to claim your authority, which is essential in arguing to persuade.

Represent other positions accurately and fairly; then present evidence that defeats those positions or show that the reasoning is inadequate or inconsistent. Don't be afraid to agree with parts of other opinions when they are consistent with your own. Such partial agreements can play a major role in overcoming reader resistance to your own position.

It is generally not a good idea to subject other positions to ridicule. Some of your readers may sympathize with all or part of the position you are attacking and take offense. Even readers gratified by your attack may feel that you have gone too far. Concentrate on the merits of your own case rather than the faults of others.

Coping with your readers' concerns and objections should present no special problems, assuming that you have found an appropriate audience and thought seriously about both the common ground you share and how their outlook differs from yours. You can ultimately handle concerns and objections in one of two ways: (1) by adjusting your case—your thesis and supporting reasons—so that the concerns or objections do not arise or (2) by taking up the more significant objections one by one and responding to them in a way that reduces reader resistance. Of course, doing one does not preclude doing the other: you can adjust your case and also raise and answer whatever objections remain. What matters is never to ignore any likely and weighty objection to what you are advocating.

Responding to objections patiently and reasonably will also help with the last and perhaps most important impression that readers have of you—that you value what they value. Being sensitive to the reasoning and moral and emotional commitments of others is one of those values you can and must share with your readers.

If you are to have any chance of persuading at all, your readers must feel that you would not deceive them, so you must conform to the standards of honesty readers will expect. Leaving readers with the impression of your honesty requires much more than simply not lying. Rather, honesty requires reporting evidence accurately and with regard for the original context; acknowledging significant counterevidence to your case, pointing to its existence and explaining why it does not change your argument; and pointing out areas of doubt and uncertainty that must await future events or study.

Following Through

The "Following Through" assignment on page 142 asked you to prepare an audience profile and explore your key areas of difference. Now use the results of that work to help you think through how you could appeal to these readers. Use the questions on page 116 to help establish commonality with your audience and to formulate strategies for bringing you and your readership closer together.

Appealing to Emotion

In both convincing and persuading, your case determines largely what you have to say and the order of your presentation. As in King's essay, argument is the center, the framework, while emotional appeal plays a supporting role to rational appeal, taking center stage only here and there. Consequently, your decisions must take the following into account:

What emotions to arouse and by what means,
The frequency and intensity of emotional appeals,
Where to introduce emotional appeals.

The first of these decisions is usually the easiest. Try to arouse emotions that you yourself have genuinely felt; whatever moved you will probably also move your readers. If your emotions come from direct experience, draw upon that experience for concrete descriptive detail, as King did. Study whatever you heard or read that moved you; you can probably adapt your sources' tactics for your own purposes. (The best strategy for arousing emotions is often to avoid emotionalism yourself. Let the facts, the descriptive detail, the concrete examples do the work, just as King did.)

Deciding how often, at what length, and how intensely to make emotional appeals presents a more difficult challenge. Much depends on the topic, the audience, and your own range and intensity of feeling. In every case you must estimate as best you can what will be appropriate, but the following suggestions may help.

As always in persuasion, your primary consideration is your audience. What attitudes and feelings do they have already? Which of these lend emotional support to your case? Which work against your purposes? You will want to emphasize those feelings that are consistent with your position and show why any others are understandable but inappropriate.

Then ask a further question: What does my audience not feel or not feel strongly enough that they must feel or feel more strongly if I am to succeed in persuading them? King, for example, decided that his readers' greatest emotional deficit was their inability to feel what victims of racial discrimination feel—hence paragraph 14, the most intense emotional appeal in his letter. Simply put, devote space and intensity to arousing emotions central to your case that are lacking or only weakly felt by your readers.

The questions of how often and where to include emotional appeals are both worth careful consideration. Regarding frequency, the best principle is to take your shots sparingly, getting as much as you can out of each effort. Positioning emotional appeals depends on pacing: use them to lead into or to clinch a key point. So positioned, they temporarily relieve the audience of the intellectual effort required to follow your argument.

It is generally not a good idea to begin an essay with your longest and most intense emotional appeal; you don't want to peak too early. Besides that, you need to concentrate in your introduction on establishing your tone and authority, providing needed background information, and making a clear and forceful statement of your thesis. The conclusion can be an effective position for emotional appeals, because your audience is left with something memorable to carry away from the reading. But in most cases it is best to concentrate emotional appeals in the middle or near the end of an essay.

Following Through

After you have a first draft of your essay, reread it with an eye to emotional appeal. Highlight the places where you have deliberately sought to rouse the audience's emotions. (You might also ask a friend to read the draft, or exchange drafts with another student in your class.)

Decide if you need to devote more attention to your emotional appeal through additional concrete examples, direct quotations, or something else. Consider also how you could make each appeal more effective and intense and whether each appeal is in the best possible location in the essay.

Appealing through Style

As we have seen, the style of your argument evolves with every choice you make, even in the prewriting stages. As you draft, think consciously about how stylistic choices can work for you, but don't agonize over them. In successive revisions, you will be able to make refinements and experiment for different effects.

In the first draft, however, set an appropriate level of formality. Most persuasive writing is neither chatty and familiar nor stiff and distant. Rather, persuasive prose is like dignified conversation, the way people talk when they care about and respect one another but do not know each other well. We can see some of the hallmarks of persuasive prose in King's letter:

It uses *I, you,* and *we.*
It avoids both technical jargon and slang.
It inclines toward strong, action verbs.
It chooses examples and images familiar to the reader.
It takes care to connect sentence to sentence and paragraph to paragraph with transitional words and phrases like "however," "moreover," "for instance," and the like.

All of these and many other features characterize the middle style of most persuasive writing.

As we discovered in King's letter, this middle style can cover quite a range of choices. King varies his style from section to section, depending on his purpose. Notice how King sounds highly formal in his introductory paragraphs (1–5), where he wants to establish authority, but more plainspoken when he narrates the difficulties he and other black leaders had in their efforts to negotiate with the city's leaders (paragraphs 6–9). Notice as well how his sentences and paragraphs shorten on average in the passage comparing just and unjust laws (paragraphs 15–22). And we have already noted the use of sound and images in the passages of highest emotional appeal, such as paragraphs 14 and 47.

Just as King matches style with function, so you need to vary your style based on what each part of your essay is doing. This variation creates pacing, or the sense of overall rhythm in your essay. Readers need places where they can relax a bit between points of higher intensity, such as lengthy arguments and passionate pleas.

As you prepare to write your first draft, then, concern yourself with matching your style to your purpose from section to section, depending on whether you are providing background information, telling a story, developing a reason in your case, mounting an emotional appeal, or something else. Save detailed attention to style (as explained in Appendix B) for later in the process, while editing a second or third draft.

Following Through

Once you have completed the first draft of an argument to persuade, select one paragraph in which you have consciously made stylistic choices to create images, connotations, sound patterns, and so on. It may be the introductory paragraph, the conclusion, or a body paragraph where you are striving for emotional effect. Be ready to share the paragraph with your class, describing your choices as we have done with many passages from Martin Luther King's letter.

READING A DRAFT OF A PERSUASIVE ESSAY WITH AN EYE TOWARD REVISION: A CHECKLIST

The following list will direct you to specific features of a good persuasive essay. You and a peer may want to exchange drafts; having someone else give your paper a critical reading often helps find weaknesses you may have overlooked. After you have revised your draft, use the suggestions in Appendix B to edit for style and check for errors at the sentence level.

1. Read the audience profile for this essay. Then read the draft all the way through, projecting yourself as much as possible into the role of the target audience. After reading the draft, find and mark the essay's natural divisions. You may also want to number the paragraphs so that you can refer to them easily.

2. Persuasive arguments must be based on careful inquiry and strategic case-making. Inspect the case first. Begin by underlining the thesis and marking the main reasons in support. You might write "Reason 1," "Reason 2," and so forth in the margins. Circle any words that need clearer definition. Also note any reasons that need more evidence or other support, such as illustrations or analogies.

3. Evaluate the plan for organizing the case. Are the reasons presented in a compelling and logical order? Does the argument build to a strong conclusion? Can you envision an alternative arrangement? Make suggestions for improvement, referring to paragraphs by number.

4. Persuasion demands that the writer make an effort to present himself or herself as worthy of the reader's trust and respect. Reread the draft with a highlighter or pen in hand, marking specific places where

Following Through

Read the following argument, and be ready to discuss its effectiveness as persuasion. You might build your evaluation around the suggestions listed in the box "Reading a Draft of a Persuasive Essay with an Eye Toward Revision: A Checklist."

Student Sample: An Essay to Persuade

The following essay was written in response to an assignment for a first-year rhetoric course. The intended readers were other students, eighteen to twenty-two years old and for the most part middle-class, who attended the same large, private university as the writer. Within this group, Shanks was the writer has sought the identification of the target audience. Has the writer made an effort to find common ground with readers by using any of the ideas listed on page 116? Make suggestions for improvement.

5. Persuasion also requires that the writer make conscious efforts to gain the audience's emotional support through concrete examples and imagery, analogies and metaphors, first-person reporting, quotations, and so on. How many instances of conscious emotional appeal are there? Are the efforts at emotional appeal uniformly successful? What improvements can you suggest? Has the writer gone too far with emotional appeal? Or should more be done?

6. Conscious stylistic appeals may be added later, in the editing stage, because style involves refinements in word choice and sentence patterns. However, look now to see if the draft exhibits a middle style appropriate to the targeted audience. Mark any instances of the following:

Poor transitions between sentences or paragraphs

Wordy passages, especially those containing the passive voice (see Appendix B, "Editing for Clarity and Conciseness")

Awkward sentences

Poor diction—that is, the use of incorrect or inappropriate words

7. Note any examples of effective style—good use of metaphor, repetition, or parallelism, for example.

8. Describe the general tone. Does it change from section to section? How appropriate and effective is the tone in general and in specific sections of the essay?

9. After studying the argument, are you sure what the writer wants or expects of the audience? Has the writer succeeded in persuading the audience? Why or why not?

---

trying to reach those who might sit in class and disagree with the opinions of more outspoken students but, for whatever reasons, fail to express their own dissenting viewpoints.

JOEY SHANKS

An Uncomfortable Position

I SAT quietly in my uncomfortable chair. Perhaps it was my position, I thought, and not the poly-wood seat that tormented me; so I sat upright, realizing then that both the chair and my position were probably responsible for my disposition. But I could do nothing to correct the problem.

Or maybe it was the conversation. I sat quietly, only for a lack of words. Usually I rambled on any subject, even if I knew nothing about it. No one in my rhetoric class would ever accuse me of lacking words, but today I was silent. The opinions of my classmates flew steadily across the room with occasional "I agree's" and "that's the truth's." My teacher shook her head in frustration.

She mediated the debate, if it was a debate. I could not imagine that a group of white college students angrily confessing that we all were constantly victims of reverse racism could provide much of a debate. In order for our generalizations to have formed a legitimate debate, there should have been two opposing sides, but the power of the majority had triumphed again. I sat quietly, knowing that what I heard was wrong. The little I said only fueled the ignorance and the guarded, David Duke-like articulations.

Did everyone in the class really think America had achieved equal opportunity? I could only hope that someone else in the classroom felt the same intimidation that I felt. I feared the majority. If I spoke my mind, I would only give the majority a minority to screw with.

But what about the young woman who sat next to me? She was His-   5 panic with glasses and no name or voice that I knew of. She was the visible minority in a class full of Greek letters and blonde hair. She must have been more uncomfortable than I was. She sat quietly every day.

The individual in society must possess the courage and the confidence to challenge and oppose the majority if he or she feels it necessary. In the classroom I had not seen this individualism. My classmates may have had different backgrounds and interests, but eventually in every discussion, a majority opinion dominated the debate and all personalities were lost in a mob mentality. In rhetoric class, we read and discussed material designed to stimulate a debate with many sides; however, the debate was rendered useless because the power of the majority stifled open discussion and bullied the individual to submit or stay quiet.

De Tocqueville wrote of the dangerous power of the majority in his book *Democracy in America:* "The moral authority of the majority is partly based upon the notion that there is more intelligence and wisdom in a number of men united than in a single individual" (113). De Tocqueville illustrated a point that I witnessed in class and that history has witnessed for ages. The majority rules through the power of numbers. No matter how wrong, an opinion with many advocates becomes the majority opinion and is difficult to oppose. The majority makes the rules; therefore, we accept that "might makes right."

The true moral authority, however, lies in the fundamental acceptance that right and wrong are universal and not relative to time and place. Thomas Nagel, a contemporary philosopher, states, "Many things that you probably think are wrong have been accepted as morally correct by large groups of people in the past" (71). The majority is not right simply because it is a large group. An individual is responsible for knowing right from wrong, no matter how large the group appears. Ancient philosophers such as Aristotle and Socrates have defied generations of majorities. They preached that morality is universal and that the majority is not always right.

In our classroom after the first week, all the students chose their chairs in particular areas. Certain mentalities aligned, acknowledging similar philosophies on politics, hunting, sports, African Americans, welfare, and women. Debate on *The Awakening* awoke the beefcake majority with confused exclamations: "She's crazy! Why did the chick kill herself?" The majority either misunderstood the book or was not willing to accept another opinion.

Mark Twain, a pioneer of American literature, fought an empire of slav-   *10* ery with his book *The Adventures of Huckleberry Finn*. Twain saw through the cruelty of racism and spoke against a nation that treated men and women like animals because of the color of their skin. Twain possessed the confidence and individualism to fight the majority, despite its power. Mark Twain protected individualism when he opposed racism and the institution of slavery. He proved that the single individual is sometimes more intelligent than men united.

Ramsey Clark, a former attorney general and now a political activist, expressed a great deal of distress over the Persian Gulf war. He spoke for the minority, a position of peace. In an interview in *The Progressive,* Clark stated, "We really believe that might makes right, and that leads us to perpetual war" (qtd. in Dreifus 32). Clark was referring to the United States' foreign policy of peace through intimidation, but his words can be taken on a universal level. We will never accomplish anything if might makes right and humanity is in a perpetual war of opinions. Clark is an example of individualism against the majority, though he will never be considered an American hero; few may remember his words, but like Mark Twain, he fought the majority's "moral authority."

In the classroom, or in the post-slavery South, or in the deserts of the Middle East, the majority has the power, and whoever has the power controls the world and may even seem to control all the opinions in it. As a country we abuse the power of the majority. America, the spokesperson for the world majority, manipulates its position while flexing and growling, "Might makes right!" This situation is a large scale version of a rhetoric seminar in which students too frequently align with or submit to the majority opinion. In rhetoric seminar we lack champions, individuals who see wrong and cry, "Foul!" Maybe the young Hispanic woman who quietly sits is just waiting for the right moment. Perhaps I had my chance and lost it, or maybe the majority has scared all the individuals into sitting quietly in their uncomfortable chairs.

WORKS CITED

De Tocqueville, Alexis. *Democracy in America.* 1835. New York: Penguin, 1956.

Dreifus, Claudia. "An Interview with Ramsey Clark." *The Progressive* Apr. 1991: 32–35.

Nagel, Thomas. *What Does It All Mean?* Oxford: Oxford UP, 1987.

THE APPEALS OF PERSUASION
IN VISUAL ARGUMENTS

Arguments to persuade are often primarily visual. Advertisements, editorial cartoons, news photographs, and some art works—paintings, films, sculpture, architecture—are fundamentally arguments. Their creators' aim is to make the audience see their subject as they do—and often to act in accord with a particular point of view. As we become familiar with the images and styles used in a particular visual medium, such as photography, we become more adept at "reading" the images critically, just as we read written texts critically.

As with critical reading, our understanding of a visual argument depends on certain prior knowledge as well as on our ability to see the image in a rhetorical context. Further, we should be able to inquire into a visual argument just as we do a written text, seeing not just surface features but also the rhetorical appeals to reason, character, emotion, and style.

An Example from Advertising

The advertisement for Silver Jeans on page 153 is a good example of how the appeals of persuasion apply to nonverbal arguments. The prior knowledge that helps us understand this advertisement is based both in current events within our culture and in current advertising trends, particularly trends in clothing advertisements. First, we recognize that in the United States the image touches on current issues involving racial tension and ethnic separatism,[1] and we understand the idea being sold as something more specific and contemporary than "Peace on Earth": the embrace shared by the young couple suggests that romantic love is, or should be, blind to differences of race. Second, we know from experience that contemporary clothing advertising often argues indirectly, selling an idea in order to sell a product, so we have no difficulty understanding that this is an argument for buying a particular brand of jeans.

The rhetorical context that helps us understand the ad is that it appeared in the December 1993/January 1994 issue of *Vibe* magazine, which is aimed at an audience of men and women of all races in their late teens and early twenties and which focuses on popular African-American music. The magazine has a liberal perspective, appealing to people interested in the arts.

While the advertisement argues that the readers should buy Silver Jeans, it does not make a case, either verbally or visually, with reasons for doing so. It does not state or show that Silver offers good fit or good value. In fact, the viewer could almost miss the jeans hanging on a clothesline in the background.

Instead of using rational appeal, the Silver advertisement sells the product by associating it with values and emotions that would appeal to *Vibe* readers. Just as verbal persuasion may appeal through character, with the writer presenting himself or herself as sharing some common ground with readers, so may visual advertisements depict the product as having something in common

[1] We should note, however, that this is a Canadian advertisement for a Canadian product. Readers in Canada, which has a more culturally diverse society, would be unlikely to see the image as a strong political statement.

with the target audience's lives and values. The Silver advertisement identifies the product with youth and racial tolerance. While nondenominational, the verbal text "Peace on Earth" reiterates the message of brotherly love.

As a visual representation of these values, the couple photographed must appeal to *Vibe* readers, and there are several factors that present the couple sympathetically. First, the advertisement suggests that these are real lovers, not models striking a pose. They are attractive but not glamorous; for example, the freckles on the woman's arm have not been airbrushed away. Also, the camera seems to have intruded upon a private moment. Notably, it is a sexual moment, but the couple is not blatantly sexy in either pose or dress.

As in verbal persuasion, style pervades all of the other appeals, affecting selection, arrangement, emphasis, tone, and so on. In this advertisement, some stylistic choices seem deliberately artistic, such as the decision to print the ad in black and white rather than in color. We might also notice how the arrangement of text, the inset oval photograph, and the couple's forehead-to-forehead pose emphasize the man's and woman's eyes; as the viewer looks at the couple, they seem to be looking back. Their gazes invite interpretation. The most notable thing about the style, however, is the decision to sell jeans indirectly, rather than directly, to a young, sophisticated audience.

Following Through

Find other advertisements that use an indirect approach, selling an idea in order to promote a product. For each, determine the audience, and write an analysis of how the ad appeals to that audience through reason, character, emotion, and style.

Two Examples from Public Art

Public sculptures, such as war memorials, are rhetorical; they aim to teach an audience about a nation's past and to represent the values for which its citizens were willing to die. Consider, for example, the Marine Corps

Memorial (better known as the Iwo Jima Memorial), which was erected in 1954 on the Mall in Washington, D.C. (see the photograph on page 154). The Marine Corps Memorial honors all Marines who have given their lives for their country through a literal depiction of one specific act of bravery, the planting of the American flag on Iwo Jima, a Pacific island that the United States captured from the Japanese in 1945. The argument of the statue is unambiguous. Charles Griswold, a philosopher, describes the Iwo Jima Memorial as ". . . a classic war memorial. The soldiers strain every muscle toward one end only, the raising of the flag. The monument shouts this imperative: Honor your country, act as nobly as these men have."

In addition to the reasoned argument, the monument stirs patriotic feelings by its choice of subject matter—the raising of the flag, a symbol of Americans' common values and identity, on what was formerly enemy soil. Through our citizenship, we share in the victory and the glory that is depicted. The Marine Corps Memorial has emotional appeal as well because it portrays real people, their faces and bodies straining to the task. It invites the viewer to relive the experience. Style is an important consideration here, because the sculpture is a realistic representation of the people and the event.

In November 1982, a very different memorial was dedicated in Washington—the Vietnam War Memorial, which has become popularly known as "the Wall" (see the photographs on this page and the next). Designed by Maya Lin when she was an undergraduate architecture student at Yale, the monument

aroused controversy because it was so untraditional in its design and its argument. However, the context for this visual argument was also untraditional; it
did not honor a victory but rather those who died in a war that tore the nation
apart. Abstract rather than literal, ambiguous rather than direct, it nevertheless
makes an argument with the appeals of reason, character, style, and, perhaps
above all, emotion.

Following Through

The Vietnam War Memorial invites interpretation and analysis. How do you
"read" the argument of the Wall? How would you describe the visual argument in terms of its thesis and its appeals of style, reason, character, and
emotion?

Two Editorial Cartoons

Unlike most cartoons on the comics pages, editorial cartoons comment
on issues in the news. They can be seen as brief arguments, expressing the
cartoonist's opinion, along with a reason or reasons in support of it. While

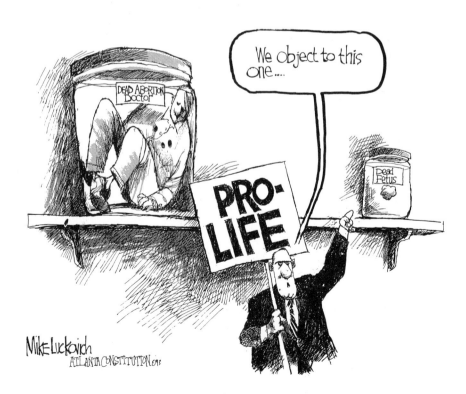

editorial cartoons often make their point very effectively, we might question how persuasive they are. The cartoonist's aim may be merely to express his or her opinion with creativity and humor. Editorial cartoonists prefer to mock their opposition rather than appeal to it, and their humor can be biting, as the two cartoons reproduced on page 157 illustrate.

One comments on extremists of the antiabortion movement, some of whom expressed no regrets over the shooting death of a Florida doctor by a fanatic protester in 1993. The other comments on pro-choice advocates who deplore such violence, yet express no regrets over the loss of life caused by abortion itself.

Following Through

How do you read the arguments made by the two editorial cartoons reproduced here? Would either be at all persuasive to a reader who disagreed with the perspective of the cartoonist? Why, or why not?

CHAPTER EIGHT

Negotiation and Mediation: Resolving Conflict

Argument with the aims of convincing and of persuading is a healthy force within a community. Whatever the issue, people hold a range of positions, and debate among advocates of these various positions serves to inform the public and draw attention to problems that need solution. Yet, while some issues seem to be debated endlessly—the death penalty, abortion, gun control, the U.S. role in the affairs of other nations—a time comes when the conflict must be resolved and a particular course of action pursued.

But what happens after each side has made its best effort to convince and persuade yet no one position has won general assent? If the conflicting parties all have equal power, the result can be an impasse, a stalemate. More often, however, one party has greater authority and is able to impose its will, as, for example, a university dean or president may impose a policy decision on students or faculty. But imposing power can be costly—especially in terms of the worsened relationships—and it is often temporary. Foes of abortion, for example, have been able to influence policy significantly under conservative administrations, only to see their policy gains eroded when more liberal politicians gain power. If conflicts are going to be resolved—and stay resolved—each side needs to move beyond advocating its own positions and start arguing with a new aim in mind: negotiation.

Arguing to negotiate aims to resolve—or at least reduce—conflict to the mutual satisfaction of all parties involved. But negotiation involves more than simply making a deal in which each side offers a few concessions while retaining a little of its initial demands. As this chapter will show, through the process of negotiating, opposing sides come to a greater understanding of their differing interests, backgrounds, and values; ideally, negotiation builds consensus and repairs relationships that may previously have been strained.

NEGOTIATION AND THE OTHER
AIMS OF ARGUMENT

You may find it difficult to think of negotiation as argument if you see argument only as presenting a case for a particular position or persuading an audience to act in accordance with that position. Both of these aims clearly involve advocating one position and addressing the argument to those with different viewpoints. But recall that one definition of argue is "to make clear." As we discussed in Chapter 5, sometimes we argue in order to learn what we should think; that is, we argue to inquire, trying out an argument, examining it critically and with as little bias as possible with an audience of nonthreatening partners in conversation such as friends or family.

Arguing to negotiate shares many of the characteristics of arguing to inquire. Like inquiry, negotiation most often takes the form of dialogue, although writing plays an important role in the process. Also, whether a party in the conflict or an outside mediator among the various parties, the negotiator must inquire into the positions of all sides. Further, anyone who agrees to enter into negotiation, especially someone who is a party to the conflict, must acknowledge his or her bias and remain open to the positions and interests of others, just as the inquirer does. Negotiation differs from inquiry, however, in that negotiation must find a mediating position that accommodates at least some of the interests of all sides. The best position in negotiation is the one all sides will accept.

As we shall see in more detail, argument as negotiation draws upon the strategies of the other aims of argument as well. Like convincing, negotiation requires an understanding of case structure, as negotiators must analyze the cases each side puts forth, and mediators often need to build a case of their own for a position acceptable to all. And like persuasion, negotiation recognizes the role of human character and emotions, both in the creation of conflict and in its resolution.

To illustrate the benefits to be gained through the process of negotiation, we will concentrate in this chapter on one of the most heated conflicts in the United States today: the debate over abortion. A wide range of positions exists on this issue. Extremists for fetal rights, who sometimes engage in violent acts of civil disobedience, and extremists for the absolute rights of women, who argue that a woman should be able to terminate a pregnancy at any time and for any reason, may not be amenable to negotiation; however, between these poles lie the viewpoints of most Americans, whose differences could possibly be resolved.

Negotiation has a chance only among people who have reasoned through their own position, through inquiry, and who have attempted to defend it, not through force, but through convincing and persuasive argumentation. And negotiation has a chance only when people see that the divisions caused by their conflict are counterproductive. They must be ready to listen to each other. They must be willing to negotiate.

THE PROCESS OF NEGOTIATION AND MEDIATION

As a student in a writing class, you can practice the process of negotiation in at least two ways. First, you and several other students who have written conflicting arguments on a common topic may negotiate among yourselves to find a resolution acceptable to all, perhaps bringing in a disinterested student to serve as a mediator. Or, your class as a whole may act as a mediator in a dispute among writers whose printed arguments offer conflicting viewpoints on the same issue. Here we illustrate the mediator approach, which is easily adapted to the more direct experience of face-to-face negotiation.

Understanding the Spirit of Negotiation

In arguing issues of public concern, it is a mistake to think of negotiation as the same thing as negotiating the price of a car or a house or even a collective bargaining agreement. In a dialogue between a buyer and seller, both sides typically begin by asking for much more than they seriously hope to get, and the process involves displays of will and power as each side tries to force the other to back down on its demands. Negotiation as rhetorical argument, how-ever, is less adversarial; in fact, it is more like collaborative problem-solving, where various opposing parties work together not to rebut one another's arguments but to understand them. Negotiation leads to the most permanent resolution of conflict when it is based on an increased understanding of differ-ence rather than on a mere exchange of concessions. Negotiators must let go of the whole notion of proving one side right and other sides wrong. Rather, the negotiator says, "I see what you are demanding, and you see what I am demanding. Now let's sit down and find out *why* we hold these positions— What are our interests in this issue? Maybe together we can work out a solu-tion that will address these interests." Unlike negotiators, mediators are impar-tial, and if they have a personal viewpoint on the issue, they must suppress it and be careful not to favor either side.

Understanding the Opposing Positions

Negotiation begins with a close look at opposing views. As in inquiry, the first stage of the process is an analysis of the positions, the thesis statements, and the supporting reasons and evidence offered on all sides. It is a good idea for each party to write a brief of his or her case, as described on pages 84–85 and 99–100. These briefs should indicate how the reasons are supported, so that disputants can see where they agree or disagree about data.

The mediator also must begin by inquiring into the arguments presented by the parties in dispute. To illustrate we will look at two reasoned arguments representing opposing views on the value of the Supreme Court's *Roe v. Wade* decision. That decision, which was handed down in 1973, ruled that the Constitution does grant to citizens a zone of personal privacy, which for women would include the decision regarding whether or not to terminate a pregnancy. The Court did stipulate, however, that the right to abortion was not unqualified and that states could regulate abortions to protect the fetus after viability.

The first argument, "Living with *Roe v. Wade*," is by Margaret Liu McConnell, a writer and mother of three, who herself had an abortion while she was in college. This experience led McConnell to decide that abortion on demand should not have become a constitutional right. To those who applaud abortion rights, McConnell argues that *Roe v. Wade* has had serious social and moral consequences for our nation. She does not call for the decision to be overturned, but she does want abortion-rights supporters to take a closer look at the issue and recognize that abortion is fundamentally an immoral choice, one that should result in a sense of guilt. This essay originally appeared in 1990 in *Commentary,* a journal published by the American Jewish Committee.

The second argument is by Ellen Willis, also a mother who once had an abortion. For Willis, abortion is very much a right, in fact, the foundation of women's equality. Willis defends *Roe v. Wade* as the "cutting edge of feminism." Her audience consists of liberals who oppose abortion—"the left wing of the right-to-life movement"—specifically, the editors of *Commonweal,* a liberal Catholic journal. Her audience could also include people like Margaret Liu McConnell, who see abortion as a moral question rather than as a political question framed in terms of equal rights. "Putting Women Back into the Abortion Debate" originally appeared in the left-leaning *Village Voice* in 1985.

MARGARET LIU MCCONNELL

Living with Roe v. Wade

THERE IS something decidedly unappealing to me about the pro-life   1
activists seen on the evening news as they are dragged away from the entrances to abortion clinics across the country. Perhaps it is that their poses remind me of sulky two-year-olds, sinking to their knees as their frazzled mothers try to haul them from the playground. Or perhaps it is because I am a little hard put to believe, when one of them cries out, often with a Southern twang, "Ma'am, don't keel your baby," that he or she could really care that deeply about a stranger's fetus. After all, there are limits to compassion and such concern seems excessive, suspect.

Besides, as pro-choice adherents like to point out, the fact that abortion is legal does not mean that someone who is against abortion will be forced to have one against her wishes. It is a private matter, so they say, between a woman and her doctor. From this it would follow that those opposed to abortion are no more than obnoxious busybodies animated by their own inner pathologies to interfere in the private lives of strangers.

Certainly this is the impression conveyed by those news clips of anti-abortion blockades being broken up by the police. We pity the woman, head sunk and afraid, humiliated in the ancient shame that all around her know she is carrying an unwanted child. Precisely because she is pregnant, our hearts go out to her in her vulnerability. It would seem that those workers from the abortion clinic, shielding arms around her shoulders, their identification vests giving them the benign look of school-crossing guards, are her protectors. They are guiding her through a hostile, irrational crowd to the cool and orderly safety of the clinic and the medical attention she needs.

But is it possible that this impression is mistaken? Is it possible that those who guide the woman along the path to the abortionist's table are not truly her protectors, shoring her up on the road to a dignified life in which she will best be able to exercise her intellectual and physical faculties free from any kind of oppression? Is it possible that they are serving, albeit often unwittingly, to keep her and millions of other women on a demeaning and rather lonely treadmill—a treadmill on which these women trudge through cycles of sex without commitment, unwanted pregnancy, and abortion, all in the name of equal opportunity and free choice?

Consider yet again the woman on the path to an abortion. She is already 5 a victim of many forces. She is living in a social climate in which she is expected to view sex as practically a form of recreation that all healthy women should pursue eagerly. She has been conditioned to fear having a child, particularly in her younger years, as an unthinkable threat to her standard of living and to the career through which she defines herself as a "real" person. Finally, since 1973, when the Supreme Court in *Roe v. Wade* declared access to abortion a constitutional right, she has been invited, in the event that she does become pregnant, not only to have an abortion, but to do so without sorrow and with no moral misgivings. As the highly vocal proabortion movement cheers her on with rallying cries of "Freedom of Choice," she may find herself wondering: "Is this the great freedom we've been fighting for? The freedom to sleep with men who don't care for us, the freedom to scorn the chance to raise a child? The freedom to let doctors siphon from our bodies that most precious gift which women alone are made to receive: a life to nurture?"

My goal here is not to persuade militant pro-choicers that abortion is wrong. Instead, it is to establish that abortion cannot and should not be seen as strictly a matter between a woman and her doctor. For the knowledge that the law allows free access to abortion affects all of us directly and indirectly by the way it shapes the social climate. Most directly and most easy to illustrate, the realization that any pregnancy, intended or accidental, may be aborted at will affects women in their so-called childbearing years. The indirect effects are more difficult to pinpoint. I would like tentatively to suggest that *Roe v. Wade* gives approval, at the highest level of judgment in this country, to certain attitudes which, when manifest at the lowest economic levels, have extremely destructive consequences.

But to begin with the simpler task of examining *Roe*'s questionable effect on the world women inhabit: I—who at thirty-two am of the age to have "benefited" from *Roe*'s protections for all my adult years—offer here some examples of those "benefits."

It was my first year at college, my first year away from my rather strict, first-generation American home. I had a boyfriend from high school whom I liked and admired but was not in love with, and I was perfectly satisfied with the stage of heavy-duty necking we had managed, skillfully avoiding the suspicious eyes of my mother. But once I got to college I could think of no good reason not to go farther. For far from perceiving any constraints around me, I encountered all manner of encouragement to become "sexually active"—from the health center, from newspapers, books, and magazines, from the behavior of other students, even from the approval of other students' parents of their children's "liberated" sexual conduct.

Yet the truth is that I longed for the days I knew only from old movies and novels, those pre-60's days when boyfriends visiting from other colleges stayed in hotels (!) and dates ended with a lingering kiss at the door. I lived in an apartment-style dormitory, six women sharing three bedrooms and a kitchen. Needless to say, visiting boyfriends did not stay in hotels. By the end of my freshman year three out of the six of us would have had abortions.

How did it come to pass that so many of us got pregnant? How has it *10* come to pass that more than one-and-one-half million women each year get pregnant in this country, only to have abortions? Nowadays it is impossible to go into a drugstore without bumping into the condoms on display above the checkout counters. And even when I was in college, contraception was freely available, and everyone knew that the health center, open from nine to four, was ready to equip us with the contraceptive armament we were sure to need.

Nevertheless, thanks to *Roe v. Wade,* we all understood as well that if anything went wrong, there would be no threat of a shotgun marriage, or of being sent away in shame to bear a child, or of a dangerous back-alley abortion. Perhaps the incredible number of "accidental" pregnancies, both at college and throughout the country, finds its explanation in just that understanding. Analogies are difficult to construct in arguments about abortion, for there is nothing quite analogous to terminating a pregnancy. That said, consider this one anyway. If children are sent out to play ball in a yard near a house, a responsible adult, knowing that every once in a while a window will get broken, will still tell them to be very careful not to break any. But what if the children are sent into the yard and told something like this: "Go out and play, and don't worry about breaking any windows. It's bound to happen, and when it does, no problem: it will be taken care of." How many more windows will be shattered?

There were, here and there, some women who seemed able to live outside these pressures. Within my apartment one was an Orthodox Jewish freshman from Queens, another a junior from Brooklyn, also Jewish, who was in the process of becoming Orthodox. They kept kosher as far as was possible in our common kitchen, and on Friday afternoons would cook supper for a group of friends, both men and women. As darkness fell they would light candles and sing and eat and laugh in a circle of light. I remember looking in at their evenings from the doorway to the kitchen, wishing vainly that I could belong to such a group, a group with a code of behavior that would provide shelter from the free-for-all I saw elsewhere. But the only group I felt I belonged to was, generically, "young American woman," and as far as I could see, the norm of behavior for a young American woman was to enjoy a healthy sex life, with or without commitment.

A few months later, again thanks to *Roe v. Wade,* I discovered that the logistics of having an abortion were, as promised, extremely simple. The school health center was again at my service. After a few perfunctory questions and sympathetic nods of the head I was given directions to the nearest abortion clinic.

A strange thing has happened since that great freedom-of-choice victory in 1973. Abortion has become the only viable alternative many women feel they have open to them when they become pregnant by accident. Young men no longer feel obligated to offer to "do the right thing." Pregnancy is most often confirmed in a medical setting. Even though it is a perfectly normal and healthy state, in an unwanted pregnancy a woman feels distressed. The situation thus becomes that of a distressed woman looking to trusted medical personnel for relief. Abortion presents itself as the simple, legal, medical solution to her distress. A woman may have private reservations, but she gets the distinct impression that if she does not take advantage of her right to an abortion she is of her own accord refusing a simple solution to her troubles.

That is certainly how it was for me, sitting across from the counselor at   *15* the health center, clutching a wad of damp tissues, my heart in my throat. The feeling was exactly parallel to the feeling I had had at the beginning of the school year: I could be defiantly old-fashioned and refuse to behave like a normal American woman, or I could exercise my sexual liberation. Here, six weeks pregnant, I could be troublesome, perverse, and somehow manage to keep the baby, causing tremendous inconvenience to everyone, or I could take the simple route of having an abortion and not even miss a single class. The choice was already made.

Physically, also, abortion has become quite a routine procedure. As one of my grosser roommates put it, comforting me with talk of her own experiences, it was about as bad as going to the dentist. My only memory of the operation is of coming out of the general anesthesia to the sound of sobbing all around. I, too, was sobbing, without thought, hard and uncontrollably, as though somehow, deep below the conscious level, below whatever superficial concerns had layered themselves in the day-to-day mind of a busy young woman, I had come to realize what I had done, and what could never be undone.

I have since had three children, and at the beginning of each pregnancy I was presented with the opportunity to have an abortion without even having to ask. For professional reasons my husband and I have moved several times, and each of our children was born in a different city with a different set of obstetrical personnel. In every case I was offered the unsolicited luxury of "keeping my options open": of choosing whether to continue the pregnancy or end it. The polite way of posing the question, after a positive pregnancy test, seems to be for the doctor to ask noncommittally, "And how are we treating this pregnancy?"

Each one of those pregnancies, each one of those expendable bunches of tissue, has grown into a child, each one different from the other. I cannot escape the haunting fact that if I had had an abortion, one of my children would be missing. Not just a generic little bundle in swaddling clothes interchangeable with any other, but a specific child.

I still carry in my mind a picture of that other child who was never born, a picture which changes as the years go by, and I imagine him growing up. For some reason I usually do imagine a boy, tall and with dark hair and eyes. This is speculation, of course, based on my coloring and build and on that of the young man involved. Such speculation seems maudlin and morbid and I do not engage in it on purpose. But whether I like it or not, every now and then my mind returns to that ghost of a child and to the certainty that for seven weeks I carried the beginnings of a being whose coloring and build and, to a large extent, personality were already determined. Buoyant green-eyed girl or shy, dark-haired boy, I wonder. Whoever, a child would have been twelve this spring.

I am not in the habit of exposing this innermost regret, this endless remorse to which I woke too late. I do so only to show that in the wake of *Roe v. Wade* abortion has become casual, commonplace, and very hard to resist as an easy way out of an unintended pregnancy, and that more unintended pregnancies are likely to occur when everyone knows there is an easy way out of them. Abortion has become an option offered to women, married as well as unmarried, including those who are financially, physically, and emotionally able to care for a child. This is what *Roe v. Wade* guarantees. For all the pro-choice lobby's talk of abortion as a deep personal moral decision, casting abortion as a right takes the weight of morality out of the balance. For, by definition, a right is something one need not feel guilty exercising.

I do not wish a return to the days when a truly desperate woman unable to get a safe legal abortion would risk her life at the hands of an illegal abortionist. Neither could I ever condemn a woman whose own grip on life is so fragile as to render her incapable of taking on the full responsibility for another life, helpless and demanding. But raising abortion to the plane of a constitutional right in order to ensure its accessibility to any woman for any reason makes abortion too easy a solution to an age-old problem.

Human beings have always coupled outside the bounds deemed proper by the societies in which they lived. But the inevitable unexpected pregnancies often served a social purpose. There was a time when many young couples found in the startling new life they had created an undeniable reason to settle down seriously to the tasks of earning a living and making a home. That might have meant taking on a nine-to-five job and assuming a mortgage, a prospect which sounds like death to many baby boomers intent on prolonging

20

adolescence well into middle age. But everyone knows anecdotally if not from straight statistics that many of these same baby boomers owe their own lives to such happy (for them) accidents.

When I became pregnant in college, I never seriously considered getting married and trying to raise a child, although it certainly would have been possible to do so. Why should I have, when the road to an abortion was so free and unencumbered, and when the very operation itself had been presented as a step on the march to women's equality?

I know that no one forced me to do anything, that I was perfectly free to step back at any time and live by my own moral code if I chose to, much as my Orthodox Jewish acquaintances did. But this is awfully hard when the society you consider yourself part of presents abortion as a legal, morally acceptable solution. And what kind of a world would it be if all those in need of a moral structure stepped back to insulate themselves, alone or in groups— ethnic, religious, or economic—each with its own exclusive moral code, leaving behind a chaos at the center? It sounds like New York City on a bad day.

This is not, of course, to ascribe the chaos reigning in our cities directly to *Roe v. Wade*. That chaos is caused by a growing and tenacious underclass defined by incredibly high rates of drug abuse, and dependence on either crime or welfare for financial support. But sometimes it does seem as though the same attitude behind abortion on demand lies behind the abandonment of parental responsibility which is the most pervasive feature of life in the underclass and the most determinative of its terrible condition.

Parental responsibility can be defined as providing one's offspring at every level of development with that which they need to grow eventually into independent beings capable of supporting themselves emotionally and financially. Different parents will, of course, have different ideas about what is best for a child, and different parents will have different resources to draw upon to provide for their children. But whatever the differences may be, responsible parents will try, to the best of their ability and in accordance with their own rights, to raise their children properly. It is tedious, expensive, and takes a long, long time. For it is not a question of fetal weeks before a human being reaches any meaningful stage of "viability" (how "viable" is a two-year-old left to his own devices? A five-year-old?). It is a question of years, somewhere in the neighborhood of eighteen.

Why does any parent take on such a long, hard task? Because life is a miracle that cannot be denied? Because it is the right thing to do? Because there is a certain kind of love a parent bears a child that does not require a calculated return on investment? Because we would hate ourselves otherwise? All these factors enter into the powerful force that compels parents to give up years of their free time and much of their money to bring up their children. Yet the cool, clinical approach *Roe v. Wade* allows all of us—men no less than women— in deciding whether or not we are "ready" to accept the responsibility of an established pregnancy seems to undermine an already weakening cultural expectation that parents simply have a duty to take care of their children.

25

A middle- or upper-class woman may have high expectations of what she will achieve so long as she is not saddled with a baby. When she finds herself pregnant she is guaranteed the right under *Roe v. Wade* to opt out of that long and tedious responsibility, and does so by the hundreds of thousands each year. By contrast, a woman in the underclass who finds herself pregnant is not likely to have great expectations of what life would be like were she free of the burden of her child; abortion would not broaden her horizons and is not usually her choice. Yet she often lacks the maternal will and the resources to take full responsibility for the well-being of her child until adulthood.

To be sure, these two forms of refusing parental responsibility have vastly different effects. But how can the government hope to devise policies that will encourage parental responsibility in the underclass when at the highest level of judgment, that of the Supreme Court, the freedom to opt out of parental responsibility is protected as a right? Or, to put the point another way, perhaps the weakening of the sense of duty toward one's own offspring is a systemic problem in America, present in all classes, with only its most visible manifestation in the underclass.

The federal Family Support Act of 1988 was the result of much study   *30* and debate on how to reform the welfare system to correct policies which have tended to make it easier for poor families to qualify for aid if the father is not part of the household. Among other provisions intended to help keep families from breaking up, states are now required to pay cash benefits to two-parent families and to step up child-support payments from absent fathers. New York City, for example, has this year begun to provide its Department of Health with information, including Social Security numbers, on the parents of every child born in the city. Should the mother ever apply for aid, the father can be tracked down and child-support payments can be deducted from his paycheck. Such a strict enforcement of child-support obligations is a powerful and exciting legal method for society to show that it will not tolerate the willful abandonment of children by their fathers.

It is evident that there is a compelling state interest in promoting the responsibility of both parents toward their child. The compelling interest is that it takes a great deal of money to care for a child whose parents do not undertake the responsibility themselves. For whatever else we may have lost of our humanity over the last several decades, however hardened we have been by violence and by the degradation witnessed daily in the lost lives on the street, we still retain a basic decent instinct to care for innocent babies and children in need.

It is also evident that parental responsibility begins well before the child is born. Thus, the Appellate Division of the State Supreme Court of New York in May of this year ruled that a woman who uses drugs during pregnancy and whose newborn has drugs in its system may be brought before Family Court for a hearing on neglect. Yet how can we condemn a woman under law for harming her unborn child while at the same time protecting her right to destroy that child absolutely, for any reason, through abortion? Is the only difference that the first instance entails a monetary cost to society while the second does not?

There is another kind of behavior implicitly condoned by *Roe v. Wade,* which involves the value of life itself, and which also has its most frightening and threatening manifestation in the underclass. Consensus on when human life begins has yet to be established and perhaps never will be. What is clear, however, is that abortion cuts short the development of a specific human life; it wipes out the future years of a human being, years we can know nothing about. Generally we have no trouble conceiving of lost future years as real loss. Lawsuits routinely place value on lost future income and lost future enjoyment, and we consider the death of a child or a young person to be particularly tragic in lost potential, in the waste of idealized years to come. Yet under *Roe v. Wade* the value of the future years of life of the fetus is determined by an individual taking into account only her own well-being.

Back in 1965, justifying his discovery of a constitutional right to privacy which is nowhere mentioned in the Constitution itself, and which helped lay the groundwork for *Roe v. Wade,* Justice William O. Douglas invoked the concept of "penumbras, formed by emanations" of constitutional amendments. Is it far-fetched to say that there are "penumbras, formed by emanations" of *Roe v. Wade* that grant the right to consider life in relative terms and to place one's own interest above any others? This same "right" when exercised by criminals is a terrifying phenomenon: these are people who feel no guilt in taking a victim's life, who value the future years of that life as nothing compared with their own interest in the victim's property. Of course, one might argue that a fetus is not yet cognizant of its own beingness and that, further, it feels no pain. Yet if a killer creeps up behind you and blows your head off with a semi-automatic, you will feel no pain either, nor will you be cognizant of your death.

Roe v. Wade was a great victory for the women's movement. It seemed   *35* to promote equality of opportunity for women in all their endeavors by freeing them from the burden of years of caring for children conceived unintentionally. But perhaps support for *Roe v. Wade* should be reconsidered in light of the damage wrought by the kind of behavior that has become common in a world in which pregnancy is no longer seen as the momentous beginning of a new life, and life, by extension, is no longer held as sacred.

At any rate, even if one rejects my speculation that *Roe v. Wade* has at least some indirect connection with the degree to which life on our streets has become so cheap, surely there can be no denying the direct connection between *Roe v. Wade* and the degree to which sex has become so casual. Surely, for example, *Roe v. Wade* will make it harder for my two daughters to grow gracefully into womanhood without being encouraged to think of sex as a kind of sport played with a partner who need feel no further responsibility toward them once the game is over.

For me, that is reason enough not to support this elevation of abortion to the status of a constitutional right.

ELLEN WILLIS

Putting Women Back into the Abortion Debate

SOME YEARS ago I attended a New York Institute for the Humanities   *1*
seminar on the new right. We were a fairly heterogeneous group of liberals
and lefties, feminists and gay activists, but on one point nearly all of us agreed:
The right-to-life movement was a dangerous antifeminist crusade. At one
session I argued that the attack on abortion had significance far beyond itself,
that it was the linchpin of the right's social agenda. I got a lot of supporting
comments and approving nods. It was too much for Peter Steinfels, a liberal
Catholic, author of *The Neoconservatives,* and executive editor of *Commonweal.*
Right-to-lifers were not all right-wing fanatics, he protested. "You have to
understand," he said plaintively, "that many of us see abortion as a *human life
issue.*" What I remember best was his air of frustrated isolation. I don't think
he came back to the seminar after that.

Things are different now. I often feel isolated when I insist that abortion
is, above all, a *feminist issue.* Once people took for granted that abortion was
an issue of sexual politics and morality. Now, abortion is most often discussed
as a question of "life" in the abstract. Public concern over abortion centers
almost exclusively on fetuses; women and their bodies are merely the stage on
which the drama of fetal life and death takes place. Debate about abortion—if
not its reality—has become sexlessly scholastic. And the people most responsible for this turn of events are, like Peter Steinfels, on the left.

The left wing of the right-to-life movement is a small, seemingly eccen-
tric minority in both "progressive" and antiabortion camps. Yet it has played
a critical role in the movement: By arguing that opposition to abortion can be
separated from the right's antifeminist program, it has given antiabortion sentiment legitimacy in left-symp and (putatively) profeminist circles.[1] While left
antiabortionists are hardly alone in emphasizing fetal life, their innovation has
been to claim that a consistent "pro-life" stand involves opposing capital punishment, supporting disarmament, demanding government programs to end
poverty, and so on. This is of course a leap the right is neither able nor willing
to make. It's been liberals—from Garry Wills to the Catholic bishops—who
have supplied the mass media with the idea that prohibiting abortion is part of
a "seamless garment" of respect for human life.

Having invented this countercontext for the abortion controversy, left
antiabortionists are trying to impose it as the only legitimate context for debate. Those of us who won't accept their terms and persist in seeing opposition to abortion, antifeminism, sexual repression, and religious sectarianism as
the real seamless garment have been accused of obscuring the issue with dem-
agoguery. Last year *Commonweal*—perhaps the most important current forum
for left antiabortion opinion—ran an editorial demanding that we shape up:

[1] *Left-symp:* sympathetic to the left.

"Those who hold that abortion is immoral believe that the biological dividing lines of birth or viability should no more determine whether a developing member of the species is denied or accorded essential rights than should the biological dividing lines of sex or race or disability or old age. This argument is open to challenge. Perhaps the dividing lines are sufficiently different. Pro-choice advocates should state their reasons for believing so. They should meet the argument on its own grounds. . . ."

In other words, the only question we're allowed to debate—or the only   *5*
one *Commonweal* is willing to entertain—is "Are fetuses the moral equivalent of born human beings?" And I can't meet the argument on its own grounds because I don't agree that this is the key question, whose answer determines whether one supports abortion or opposes it. I don't doubt that fetuses are alive, or that they're biologically human—what else would they be? I do consider the life of a fertilized egg less precious than the well-being of a woman with feelings, self-consciousness, a history, social ties; and I think fetuses get closer to being human in a moral sense as they come closer to birth. But to me these propositions are intuitively self-evident. I wouldn't know how to justify them to a "nonbeliever," nor do I see the point of trying.

I believe the debate has to start in a different place—with the recognition that fertilized eggs develop into infants inside the bodies of women. Pregnancy and birth are active processes in which a woman's body shelters, nourishes, and expels a new life; for nine months she is immersed in the most intimate possible relationship with another being. The growing fetus makes consider-able demands on her physical and emotional resources, culminating in the cataclysmic experience of birth. And child-bearing has unpredictable conse-quences; it always entails some risk of injury or death.

For me all this has a new concreteness: I had a baby last year. My much-desired and relatively easy pregnancy was full of what antiabortionists like to call "inconveniences." I was always tired, short of breath; my digestion was never right; for three months I endured a state of hormonal siege; later I had pains in my fingers, swelling feet, numb spots on my legs, the dread hemor-rhoids. I had to think about everything I ate. I developed borderline glucose intolerance. I gained fifty pounds and am still overweight; my shape has changed in other ways that may well be permanent. Psychologically, my pregnancy con-sumed me—though I'd happily bought the seat on the roller coaster, I was still terrified to be so out of control of my normally tractable body. It was all bearable, even interesting—even, at times, transcendent—because I wanted a baby. Birth was painful, exhausting, and wonderful. If I hadn't wanted a baby it would only have been painful and exhausting—or worse. I can hardly imagine what it's like to have your body and mind taken over in this way when you not only don't look forward to the result, but positively dread it. The thought appalls me. So as I see it, the key question is "Can it be moral, under any circumstances, to make a woman bear a child against her will?"

From this vantage point, *Commonweal*'s argument is irrelevant, for in a society that respects the individual, no "member of the species" in *any* stage of development has an "essential right" to make use of someone else's body, let alone in such all-encompassing fashion, without that person's consent. You can't make a case against abortion by applying a general principle about everybody's human rights; you have to show exactly the opposite—that the relationship between fetus and pregnant woman is an exception, one that justifies depriving women of their right to bodily integrity. And in fact all antiabortion ideology rests on the premise—acknowledged or simply assumed—that women's unique capacity to bring life into the world carries with it a unique obligation that women cannot be allowed to "play God" and launch only the lives they welcome.

Yet the alternative to allowing women this power is to make them impotent. Criminalizing abortion doesn't just harm individual women with unwanted pregnancies, it affects all women's sense of themselves. Without control of our fertility we can never envision ourselves as free, for our biology makes us constantly vulnerable. Simply because we are female our physical integrity can be violated, our lives disrupted and transformed, at any time. Our ability to act in the world is hopelessly compromised by our sexual being.

Ah, sex—it does have a way of coming up in these discussions, despite   *10* all. When pressed, right-to-lifers of whatever political persuasion invariably point out that pregnancy doesn't happen by itself. The leftists often give patronizing lectures on contraception (though some find only "natural birth control" acceptable), but remain unmoved when reminded that contraceptives fail. Openly or implicitly they argue that people shouldn't have sex unless they're prepared to procreate. (They are quick to profess a single standard—men as well as women should be sexually "responsible." Yes, and the rich as well as the poor should be allowed to sleep under bridges.) Which amounts to saying that if women want to lead heterosexual lives they must give up any claim to self-determination, and that they have no right to sexual pleasure without fear.

Opposing abortion, then, means accepting that women must suffer sexual disempowerment and a radical loss of autonomy relative to men: If fetal life is sacred, the self-denial basic to women's oppression is also basic to the moral order. Opposing abortion means embracing a conservative sexual morality, one that subordinates pleasure to reproduction: If fetal life is sacred, there is no room for the view that sexual passion—or even sexual love—for its own sake is a human need and a human right. Opposing abortion means tolerating the inevitable double standard, by which men may accept or reject sexual restrictions in accordance with their beliefs, while women must bow to them out of fear . . . or defy them at great risk. However much *Commonweal*'s editors and those of like mind want to believe their opposition to abortion is simply about saving lives, the truth is that in the real world they are shoring up a particular sexual culture, whose rules are stacked against women. I have yet to hear any left right-to-lifers take full responsibility for that fact or deal seriously with its political implications.

Unfortunately, their fuzziness has not lessened their appeal—if anything it's done the opposite. In increasing numbers liberals and leftists, while opposing antiabortion laws, have come to view abortion as an "agonizing moral issue" with some justice on both sides, rather than an issue—however emotionally complex—of freedom versus repression, or equality versus hierarchy, that affects their political self-definition. This above-the-battle stance is attractive to leftists who want to be feminist good guys but are uneasy or ambivalent about sexual issues, not to mention those who want to ally with "progressive" factions of the Catholic church on Central America, nuclear disarmament, or populist economics without that sticky abortion question getting in the way.

Such neutrality is a way of avoiding the painful conflict over cultural issues that continually smolders on the left. It can also be a way of coping with the contradictions of personal life at a time when liberation is a dream deferred. To me the fight for abortion has always been the cutting edge of feminism, precisely because it denies that anatomy is destiny, that female biology dictates women's subordinate status. Yet recently I've found it hard to focus on the issue, let alone summon up the militance needed to stop the antiabortion tanks. In part that has to do with second-round weariness—do we really have to go through all these things twice?—in part with my life now.

Since my daughter's birth my feelings about abortion—not as a political demand but as a personal choice—have changed. In this society, the difference between the situation of a childless woman and of a mother is immense; the fear that having a child will dislodge one's tenuous hold on a nontraditional life is excruciating. This terror of being forced into the sea-change of motherhood gave a special edge to my convictions about abortion. Since I've made that plunge voluntarily, with consequences still unfolding, the terror is gone; I might not want another child, for all sorts of reasons, but I will never again feel that my identity is at stake. Different battles with the culture absorb my energy now. Besides, since I've experienced the primal, sensual passion of caring for an infant, there will always be part of me that does want another. If I had an abortion today, it would be with conflict and sadness unknown to me when I had an abortion a decade ago. And the antiabortionists' imagery of dead babies hits me with new force. Do many women—left, feminist women— have such feelings? Is this the sort of "ambivalence about abortion" that in the present atmosphere slides so easily into self-flagellating guilt?

Some left antiabortionists, mainly pacifists—Juli Loesch, Mary Meehan, *15* and other "feminists for life"; Jim Wallis and various writers for Wallis's radical evangelical journal *Sojourners*—have tried to square their position with concern for women. They blame the prevalence of abortion on oppressive conditions— economic injustice, lack of child care and other social supports for mothers, the devaluation of childrearing, men's exploitative sexual behavior and refusal to take equal responsibility for children. They disagree on whether to criminalize abortion now (since murder is intolerable no matter what the cause) or to build a long-term moral consensus (since stopping abortion requires a general social transformation), but they all regard abortion as a desperate solution to desperate problems, and the women who resort to it as more sinned against than sinning.

This analysis grasps an essential feminist truth: that in a male-supremacist society no choice a woman makes is genuinely free or entirely in her interest. Certainly many women have had abortions they didn't want or wouldn't have wanted if they had any plausible means of caring for a child; and countless others wouldn't have gotten pregnant in the first place were it not for inadequate contraception, sexual confusion and guilt, male pressure, and other stigmata of female powerlessness. Yet forcing a woman to bear a child she doesn't want can only add injury to insult, while refusing to go through with such a pregnancy can be a woman's first step toward taking hold of her life. And many women who have abortions are "victims" only of ordinary human miscalculation, technological failure, or the vagaries of passion, all bound to exist in any society, however utopian. There will always be women who, at any given moment, want sex but don't want a child; some of these women will get pregnant; some of them will have abortions. Behind the victim theory of abortion is the implicit belief that women are always ready to be mothers, if only conditions are right, and that sex for pleasure rather than procreation is not only "irresponsible" (i.e., bad) but something men impose on women, never something women actively seek. Ironically, left right-to-lifers see abortion as always coerced (it's "exploitation" and "violence against women"), yet regard motherhood—which for most women throughout history has been inescapable, and is still our most socially approved role—as a positive choice. The analogy to the feminist antipornography movement goes beyond borrowed rhetoric: the antiporners, too, see active female lust as surrender to male domination and traditionally feminine sexual attitudes as expressions of women's true nature.

This Orwellian version of feminism, which glorifies "female values" and dismisses women's struggles for freedom—particularly sexual freedom—as a male plot, has become all too familiar in recent years. But its use in the abortion debate has been especially muddleheaded. Somehow we're supposed to leap from an oppressive patriarchal society to the egalitarian one that will supposedly make abortion obsolete without ever allowing women to see themselves as people entitled to control their reproductive function rather than be controlled by it. How women who have no power in this most personal of areas can effectively fight for power in the larger society is left to our imagination. A "New Zealand feminist" quoted by Mary Meehan in a 1980 article in *The Progressive* says, "Accepting short-term solutions like abortion only delays the implementation of real reforms like decent maternity and paternity leaves, job protection, high-quality child care, community responsibility for dependent people of all ages, and recognition of the economic contribution of childminders"—as if these causes were progressing nicely before legal abortion came along. On the contrary, the fight for reproductive freedom is the foundation of all the others, which is why antifeminists resist it so fiercely.

As "pro-life" pacifists have been particularly concerned with refuting charges of misogyny, the liberal Catholics at *Commonweal* are most exercised by the claim that antiabortion laws violate religious freedom. The editorial quoted above hurled another challenge at the proabortion forces:

> It is time, finally, for the pro-choice advocates and editorial writers to abandon, once and for all, the argument that abortion is a religious "doctrine" of a single or several churches being imposed on those of other persuasions in violation of the First Amendment. . . . Catholics and their bishops are accused of imposing their "doctrine" on abortion, but not their "doctrine" on the needs of the poor, or their "doctrine" on the arms race, or their "doctrine" on human rights in Central America. . . .
>
> The briefest investigation into Catholic teaching would show that the church's case against abortion is utterly unlike, say, its belief in the Real Presence, known with the eyes of faith alone, or its insistence on a Sunday obligation, applicable only to the faithful. The church's moral teaching on abortion . . . is for the most part like its teaching on racism, warfare, and capital punishment, based on ordinary reasoning common to believers and nonbelievers. . . .

This is one more example of right-to-lifers' tendency to ignore the sexual ideology underlying their stand. Interesting, isn't it, how the editorial neglects to mention that the church's moral teaching on abortion jibes neatly with its teaching on birth control, sex, divorce, and the role of women. The traditional, patriarchal sexual morality common to these teachings is explicitly religious, and its chief defenders in modern times have been the more conservative churches. The Catholic and evangelical Christian churches are the backbone of the organized right-to-life movement and—a few Nathansons and Hentoffs notwithstanding—have provided most of the movement's activists and spokespeople.

Furthermore, the Catholic hierarchy has made opposition to abortion a *20* litmus test of loyalty to the church in a way it has done with no other political issue—witness Archbishop O'Connor's harassment of Geraldine Ferraro during her vice-presidential campaign. It's unthinkable that a Catholic bishop would publicly excoriate a Catholic officeholder or candidate for taking a hawkish position on the arms race or Central America or capital punishment. Nor do I notice anyone trying to read William F. Buckley out of the church for his views on welfare. The fact is there is no accepted Catholic "doctrine" on these matters comparable to the church's absolutist condemnation of abortion. While differing attitudes toward war, racism, and poverty cut across religious and secular lines, the sexual values that mandate opposition to abortion are the bedrock of the traditional religious world view, and the source of the most bitter conflict with secular and religious modernists. When churches devote their considerable political power, organizational resources, and money to translating those values into law, I call that imposing their religious beliefs on me—whether or not they're technically violating the First Amendment.

Statistical studies have repeatedly shown that people's views on abortion are best predicted by their opinions on sex and "family" issues, not on "life" issues like nuclear weapons or the death penalty. That's not because we're inconsistent but because we comprehend what's really at stake in the abortion fight. It's the antiabortion left that refuses to face the contradiction in its own position: you can't be wholeheartedly for "life"—or for such progressive aspirations as freedom, democracy, equality—and condone the subjugation of women. The seamless garment is full of holes.

These preceding essays by McConnell and Willis represent the two sides on which most Americans fall regarding the issue of legalized abortion. Since abortion is likely to stay legal, what is the point of trying to reconcile these positions? One benefit is that doing so might help put to rest the controversy surrounding abortion—a controversy that rages at abortion clinics and in the media, distracting Americans from other issues of importance and causing divisiveness and distrust, and that also rages within millions of Americans who want abortion to remain legal but at the same time disapprove of it. In addition, reaching some consensus on abortion might resolve the contradiction of its being legal but unavailable to many women, as extremist opponents have caused many doctors to refuse to perform abortions and the access of poor women is limited by restrictions on public funding for abortion. Finally, some consensus on abortion will be necessary to formulate decisions of public policy: What restrictions, if any, are appropriate? Should parental notification or consent be required for women under eighteen? Should public funds be available for an abortion when a woman cannot otherwise afford one?

We have said that the first step in resolving conflict is to understand what the parties in conflict are claiming and why. Using the following outline form, or brief, we can describe the positions of each side:

McConnell's position: She is against unrestricted abortion as a woman's right.

Claim (or thesis):   The right to abortion has hurt the moral and social climate of our nation.

> *Reason:* It has put pressure on young single women to adopt a "liberated" lifestyle of sex without commitment.
> *Evidence:* Her own college experiences.

> *Reason:* It has caused an increase in unintended pregnancies.
> *Evidence:* The analogy of children playing ball.

> *Reason:* It has taken questions about morality out of the decision to end a pregnancy.
> *Evidence:* Her own experiences with doctors and clinics.

Reason: It has allowed middle- and upper-class men and women to avoid the consequences of their sex lives and to evade the responsibilities of parenthood.
> *Evidence:* None offered.

Reason: It has reduced people's sense of duty toward their offspring, most noticeably in the lower classes.
> *Evidence:* Legislation has become necessary to make fathers provide financial support for their children and to hold women legally culpable for harming their fetuses through drug use.

Willis's position: She is for unrestricted abortion as a woman's right.

Claim (or thesis): The right to abortion is an essential part of feminism.

Reason: Without control of their reproductive lives, women constantly fear having their lives disrupted.
> *Evidence:* A fetus makes immense demands on a woman's physical and mental resources. Her own pregnancy is an example.

Reason: Without abortion, women must live according to a sexual double standard.
> *Evidence:* Sex always carries the risk of pregnancy. The fear of pregnancy puts restrictions on women's ability to enjoy sex for pleasure or passion, rather than procreation.

Following Through

If you and some of your classmates have written arguments taking opposing views on the same issue, prepare briefs of your respective positions to share with each other. (You each might also create briefs of your opponents' positions to see how well you have understood one another's written arguments.)

Alternatively, write briefs summarizing the opposing positions offered in several published arguments as a first step toward mediating these viewpoints.

Locating the Areas of Disagreement

Areas of disagreement generally involve differences over facts and differences in interests.

Differences over Facts

Any parties involved in negotiation, as well as any mediator in a dispute, should consider both the reasons and evidence offered on all sides in order to locate areas of factual agreement and, particularly, disagreement. Parties genuinely interested in finding the best solution to a conflict rather than in advocating their own positions ought to be able to recognize where more evidence is needed, no matter the side. Negotiators and mediators should also consider the currency and the authority of any sources. If new or better research could help resolve factual disparities, the parties should do it collaboratively rather than independently.

Following Through

In the preceding arguments on abortion, the writers do not present much factual evidence, as their arguments are relatively abstract. Are there any facts that they agree on? Would more facts make a difference in getting either side to reconsider her position? How could you gather more solid evidence or hard data?

Differences in Interests

Experts in negotiation have found that conflicts most often result from interpretive differences rather than from factual differences; that is, people in conflict look at the same situation differently depending on their values, their beliefs, and their interests. McConnell opens her argument with this very point by showing, first, how most women's rights advocates would interpret the scene at a typical antiabortion protest and then offering a second perspective, affected by her view that legalized abortion has victimized women.

What kinds of subjective differences cause people to draw conflicting conclusions from the same evidence? To identify these differences, we can ask the same questions that are useful in persuasion to identify what divides us from our audience (see the box "Questions about Difference"). In negotiation and mediation, these questions can help uncover the real interests that any resolution must address. It is in identifying these interests that the dialogue of negotiation begins, because only when the interests that underlie opposing positions are identified can creative solutions be formulated. Often, uncovering each party's real interests leads to the discovery of previously ignored common ground. Finding these interests should be a collaborative project, one that negotiation experts compare to problem-solving through teamwork.

Here we apply the questions about difference to McConnell's and Willis's positions on abortion rights.

Is the Difference a Matter of Assumptions?
Both arguments make the assumption that legalizing abortion removed constraints on women's sexuality. McConnell blames abortion for this presumed effect, but Willis credits abortion with enabling women to enjoy sex as men have traditionally been able to do. A mediator could begin by pointing out that this assumption itself could

---

QUESTIONS ABOUT DIFFERENCE

1. Is the difference a matter of *assumptions*? As we discussed in Chapter 4 on the Toulmin method of analysis and in Chapter 5 on inquiry, all arguments are based on some assumptions.

2. Is the difference a matter of *principle*? Are some parties to the dispute following different principles, or general rules, than others?

3. Is the difference a matter of *values* or a matter of having the same values but giving them different *priorities*?

4. Is the difference a matter of *ends or means*? That is, do people want to achieve different goals, or do they have the same goals in mind but disagree on the means to achieve them?

5. Is the difference a matter of *interpretation*?

6. Is the difference a matter of *implications* or *consequences*?

7. Is the difference a result of *personal background, basic human needs, or emotions*? To our list of questions about difference in persuasive writing we add this further question, because negotiation requires the parties involved to look not just at one another's arguments but also at one another as people, with histories and feelings. It is not realistic to think that human problems can be solved without taking human factors into consideration. Negotiators must be open about their emotions and such basic human needs as personal security, economic well-being, and a sense of belonging, recognition, and control over their own lives. They can be open with each other about such matters only if their dialogue up to this point has established trust between them. If you are mediating among printed texts, you must use the texts themselves as evidence of these human factors.

---

be wrong, that it is possible, for example, that the introduction of birth control pills and the political liberalism of the 1970s contributed more to the increased sexual activity of women. McConnell wants young women not to feel pressured to have sex, while Willis's interest is in freeing women from a sexual double standard.

McConnell also assumes that abortion becomes guilt-free for most women because it is legal. Willis insists that women should not feel guilty. A mediator might ask what interest McConnell has in making women feel guilty and what Willis means when she says she would now feel "conflict and sadness" (paragraph 14) over choosing an abortion. What is the difference between "conflict and sadness" and "guilt"?

The main assumption these writers do not share concerns the motives of those who cast abortion as a moral issue. Willis assumes that any question about the morality of abortion is part of an effort to repress and subordinate women. This assumption makes Willis see those who disagree with her as a threat to her chief interest—women's rights. McConnell, on the other hand, challenges the feminist assumption that abortion has liberated women. To her, the legalization of abortion, rather than protecting women's rights, has actually contributed to the further exploitation of women sexually, which she sees as immoral.

Is the Difference a Matter of Principle?   The principle of equal rights for all individuals is featured in both arguments but in different ways. Willis is interested in equal rights among men and women. McConnell is concerned with the equal rights of the fetus as a potential human being.

Is the Difference a Matter of Values or of Priorities?   The question of priorities brings us to a key difference underlying the positions of McConnell and Willis. Willis puts the value of a woman's well-being above the value of a fetus's life (paragraph 5). In paragraph 8, she states, ". . . in a society that respects the individual, no [fetus] in *any* stage of development has an 'essential right' to make use of someone else's body . . . without that person's consent." For Willis, it is immoral to force any woman to bear a child against her will. For McConnell, however, the interests of the fetus have priority over the interests of the pregnant woman. Denying the fetus's rights in this case is denying nothing less than life itself; therefore, the woman has a duty and responsibility to bear the child, even at great sacrifice to her well-being. For McConnell, it is immoral for a woman to refuse this obligation (paragraphs 4 and 33).

In addition, these two writers have very different values regarding sex. For McConnell, sex for pleasure, without commitment, is demeaning to women, something that they acquiesce to only because they have been told that it is normal and healthy. For Willis, sexual passion "for its own sake is a human need and a human right" (paragraph 11); she seems to be responding directly to McConnell in paragraph 16: "Behind the victim theory of abortion is the implicit belief . . . that sex for pleasure is not only 'irresponsible' (i.e., bad) but something men impose on women, never something women actively seek."

Is the Difference a Matter of Ends or Means?   McConnell and Willis both claim to have the same end in mind—a society in which women are truly free and equal, able to live dignified and uncompromised lives. However, they differ over legalized abortion as a means to this end. McConnell does not argue that *Roe v. Wade* should be overturned; rather, she wants her audience to recognize that abortion has cheapened both sex and life, allowing women to be victimized by men who want sex without commitment and encouraging a society that wants rights without responsibilities. Her ultimate goal is higher moral standards for the community. Willis, on the other hand, wants to make sure that freedom and equality for women stay in the forefront of the abortion debate. She resists any compromise on the abortion issue—even the concession that women should feel guilt over having abortions—because she sees the issue of morality as a slope down which women could slide back into a subordinate societal role.

Is the Difference a Matter of Interpretation?   These two writers interpret abortion from polar extremes. McConnell sees it as totally negative; to her, abortion is a convenience, a way of avoiding responsibility after an act of sexual carelessness. Willis's definition of abortion stresses its positive political value; it is the "cutting edge of feminism" because it guarantees to women absolute control over their reproductive freedom. Further, as we have seen, they interpret individualism differently: for Willis individualism is positive, the autonomy and freedom to reach one's goals, while for McConnell it is more negative, with connotations of selfishness and immaturity.

Is the Difference a Matter of Implications or Consequences?   Both writers are concerned with consequences, but neither entertains the other's concerns. Willis sees the results of legalized abortion as a more just society. McConnell argues that the positive consequences Willis would claim for women are illusory and that women have been harmed by the easy availability of abortion.

Is the Difference a Result of Personal Background, Basic Human Needs, or Emotions?   In their arguments about abortion, both writers are fairly open about some of their emotions. McConnell is quite frank about her "remorse" over her abortion in her first year of college. In her description of that experience, she suggests that she was coerced by the university's health counselors. Notice, too, that she describes herself as the child of "first-generation" Americans, with strict moral standards, a fact that surely influenced her perception of liberated sexual morals.

Willis expresses anger that the arena of debate over abortion has moved from its original focus on women's rights to a new focus on the rights of the fetus. She fears that hard-won ground on women's rights could be slipping. Yet in discussing her own child, she reveals an emotional vulnerability that could possibly make her rethink her position on the morality of abortion. Note, for example, that she mentions her own abortion only once, in paragraph 14.

In face-to-face negotiation and mediation, having a conversation about underlying differences can go a long way toward helping opposing parties understand each other. Each side must "try on" the position of those who see the issue from a different perspective. They may still not agree or let go of their positions, but at this point each side ought to be able to say to the other, "I see what your concerns are." Progress toward resolution begins when people start talking about their underlying concerns, or interests, rather than their positions.

As a student mediating among written texts, you must decide what you could say to help each side see other viewpoints and to loosen the commitment each has to his or her own position.

Following Through

If you are negotiating between your own position and the arguments of classmates, form groups and use the questions on page 179 to identify the interests of each party. You may ask an outside student to mediate the discussion. As a group, prepare a report on your conversation: What are the main interests of each party?

If you are mediating the views of printed arguments, write an analysis based on applying the questions to two or more arguments. You could write out your analysis in list form, as we did in analyzing the differences between McConnell and Willis, or you could treat it as an exploratory essay (see page 61).

As a creative variation for your analysis, write a dialogue with yourself as mediator, posing questions to each of the opposing parties. Have each side respond to your questions just as we demonstrated in our sample dialogue in Chapter 5 (pages 48–52).

Defining the Problem in Terms of the Real Interests

As we have said, while it is important in negotiating to see clearly what each side is demanding, successful negotiation looks for a solution that addresses the interests that underlie the positions of each side. Uncovering those interests is the first step. The next is summing them up, recognizing the most important ones a solution must address. Meeting these underlying interests is the task that negotiators undertake collaboratively.

To illustrate, let's look at the two arguments over legalized abortion. While McConnell criticizes abortion and those who choose it, she admits that she would keep it legal. Her real interest is in reducing what she sees as the consequences of legalized abortion: irresponsible sex and a disregard for life.

Willis is not totally unwilling to consider the moral value of the fetus as human life, admitting that it begins to acquire moral value as it comes to term; her problem with the moral question is the possibility that considering it at all will endanger women's right to choose for—or against—having an abortion. Her real interest is in equality of the sexes.

A mediator between these two positions would have to help resolve the conflict in a way that guarantees women's autonomy and control over their reproductive lives and that promotes responsibility and respect for the value of life. Any resolution here must ensure the rights of the individual and the good of the community at the same time.

Following Through

For the conflict among classmates' positions that you have been negotiating or the conflict among written texts that you have been mediating, write a description of the problem that a resolution must solve: What are the key interests that must be addressed? If you are negotiating, come to a collaborative statement.

_____

Inventing Creative Options

Parties can work toward solutions to a problem collaboratively, each party can brainstorm solutions alone, or an individual mediator can take on this task. Collaboration can either help or hinder the invention process, depending on the relationship of the negotiators, and since coming up with possible solutions means making some concessions, you might want to do so privately rather than state publicly what you would be willing to give up. Whether you are a mediator or a negotiator, this is the stage for opening the options, for exploring wild ideas, for experimenting without making any judgments.

With respect to the abortion issue, Willis might be willing to consider counseling for women contemplating abortion and admit that the issue inevitably involves some ethical concerns. McConnell might be willing to take a less judgmental position and concede that it is not really fair to impose either motherhood or guilt on every woman with an unwanted pregnancy.

_____

Following Through

1. What do you think might be a possible compromise on the issue of legalized abortion? Your ideas should address the interests of both Willis and McConnell. How likely do you think the two writers would be to accept your compromise?
2. For a class assignment on negotiating or mediating a dispute, brainstorm possible solutions either independently or collaboratively. Try to make your list of options as long as you can, initially ruling out nothing.

_____

Gathering More Data

Once a mediator has proposed a solution or negotiators have created a tentative resolution, some or all of the parties might be thinking that they could accept it if only they had a little more information. For example, one side in the abortion issue might want to know not just that there are approximately 1.5 million abortions performed each year in the United States but that many of them are second or third abortions for the same women. If Willis learned that many women have abortions repeatedly, she might agree that the right is being abused—and that some counseling might help. If McConnell were to find out that most women have only a single abortion, she might decide that women do not interpret the right to abortion as nonchalantly as she had imagined. Professionals in the field of negotiation suggest that information-gathering at this point be done collaboratively. The trust and spirit of collaboration built so far, however, can be damaged if each side tries to gather data favorable to its own original position.

Following Through

1. If you have an idea for a compromise that would address the interests of Willis and McConnell, what additional data do you think either or both of these authors would want to have before accepting your solution?
2. If you have invented a proposal for resolving a conflict that you and some classmates have been negotiating or that you have been mediating, decide together if additional information could help you reach consensus. What questions need to be answered? Try to answer these questions collaboratively, with a joint visit to the library.

Reaching a Solution Based on Agreed-upon Principles

The kind of negotiation we have been talking about in this chapter is not of the "I-give-a-little, you-give-a-little" sort that occurs between a buyer and seller or, for example, in a hostage situation when terrorists offer to trade a number of hostages for an equal number of released prisoners; such a resolution involves no real principle other than that concessions ought to be of equal value. It brings the opposing sides no closer to understanding why they differed in the first place.

Instead, negotiated settlements on matters of public policy such as abortion or sexual harassment or gun control ought to involve some principles that both sides agree are fair. For example, Willis might agree that abortion ought to be a real choice, not something a woman is railroaded into as McConnell feels she was at age eighteen. On this principle, Willis might agree that professional counseling about ethics and options ought at least to be available to women considering abortion.

Following Through

1. If you have been mediating or negotiating a conflict with classmates, formalize your resolution, if possible. Be ready to explain what principles you have agreed on as the basis for the compromise.
2. After reading about mediatory essays in the following section, decide if the example offered, "How to End the Abortion War" by Roger Rosenblatt, would move Willis and McConnell—and others who hold similar views— closer to consensus about how to view abortion. What is Rosenblatt's proposed solution? Could you improve upon it?

THE MEDIATORY ESSAY

Arguments that appear in newspapers and popular magazines usually seek to convince or persuade an audience to accept the author's position. Sometimes, however, the writer assumes the role of mediator and attempts to negotiate a solution acceptable to the opposing sides. The writer of such an essay moves beyond the stated positions and the facts of the dispute to expose the underlying interests, values, and beliefs of those in opposition. The goal is to show what interests they may have in common, to increase each side's understanding of the other, and to propose a solution to the dispute, a new position based on interests and values that will be acceptable to both sides. The following essay by Roger Rosenblatt aims to mediate one of the most deeply entrenched conflicts of our day—the issue of legalized abortion. As you read it, keep in mind the arguments of Margaret Liu McConnell and Ellen Willis. Do you think that reading this mediatory essay might bring them closer to some consensus on the question of how to live with legalized abortion?

ROGER ROSENBLATT

How to End the Abortion War

Roger Rosenblatt is a writer who regularly contributes to the New York Times Magazine, *where this essay originally appeared.*

THE VEINS in his forehead bulged so prominently they might have been blue worms that had worked their way under the surface of his skin. His eyes bulged, too, capillaries zigzagging from the pupils in all directions. His face was pulled tight about the jaw, which thrust forward like a snowplow attachment on the grille of a truck. From the flattened O of his mouth, the word "murderer" erupted in a regular rhythm, the repetition of the r's giving the word the sound of an outboard motor that failed to catch.

She, for her part, paced up and down directly in front of him, saying nothing. Instead, she held high a large cardboard sign on a stick, showing the cartoonish drawing of a bloody coat hanger over the caption, "Never again." Like his, her face was taut with fury, her lips pressed together so tightly they folded under and vanished. Whenever she drew close to him, she would deliberately lower the sign and turn it toward him, so that he would be yelling his "murderer" at the picture of the coat hanger.

For nearly twenty years these two have been at each other with all the hatred they can unearth. Sometimes the man is a woman, sometimes the woman a man. They are black, white, Hispanic, Asian; they make their homes in Missouri or New Jersey; they are teenagers and pharmacists and college professors; Catholic, Baptist, Jew. They have exploded at each other on the steps of the Capitol in Washington, in front of abortion clinics, hospitals, and politicians' homes, on village greens and the avenues of cities. Their rage is tireless; at every decision of the United States Supreme Court or of the President or of the state legislatures, it rises like a missile seeking only the heat of its counterpart.

This is where America is these days on the matter of abortion, or where it seems to be. In fact, it is very hard to tell how the country really feels about abortion, because those feelings are almost always displayed in political arenas. Most ordinary people do not speak of abortion. Friends who gladly debate other volatile issues—political philosophy, war, race—shy away from the subject. It is too private, too personal, too bound up with one's faith or spiritual identity. Give abortion five seconds of thought, and it quickly spirals down in the mind to the most basic questions about human life, to the mysteries of birth and our relationship with our souls.

We simply will not talk about it. We will march in demonstrations, shout and carry placards, but we will not talk about it. In the Presidential election of 1992, we will cast votes for a national leader based in part on his or her position on abortion. Still, we will not talk about it.   5

The oddity in this unnatural silence is that most of us actually know what we feel about abortion. But because those feelings are mixed and complicated, we have decided that they are intractable. I believe the opposite is true: that we are more prepared than we realize to reach a common, reasonable understanding on this subject, and if we were to vent our mixed feelings and begin to make use of them, a resolution would be at hand.

Seventy-three percent of Americans polled in 1990 were in favor of abortion rights. Seventy-seven percent polled also regard abortion as a kind of killing. (Forty-nine percent see abortion as outright murder, 28 percent solely as the taking of human life.) These figures represent the findings of the Harris and Gallup polls, respectively, and contain certain nuances of opinion within both attitudes. But the general conclusions are widely considered valid. In other words, most Americans are both for the choice of abortion as a principle and against abortion for themselves. One has to know nothing else to realize how conflicted a problem we have before and within us.

The fact that abortion entails conflict, however, does not mean that the country is bound to be locked in combat forever. In other contexts, living with conflict is not only normal to America, it is often the only way to function honestly. We are for both Federal assistance and states' autonomy; we are for both the First Amendment and normal standards of propriety; we are for both the rights of privacy and the needs of public health. Our most productive thinking usually contains an inner confession of mixed feelings. Our least productive thinking, a nebulous irritation resulting from a refusal to come to terms with disturbing and patently irreconcilable ideas.

Yet acknowledging and living with ambivalence is, in a way, what America was invented to do. To create a society in which abortion is permitted and its gravity appreciated is to create but another of the many useful frictions of a democratic society. Such a society does not devalue life by allowing abortion; it takes life with utmost seriousness and is, by the depth of its conflicts and by the richness of its difficulties, a reflection of life itself.

Why, then, are we stuck in political warfare on this issue? Why can we not make use of our ambivalence and move on? *10*

The answer has to do with America's peculiar place in the history of abortion, and also with the country's special defining characteristics, both ancient and modern, with which abortion has collided. In the 4,000-year-old history extending from the Greeks and Romans through the Middle Ages and into the present, every civilization has taken abortion with utmost seriousness. Yet ours seems to be the only civilization to have engaged in an emotional and intellectual civil war over the issue.

There are several reasons for this. The more obvious include the general lack of consensus in the country since the mid-60's, which has promoted bitter divisions over many social issues—race, crime, war, and abortion, too. The sexual revolution of the 60's resulted in the heightened activity of people who declared themselves "pro-choice" *and* "pro-life"—misleading terms used here principally for convenience. The pro-life movement began in 1967, six years before *Roe v. Wade.* The women's movement, also revitalized during the 60's, gave an impetus for self-assertion to women on both sides of the abortion issue.

But there are less obvious reasons, central to America's special character, which have helped to make abortion an explosive issue in this country.

Religiosity. America is, and always has been, a religious country, even though it spreads its religiosity among many different religions. Perry Miller, the great historian of American religious thought, established that the New England colonists arrived with a ready-made religious mission, which they cultivated and sustained through all its manifestations, from charity to intolerance. The Virginia settlement, too, was energized by God's glory. Nothing changed in this attitude by the time the nation was invented. If anything, the creation of the United States of America made the desire to receive redemption in the New World more intense.

Yet individuals sought something in American religion that was different, more emotional than the religion practiced in England. One member of an early congregation explained that the reason he made the long journey to America was "I thought I should find feelings." This personalized sense of religion, which has endured to the present, has an odd but telling relationship with the national attitude toward religion. Officially, America is an a-religious country; the separation of church and state is so rooted in the democracy it has become a cliché. Yet that same separation has created and intensified a hidden national feeling about faith and God, a sort of secret, undercurrent religion, which, perhaps because of its subterranean nature, is often more deeply felt and volatile than that of countries with official or state religions. *15*

The Catholic Church seems more steadily impassioned about abortion in America than anywhere else, even in a country like Poland—so agitated, in fact, that it has entered into an unlikely, if not unholy, alliance with evangelical churches in the pro-life camp. In Catholic countries like Italy, France, and Ireland, religion is often so fluidly mixed with social life that rules are bent more quietly, without our personal sort of moral upheaval.

Americans are moral worriers. We tend to treat every political dispute that arises as a test of our national soul. The smallest incident, like the burning of the flag, can bring our hidden religion to the surface. The largest and most complex moral problem, like abortion, can confound it for decades.

Individualism. Two basic and antithetical views of individualism have grown up with the country. Emerson, the evangelist of self-reliance and non-conformity, had a quasi-mystical sense of the value of the individual self.[1] He described man as a self-sufficient microcosm: "The lightning which explodes and fashions planets, maker of planets and suns, is in him." Tocqueville had a more prosaic and practical view.[2] He worried about the tendency of Americans to withdraw into themselves at the expense of the public good, confusing self-assertion with self-absorption.

Abortion hits both of these views of the individual head on, of course; but both views are open to antipodal interpretations. The Emersonian celebration of the individual may be shared by the pro-choice advocate who sees in individualism one's right to privacy. It may be seen equally by a pro-life advocate as a justification for taking an individual stance—an antiliberal stance to boot—on a matter of conscience.

The idea of the independent individual may also be embraced by the pro-life position as the condition of life on which the unborn have a claim immediately after conception. Pro-life advocates see the pregnant woman as two individuals, each with an equal claim to the riches that American individualism offers.

Tocqueville's concern with individualism as selfishness is also available for adoption by both camps. The pro-life people claim that the pro-choice advocates are placing their individual rights above those of society, and one of the fundamental rights of American society is the right to life. Even the Supreme Court, when it passed *Roe v. Wade,* concluded that abortion "is not unqualified and must be considered against important state interests in regulation."

To those who believe in abortion rights, the "public good" consists of a society in which people, collectively, have the right to privacy and individual choice. Their vision of an unselfish, unself-centered America is one in which the collective sustains its strength by encouraging the independence of those who comprise it. Logically, both camps rail against the individual imposing his or her individual views on society at large, each feeling the same, if opposite, passion about both what society and the individual ought to be. Passion on this subject has led to rage.

[1]Ralph Waldo Emerson (1803–1882) was an essayist and leader of New England transcendentalism.

[2]Alexis de Tocqueville (1805–1859) was a French aristocrat and magistrate who toured the United States in 1831 to study the effects of democracy. His classic work *Democracy in America* was first published in 1835.

Optimism. The American characteristic of optimism, like that of individualism, is affected by abortion in contradictory ways. People favoring the pro-life position see optimism exactly as they read individual rights: Every American, born or unborn, is entitled to look forward to a state of infinite hope and progress. The process of birth is itself an optimistic activity.

Taking the opposite view, those favoring abortion rights interpret the ideas of hope and progress as a consequence of one's entitlement to free choice in all things, abortion definitely included. If the individual woman wishes to pursue her manifest destiny unencumbered by children she does not want, that is not only her business but her glory. The issue is national as well as personal. The pro-choice reasoning goes: The country may only reach its ideal goals if women, along with men, are allowed to achieve their highest potential as citizens, unburdened by limitations that are not of their own choosing.

Even the element of American "can-do" ingenuity applies. The inven-   *25* tion of abortion, like other instruments of American optimism, supports both the pro-life and pro-choice stands. Hail the procedure for allowing women to realize full control over their invented selves. Or damn the procedure for destroying forever the possibility of a new life inventing itself. As with all else pertaining to this issue, one's moral position depends on the direction in which one is looking. Yet both directions are heaving with optimism, and both see life in America as the best of choices.

Sexuality. The connection of abortion with American attitudes toward sexuality is both economic and social. The American way with sex is directly related to the country's original desire to become a society of the middle class, and thus to cast off the extremes of luxury and poverty that characterized Europe and the Old World. The structure of English society, in particular, was something the new nation sought to avoid. Not for Puritan America was the rigid English class system, which not only fixed people into economically immobile slots but allowed and encouraged free-wheeling sexual behavior at both the highest and lowest strata.

At the top of the English classes was a self-indulgent minority rich enough to ignore middle-class moral codes and idle enough to spend their time seducing servants. At the opposite end of the system, the poor also felt free to do whatever they wished with their bodies, since the world offered them so little. The masses of urban poor, created by the Industrial Revolution, had little or no hope of bettering their lot. Many of them wallowed in a kind of sexual Pandemonium, producing babies wantonly and routinely engaging in rape and incest. Between the two class extremes stood the staunch English middle class, with its hands on its hips, outraged at the behavior both above and below them, but powerless to insist on, much less enforce, bourgeois values.

This was not to be the case in America, where bourgeois values were to become the standards and the moral engine of the country. Puritanism, a mere aberrant religion to the English, who were able to get rid of it in 1660 after a brief eighteen years, was the force that dominated American social life for a century and a half. Since there has been a natural progression from Puritanism to Victorianism and from Victorianism to modern forms of fundamentalism in terms of social values, it may be said that the Puritans have really never loosened their headlock on American thinking. The Puritans offered a perfect context for America's desire to create a ruling middle class, which was to be known equally for infinite mobility (geographic, social, economic) and the severest forms of repression.

Abortion fits into such thinking more by what the issue implies than by what it is. In the 1800's and the early 1900's, Americans were able to live with abortion, even during periods of intense national prudery, as long as the practice was considered the exception that proved the rule. The rule was that abortion was legally and morally discouraged. Indeed, most every modern civilization has adopted that attitude, which, put simply, is an attitude of looking the other way in a difficult human situation, which often cannot and should not be avoided. For all its adamant middle-classedness, it was not uncomfortable for Americans to look the other way, either—at least until recently.

When abortion was no longer allowed to be a private, albeit dangerous, business, however, especially during the sexual revolution of the 60's, America's basic middle-classedness asserted itself loudly. Who was having all these abortions? The upper classes, who were behaving irresponsibly, and the lower orders, who had nothing to lose. Abortion, in other words, was a sign of careless sexuality and was thus an offense to the bourgeois dream.

The complaint was, and is, that abortion contradicts middle-class values, which dictate the rules of sexual conduct. Abortion, it is assumed, is the practice of the socially irresponsible, those who defy the solid norms that keep America intact. When *Roe v. Wade* was ruled upon, it sent the harshest message to the American middle class, including those who did not oppose abortion themselves but did oppose the disruption of conformity and stability. If they—certainly the middle-class majority—did not object to *Roe v. Wade* specifically, they did very much object to the atmosphere of lawlessness or unruliness that they felt the law encouraged. Thus the outcry; thus the warfare.

There may be one other reason for abortion's traumatic effect on the country in recent years. Since the end of the Second World War, American society, not unlike modern Western societies in general, has shifted intellectually from a humanistic to a social science culture; that is, from a culture used to dealing with contrarieties to one that demands definite, provable answers. The nature of social science is that it tends not only to identify, but to create issues that must be solved. Often these issues are the most significant to the country's future—civil rights, for example.

What social science thinking does not encourage is human sympathy. By that I do not mean the sentimental feeling that acknowledges another's pain or discomfort; I mean the intellectual sympathy that accepts another's views as both interesting and potentially valid, that deliberately goes to the heart of the thinking of the opposition and spends some time there. That sort of humanistic thinking may or may not be humane, but it does offer the opportunity to arrive at a humane understanding outside the realm and rules of politics. In a way, it is a literary sort of thinking, gone now from a post-literary age, a "reading" of events to determine layers of depth, complication, and confusion and to learn to live with them.

Everything that has happened in the abortion debate has been within the polarities that social science thinking creates. The quest to determine when life begins is a typical exercise of social science—the attempt to impose objective precision on a subjective area of speculation. Arguments over the mother's rights versus the rights of the unborn child are social science arguments, too. The social sciences are far more interested in rights than in how one arrives at what is right—that is, both their strength and weakness. Thus the abortion debate has been political from the start.

A good many pro-choice advocates, in fact, came to lament the political 35 character of the abortion debate when it first began in the 60's. At that time, political thinking in America was largely and conventionally liberal. The liberals had the numbers; therefore, they felt that they could set the national agenda without taking into account the valid feelings or objections of the conservative opposition. When, in the Presidential election of 1980, it became glaringly apparent that the feelings of the conservative opposition were not only valid but were politically ascendant, many liberals reconsidered the idea that abortion was purely a rights issue. They expressed appreciation of a more emotionally complicated attitude, one they realized that they shared themselves, however they might vote.

If the abortion debate had risen in a humanistic environment, it might never have achieved the definition and clarity of the *Roe v. Wade* decision, yet it might have moved toward a greater public consensus. One has to guess at such things through hindsight, of course. But in a world in which humanistic thought predominated, abortion might have been taken up more in its human terms and the debate might have focused more on such unscientific and apolitical components as human guilt, human choice and human mystery.

If we could find the way to retrieve this kind of conflicted thinking, and find a way to apply it to the country's needs, we might be on our way toward a common understanding on abortion, and perhaps toward a common good. Abortion requires us to think one way and another way simultaneously. Americans these days could make very good use of this bifurcated way of thinking.

This brings me back to the concern I voiced at the beginning: Americans are not speaking their true minds about abortion because their minds are in conflict. Yet living with conflict is normal in America, and our reluctance to do so openly in this matter, while understandable in an atmosphere of easy polarities, may help create a false image of our country in which we do not recognize ourselves. An America that declares abortion legal and says nothing more about it would be just as distorted as one that prohibited the practice. The ideal situation, in my view, would consist of a combination of laws, attitudes, and actions that would go toward satisfying both the rights of citizens and the doubts held by most of them.

Achieving this goal is, I believe, within reach. I know how odd that must sound when one considers the violent explosions that have occurred in places like Wichita as recently as August of last year, or when one sees the pro-life and pro-choice camps amassing ammunition for this year's Presidential campaign. But for the ordinary private citizen, the elements of a reasonably satisfying resolution are already in place. I return to the fact that the great majority of Americans both favor abortion rights and disapprove of abortion. Were that conflict of thought to be openly expressed, and were certain social remedies to come from it, we would not find a middle of the road on this issue—logically there is no middle of the road. But we might well establish a wider road, which would accommodate a broad range of beliefs and opinions and allow us to move on to more important social concerns.

What most Americans want to do with abortion is to permit but dis-   *40* courage it. Even those with the most pronounced political stands on the subject reveal this duality in the things they say; while making strong defenses of their positions, they nonetheless, if given time to work out their thoughts, allow for opposing views. I discovered this in a great many interviews over the past three years.

Pro-choice advocates are often surprised to hear themselves speak of the immorality of taking a life. Pro-life people are surprised to hear themselves defend individual rights, especially women's rights. And both sides might be surprised to learn how similar are their visions of a society that makes abortion less necessary through sex education, help for unwanted babies, programs to shore up disintegrating families and moral values, and other forms of constructive community action. Such visions may appear Panglossian, but they have been realized before, and the effort is itself salutary.

If one combines that sense of social responsibility with the advocacy of individual rights, the permit-but-discourage formula could work. By "discourage," I mean the implementation of social programs that help to create an atmosphere of discouragement. I do not mean ideas like parental consent or notification, already the law in some states, which, however well-intentioned, only whittle away at individual freedoms. The "discourage" part is the easier to find agreement on, of course, but when one places the "permit" question in the realm of respect for private values, even that may become more palatable.

Already 73 percent of America finds abortion acceptable. Even more may find it so if they can tolerate living in a country in which they may exercise the individual right not to have an abortion themselves or to argue against others having one, yet still go along with the majority who want the practice continued. The key element for all is to create social conditions in which abortion will be increasingly unnecessary. It is right that we have the choice, but it would be better if we did not have to make it.

Were this balance of thought and attitude to be expressed publicly, it might serve some of the country's wider purposes as well, especially these days when there is so much anguish over how we have lost our national identity and character. The character we lost, it seems to me, was one that exalted the individual for what the individual did for the community. It honored and embodied both privacy and selflessness. A balanced attitude on abortion would also do both. It would make a splendid irony if this most painful and trouble-some issue could be converted into a building block for a renewed national pride based on good will.

For that to happen, the country's leaders—Presidential candidates come to mind—have to express themselves as well. As for Congress, it hardly seems too much to expect our representatives to say something representative about the issue. Should *Roe v. Wade* be overturned, as may well happen, the country could be blown apart. To leave the matter to the states would lead to mayhem, a balkanization of what ought to be standard American rights. Congress used to pass laws, remember? I think it is time for Congress to make a law like *Roe v. Wade* that fully protects abortion rights, but legislates the kind of community help, like sex education, that would diminish the practice.

Taking a stand against abortion while allowing for its existence can turn out to be a progressive philosophy. It both speaks for moral seriousness and moves in the direction of ameliorating conditions of ignorance, poverty, the social self-destruction of fragmented families, and the loss of spiritual values in general. What started as a debate as to when life begins might lead to making life better.

The effort to reduce the necessity of abortion, then, is to choose life as wholeheartedly as it is to be "pro-life." By such an effort, one is choosing life for millions who do not want to be, who do not deserve to be, forever hobbled by an accident, a mistake or by miseducation. By such an effort, one is also choosing a different sort of life for the country as a whole—a more sympathetic life in which we acknowledge, privileged and unprivileged alike, that we have the same doubts and mysteries and hopes for one another.

Earlier, I noted America's obsessive moral character, our tendency to treat every question that comes before us as a test of our national soul. The permit-but-discourage formula on abortion offers the chance to test our national soul by appealing to its basic egalitarian impulse. Were we once again to work actively toward creating a country where everyone had the same health care, the same sex education, the same opportunity for economic survival, the same sense of personal dignity and worth, we would see both fewer abortions and a more respectable America.

Analyzing a Mediatory Essay

Rosenblatt's argument poses a possible resolution of the abortion contro-versy and, in so doing, analyzes the opposing positions and interests, as all mediation must. The following analysis shows how Rosenblatt takes his readers through the process of mediation.

Understanding the Spirit of Negotiation

A mediator has to be concerned with his or her own ethos as well as with helping the opposing parties achieve an attitude that will enable negotiation to begin. The mediator must sound fair and evenhanded; the opposing parties must be open-minded.

Rosenblatt, interestingly, opens his essay in a way that invites commentary. In his first two paragraphs he portrays both sides at their worst, as extremes in no frame of mind to negotiate—and, in fact, in no frame of mind even to speak to each other. In his third paragraph he relates the history of their debate, describing their emotions with words like "hatred" and "rage" and their behavior with metaphors of war and destruction. Readers who see themselves as reasonable will disassociate themselves from the people in these portraits.

Following Through

Do you think Rosenblatt's introduction is a good mediation strategy? In your writer's notebook, describe your initial response to Rosenblatt's opening. Having read the whole essay, do you think it is an effective opening? Once he has presented these warriors on both sides, do you think he goes on to discuss the opposing positions and their values in an evenhanded, neutral way? Can you cite some passages where you see either fairness or bias on his part?

Understanding the Opposing Positions

Rosenblatt establishes the opposing positions, already well known, in the first two paragraphs: the "pro-life" position that abortion is murder, the "pro-choice" position that outlawing abortion violates women's rights. Interestingly, Rosenblatt does not wait until the close of the essay to suggest his compromise position. Rather, he presents it in paragraph 9, although he goes into more detail about the solution later in the essay.

Following Through

In your writer's notebook, paraphrase Rosenblatt's compromise position on abortion. Do you think this essay would have been more effective if Rosenblatt had postponed presenting his solution?

Locating Areas of Disagreement over Facts

Rosenblatt points out that both sides' focus on the facts alone is what has made the issue intractable. As he points out in paragraph 34, the opposing sides have adopted the "objective precision" of the social sciences: The pro-life side has focused on establishing the precise moment of the beginning of life; the pro-choice side has focused on the absolute rights of women, ignoring the emotions of their conservative opponents.

Following Through

Reread paragraph 33. In your writer's notebook, paraphrase Rosenblatt's point about humanistic thinking as opposed to social science thinking. If you have taken social science courses, what is your opinion?

Locating Areas of Disagreement in Interests

Rosenblatt perceives that the disagreement over abortion may in fact be a disagreement over certain underlying interests and emotions held by each side, involving their perceptions about what life should be like in America. His aim is to help the two sides understand how these "less obvious reasons" have kept them from reaching any agreement. At the same time, he points out that many of the differences that seem to put them at odds are tied to common values deeply rooted in American culture. Thus, Rosenblatt attempts to show each side that the other is not a threat to its interests and perceptions of the American way of life.

Rosenblatt notes that both sides share an assumption that is keeping them apart: they both assume that there is one answer to the question of abortion rights, rather than a solution that accepts ambivalence. He locates the source of this assumption in what he calls "social science thinking," which leads both sides to think that problems can be objectively studied and solved apart from human subjectivity. Thus, both sides are ignoring the very thing that is so vital to the process of negotiation and mediation.

Rosenblatt further shows how different principles underlie the arguments of each side. One side bases its argument on the right to privacy and free choice, while the other bases its argument on the right to life. Both principles are fundamental to American society—and neither is completely unqualified.

In addition, Rosenblatt shows how each side values the rights of the individual but interprets these rights differently. For example, antiabortion advocates see the fetus as an individual with the right to life, while pro-choice advocates argue for the individual right of the mother to privacy. In paragraphs 18 through 22, Rosenblatt shows how two perceptions or interpretations of individualism, one positive (emphasizing self-reliance) and one more critical (emphasizing selfishness), are traceable throughout American culture. In fact, he shows how both sides embrace individualism as an element of their arguments.

In addressing the main difference between the opposing parties over values, Rosenblatt shows how legalized abortion could be perceived as a threat to traditional middle-class economic and social values, and he traces middle-class sexual repression back to the Puritans. Rosenblatt may be stepping outside of the neutral stance of a mediator here, as he suggests that antiabortionists are somewhat prudish. He makes no corresponding remarks about the sexual values of the pro-choice side.

Rosenblatt points out that both sides see different consequences of legalizing abortion. Antiabortion advocates see abortion as destabilizing society and undermining the middle-class American way of life. These people worry not just about abortion but rather about an "unruly" society. Pro-choice advocates, on the other hand, see abortion as the route to a better society; as Rosenblatt paraphrases their vision, "the country may only reach its ideal goals if women, along with men, are allowed to achieve their highest potential as citizens . . ." (paragraph 24).

In addressing the emotional characteristics of those involved in the dispute over abortion, Rosenblatt points to the role of religion in America. He explains that Americans have historically been more emotional about religion and morality than people of other nations, even ones where Catholicism is a state religion.

Following Through

Recall the chief areas of difference between Ellen Willis and Margaret Liu McConnell in their respective arguments on the value of abortion rights. In your writer's notebook, indicate which of their stated concerns correspond to points in Rosenblatt's analysis of the differences that fuel the abortion war. Does Rosenblatt say anything that might help bring Willis and McConnell closer together?

Defining the Problem in Terms of the Real Interests

Rosenblatt finds the real issue in the abortion controversy to be not whether abortion should be legal or illegal but rather how fundamental, conflicting interests in American society can be addressed—in other words, how can we create laws and institutions that reflect the ambivalence most Americans feel on the topic of abortion? How do we permit abortion legally, in order to satisfy our traditional values for privacy and individual rights, but also discourage it morally, in order to satisfy the American religious tradition that values life, respects fetal rights, and disapproves of casual and promiscuous sex?

Following Through

In your writer's notebook, give your opinion of whether or not Rosenblatt has defined the abortion debate in terms of the opposing sides' real interests. Would his definition of the problem affect related abortion rights issues, such as making the "abortion pill," or RU 486, available in the United States?

Inventing Creative Options

Rosenblatt's solution is based on what he calls humanistic thinking, that is, thinking that permits conflict and rejects simple solutions to complicated human problems. He shows that many Americans think that abortion is both right and wrong but cannot even talk about their feelings because they are so contradictory. His creative option is for us to accept this ambivalence as a society and pass legislation that would satisfy both "the rights of citizens and the doubts held by most of them" (paragraph 38). In paragraph 45, Rosenblatt suggests that Congress pass a law legalizing abortion but at the same time requiring various activities, such as sex education, that over time promote respect for life and strengthen community moral standards.

Following Through

Reread paragraphs 39 through 48, and explore in your writer's notebook your opinion of Rosenblatt's proposed solution. Should he have made it more specific?

Gathering More Data

Before opposing sides can reach an agreement based on the real issues, they often need to get more information. Rosenblatt's mediatory argument is short on actual data. In response to his proposed solution, the antiabortion side might have severe doubts that the social programs proposed could in fact reduce the number of abortions performed.

Following Through

In your writer's notebook, make suggestions as to what kind of evidence Rosenblatt might have to offer to convince the antiabortion side that sex education and other social programs could reduce the number of abortions performed.

Reaching a Solution Based on Agreed-upon Principles

Rosenblatt attempts to get those who support abortion rights and those who oppose them to reduce their differences by accepting the "permit-but-discourage" principle. This is a principle that American society applies to other areas, such as marital infidelity, which is legal but certainly discouraged through social institutions and customs.

Following Through

1. Reread, if necessary, the two arguments on abortion by McConnell and Willis. Would each writer accept the principle of "permit but discourage"?
2. Draft a letter to the editor of the *New York Times Magazine,* where Rosenblatt's argument originally appeared. In no more than three paragraphs,

evaluate the argument as an attempt at mediation. Then read the following letters to the *Times Magazine,* responding to Rosenblatt's essay.

Alternatively, write a letter or letters to the editor of the *New York Times,* playing the role of either Willis or McConnell, or both, responding as you think each would.

> Roger Rosenblatt's essay on abortion is timely and welcome ("How to End the Abortion War," Jan. 19). However, his belief that Americans can coalesce on a policy that "discourages" abortion without making it illegal is probably too optimistic. The polarization of Americans on this issue results from some pretty deep differences. Differences in life style, for one thing, can dictate profound political polarization. Many American women derive their most fundamental sense of self-worth from child-rearing and care of the family; many others find theirs in lives that include participation in the larger society, particularly the work place. For women in "traditional" families (and their husbands), untrammeled access to abortion constitutes a form of permissiveness that threatens the things they hold most dear. For women whose identities are tied to work outside the home, the right to control reproductive lives is essential.
>
> So I'm afraid these wars will continue. Rosenblatt and others should not tire in their efforts to find middle ground, but it would be unrealistic to think that we will be able to occupy it together anytime soon.
>
> —PHILIP D. HARVEY *Cabin John, Md.*

> I don't want to "permit but discourage" abortion. I want to stop abortion the way the abolitionists wanted to stop slavery. I believe slavery is wrong: that no one has the right to assure his or her quality of life by owning another. In the same way, and for the same reasons, I believe abortion is wrong: that no one has the right to assure her quality of life by aborting another.
>
> —ANITA JANDA *Kew Gardens, Queens*

> Your article states that "most of us actually know what we feel about abortion." It is true that most people have a position on abortion, but that position is seldom an informed one in this era of the 10-second sound bite and the oversimplification of issues.
>
> Few people understand that *Roe v. Wade* gives the interests of the woman precedence over those of the embryo early in the pregnancy, but allows Government to favor the fetus once it has attained viability.
>
> Were a poll to propose full freedom of choice for women during the early stages of pregnancy, and prohibition of abortion during the later stages, except in cases of fetal deformity or a threat to a woman's life, I believe that the response of the American public would be overwhelmingly positive. Rosenblatt is right on the mark in saying that the public "simply will not talk about abortion." With thoughtful

and dispassionate discussion, we might lay aside the all-or-nothing attitude that currently prevails.

—RICHARD A. KELLEY *Rumson, N.J.*

Following Through

Analyze the preceding letters to the *New York Times Magazine* critiquing Rosenblatt's article. What values does each contribute to the debate? How might Rosenblatt respond to each?

Writing a Mediatory Essay

Prewriting

If you have been mediating the positions of two or more groups of classmates or two or more authors of published arguments, you may be assigned to write a mediatory essay in which you argue for a compromise position, appealing to an audience of people on all sides. In preparing to write such an essay, you should work through the steps of negotiation and mediation, as described on pages 161–162. In your writer's notebook, prepare briefs of the various conflicting positions, and note areas of disagreement; think hard about the differing interests of the conflicting parties, and respond to the questions about difference on page 179.

If possible, give some thought to each party's background—age, race, gender, and so forth—and how it might contribute to his or her viewpoint on the issue. For example, in a debate about whether *Huckleberry Finn* should be taught and read aloud in U.S. high schools, an African-American parent whose child is the only minority student in her English class might well have a different perspective from that of a white teacher. Can the white teacher be made to understand the embarrassment that a sole black child might feel when the white characters speak with derision about "niggers"?

In your notebook describe the conflict in terms of the opposing sides' real interests rather than the superficial demands each side might be stating. For example, considering the controversy over *Huckleberry Finn,* you might find some arguments in favor of teaching it anytime, others opposed to teaching it at all, others suggesting that it be an optional text for reading outside of class, and still others proposing that it be taught only in twelfth grade, when students are mature enough to understand Mark Twain's satire. However, none of these suggestions addresses the problem in terms of the real interests involved: a desire to teach the classics of American literature for what they tell us about the human condition and our country's history and values; a desire to promote respect for African-American students; a desire to ensure a comfortable learning climate for all students; and so on. You may be able to see that people's real interests are not as far apart as they might seem. For example, those who advocate teaching *Huckleberry Finn* and those who are opposed may both have in mind the goal of eliminating racial prejudice.

At this point in the prewriting process, think of some solutions that would satisfy at least some of the real interests on all sides. It might be necessary for you to do some additional research. What do you anticipate any of the opposing parties might want to know more about in order to accept your solution?

Finally, write up a clear statement of your compromise. Can you explain what principles it is based on? In the *Huckleberry Finn* debate, we might propose that the novel be taught at any grade level provided that it is presented as part of a curriculum to educate students about the African-American experience, with the involvement of African-American faculty or visiting lecturers.

Drafting

There is no set form for the mediatory essay. In fact, it is an unusual, even somewhat experimental, form of writing. The important thing, as with any argument, is that you have a plan for arranging your points and that you provide clear signals to your readers. One logical way to organize a mediatory essay is in three parts:

> *Overview of the conflict.* The introductory paragraphs should describe the conflict and the opposing positions.
>
> *Discussion of differences underlying the conflict.* Here your goal is to make all sides more sympathetic to each other as well as to sort out the important real interests that must be addressed by the solution.
>
> *Proposed solution.* Here you make a case for your compromise position, giving reasons why it should be acceptable to all—that is, showing that it does serve at least some of their interests.

Revising

When revising a mediatory essay, you should look for the usual problems of organization and development that you would be looking for in any essay to convince or persuade. You want to be sure that you have inquired carefully and fairly into the conflict and that you have clearly presented the cases for all sides, including your proposed solution. At this point, you also need to consider how well you have used the persuasive appeals:

> *The Appeal to Character.* What kind of character have you projected as a mediator? Have you maintained neutrality? Do you model open-mindedness and genuine concern for the sensitivities of all sides?
>
> *The Appeal to Emotions.* To arouse sympathy and empathy, which we have said are needed in negotiation, you should take into account the emotional appeals discussed in Chapter 7 (pages 135–138). Your mediatory essay should be a moving argument for understanding and overcoming difference.
>
> *The Appeal through Style.* As in persuasion, you should put the power of language to work for you. Pay attention to concrete word choice,

striking metaphors, and phrases that stand out because of repeated sounds and rhythms.

For suggestions about editing and proofreading, see Appendix B.

Student Sample: A Mediatory Essay

The following mediatory essay was written by Angi Grellhesl, a first-year student at Southern Methodist University. Her essay examines opposing written views on the institution of speech codes at various U.S. colleges and its effect on freedom of speech.

ANGI GRELLHESL

Mediating the Speech Code Controversy

THE RIGHT to free speech has raised many controversies over the years. Explicit lyrics in rap music and marches by the Ku Klux Klan are just some examples that test the power of the First Amendment. Now, students and administrators are questioning if, in fact, free speech ought to be limited on university campuses. Many schools have instituted speech codes to protect specified groups from harassing speech.

Both sides in the debate, the speech code advocates and the free speech advocates, have presented their cases in recent books and articles. Columnist Nat Hentoff argues strongly against the speech codes, his main reason being that the codes violate students' First Amendment rights. Hentoff links the right to free speech with the values of higher education. In support, he quotes Yale president Benno Schmidt, who says, "Freedom of thought must be Yale's central commitment. . . . [U]niversities cannot censor or suppress speech, no matter how obnoxious in content, without violating their justification for existence. . . ." (qtd. in Hentoff 223). Another reason Hentoff offers against speech codes is that universities must teach students to defend themselves in preparation for the real world, where such codes cannot shield them. Finally, he suggests that most codes are too vaguely worded; students may not even know they are violating the codes (216).

Two writers in favor of speech codes are Richard Perry and Patricia Williams. They see speech codes as a necessary and fair limitation on free speech. Perry and Williams argue that speech codes promote multicultural awareness, making students more sensitive to the differences that are out there in the real world. These authors do not think that the codes violate First Amendment rights, and they are suspicious of the motives of those who say they do. As Perry and Williams put it, those who feel free speech rights are being threatened "are apparently unable to distinguish between a liberty interest on the one hand and, on the other, a quite specific interest in being able to

1

spout racist, sexist, and homophobic epithets completely unchallenged—without, in other words, the terrible inconvenience of feeling bad about it" (228).

Perhaps if both sides trusted each other a little more, they could see that their goals are not contradictory. Everyone agrees that students' rights should be protected. Hentoff wishes to ensure that students have the right to speak their minds. He and others on his side are concerned about freedom. Defenders of the codes argue that students have the right not to be harassed, especially while they are getting an education. They are concerned about opportunity. Would either side really deny that the other's goal had value?

Also, both sides want to create the best possible educational environment. Here, the difference rests on the interpretation of what benefits the students. Is the best environment one most like the real world, where prejudice and harassment occur? Or does the university have an obligation to provide an atmosphere where potential victims can thrive and participate freely without intimidation?

I think it is possible to reach a solution that everyone can agree on. Most citizens want to protect constitutional rights; but they also agree that those rights have limitations, the ultimate limit being when one person infringes on the rights of others to live in peace. All sides should agree that a person ought to be able to speak out about his or her convictions, values, and beliefs. And most people can see a difference between that protected speech and the kind that is intended to harass and intimidate. For example, there is a clear difference between expressing one's view that Jews are mistaken in not accepting Christ as the son of God, on the one hand, and yelling anti-Jewish threats at a particular person in the middle of the night, on the other. Could a code not be worded in such a way as to distinguish between these two kinds of speech?

Also, I don't believe either side would want the university to be an artificial world. Codes should not attempt to ensure that no one is criticized or even offended. Students should not be afraid to say controversial things. But universities do help to shape the future of the real world, so shouldn't they at least take a stand against harassment? Can a code be worded that would protect free speech and prevent harassment?

The current speech code at Southern Methodist University is a compromise that ought to satisfy free speech advocates and speech code advocates. It prohibits hate speech at the same time that it protects an individual's First Amendment rights.

First, it upholds the First Amendment by including a section that reads, "due to the University's commitment to freedom of speech and expression, harassment is more than mere insensitivity or offensive conduct which creates an uncomfortable situation for certain members of the community" (*Peruna* 92). The code therefore should satisfy those, like Hentoff, who place a high value on the basic rights our nation was built upon. Secondly, whether or not there is a need for protection, the current code protects potential victims from hate speech or "any words or acts deliberately designed to disregard the safety or rights of another, and which intimidate, degrade, demean, threaten, haze, or otherwise interfere with another person's rightful action" (*Peruna* 92). This part of the code should satisfy those who recognize that some hurts cannot be overcome. Finally, the current code outlines specific acts that constitute harassment: "Physical, psychological, verbal and/or written acts directed toward an individual or group of individuals which rise to the level of 'fighting words' are prohibited" (*Peruna* 92).

The SMU code protects our citizens from hurt and from unconstitutional censorship. Those merely taking a position can express it, even if it hurts. On the other hand, those who are spreading hatred will be limited as to what harm they may inflict. Therefore, all sides should respect the code as a safeguard for those who use free speech but a limitation for those who abuse it. *10*

WORKS CITED

Hentoff, Nat. "Speech Codes on the Campus and Problems of Free Speech." *Debating P.C.* Ed. Paul Berman. New York: Bantam, 1992. 215–224.

Perry, Richard, and Patricia Williams. "Freedom of Speech." *Debating P.C.* Ed. Paul Berman. New York: Bantam, 1992. 225–230.

Peruna Express 1993–1994. Dallas: Southern Methodist University, 1993.

Researching Arguments

This appendix is intended to help you with any argument you write. Research, which simply means "careful study," is essential to serious inquiry and most well-constructed cases. Before you write, you need to investigate the ongoing conversation regarding your issue. As you construct your argument, you will need specific evidence and the support of authorities to make a convincing case to a skeptical audience.

Your high school experience may have led you to regard the "research paper" as different from other papers, but this distinction between researched and non-researched writing does not usually apply to argumentation. An argument with no research behind it is generally a weak one indeed. Many of the arguments you read may not appear to be "researched" because the writers have not cited their sources—most likely because they were writing for the general public rather than for an academic or professional audience. In college writing, however, students are usually required to document all sources of ideas, as we will demonstrate later in this section.

Research for argumentation usually begins not as a search for evidence but rather as inquiry into an issue you have chosen or been assigned. Your task in inquiry is to discover information about the issue and, more importantly, to find arguments that address the issue and to familiarize yourself with the range of positions and the cases people make for them. You should inquire into these arguments using your critical reading skills and entering into dialogues with the authors until you feel satisfied with and confident about the position you take.

Sometimes, however, research must begin at an even earlier stage—when, for example, your instructor asks you to select an issue to write about. So we begin with suggestions on how to find an issue.

FINDING AN ISSUE

Let's say you have been assigned an essay on any issue of current public concern, ranging from one debated on your campus to one rooted in international affairs. If you have no ideas about what to write, what should you do?

Understand That an Issue Is More Than Just a Topic

You must look for a subject over which people genuinely disagree. For example, homelessness is a *topic:* you could report on many different aspects of it—from the number of homeless people in our country to profiles of individual homeless people. But homelessness in itself is not really an issue because virtually everyone agrees that the problem exists. However, once you start considering solutions to the problem of homelessness, you are dealing with an *issue,* because people will disagree about how to solve the problem.

Keep Abreast of Current Events

Develop the habit of reading newspapers and magazines regularly to keep informed of debates on current issues. It is best to write on issues of genuine concern to you rather than to manufacture concern at the last minute because a paper is due. Keep a record of your responses to your reading in your writer's notebook so that you have a readily available source of ideas.

Research the News

Visit the current periodicals shelves of your library or local newsstand. Consult the front page and the editorial/opinion columns of your city's daily paper. In addition, most newsstands and libraries carry the *New York Times* and other large-city dailies that offer thorough coverage of national and international events. Remember that you are looking for an issue, so if you find an article on the front page that interests you, think about how people might disagree over some question it raises. For example, an article announcing that health care costs rose a record fourteen percent in the last year might suggest the issue of government control over the medical profession; a campus-newspaper article about a traditionally African-American fraternity could raise the issue of colleges tolerating racial segregation in the Greek system. In addition to newspapers, such magazines as *Time, Newsweek,* and *U.S. News and World Report* cover current events; and others, such as *Harper's, Atlantic Monthly, New Republic, National Review,* and *Utne Reader* offer essays, articles, and arguments on important current issues.

Research Your Library's Periodicals Indexes

Indexes are lists of articles in specific publications or groups of publications. You are most likely familiar with one index, the *Readers' Guide to Periodical Literature.* (For names of other indexes, see the section "Finding Sources" later in this appendix.) If you have a vague subject in mind, such as gender discrimination, consulting an index for articles and arguments on the topic can help you narrow your focus to a more concrete issue. Of course, if you don't have an issue in mind, looking through the *Readers' Guide* won't be very helpful, so we offer some suggestions for using indexes more efficiently.

You can, for example, look in a newspaper index (some are printed and bound, while others are computerized) under "editorial" for a list of topics on which the editors have stated positions, or you can look under the name of a columnist—such as William F. Buckley, Anna Quindlen, or A. M. Rosenthal—whose views on current issues regularly appear in that paper. The bonus to using a newspaper index in this way is that it will lead you directly to arguments on an issue.

Another resource for finding arguments on an issue when you have a topic in mind is *InfoTrac,* a computerized index to magazines, journals, and selected current articles in the *New York Times.* After you type in an appropriate subject word or key word, *InfoTrac* allows you to narrow your search further. If you type in the key word of your subject followed by "and editorial" or "and opinion," only argumentative columns and editorials will appear on your screen.

A further possibility is to browse through an index dedicated solely to periodicals that specialize in social issues topics, such as the *Journal of Social Issues* and *Vital Speeches of the Day.* Finally, *Speech Index* will help you find speeches that have been printed in books.

Inquire into the Issue

Once you have determined an issue, you can begin your inquiry into the positions already articulated in the public conversation. You may yourself already hold a position, but during inquiry you should be as open as possible to the full range of viewpoints on the issue; you should look for informative articles and for arguments about the issue.

Inquiring into an issue also involves evaluating sources. Remember that research means "careful study," and being careful as you perform these initial steps will make all the difference in the quality of the argument you eventually write. And, the more care you take now, the more time you'll save in the long run.

FINDING SOURCES

Sources for developing an argument can be found through several kinds of research. Library research is usually essential, but don't overlook what social scientists call field research. Also, the Internet and electronic mail offer rapidly expanding avenues for researching almost any topic. All research requires time and patience, as well as a knowledge of tools and techniques.

Field Research

Research "in the field" means studying the world directly through observations, questionnaires, and interviews.

Observations

Do not discount the value of your own personal experiences as evidence in making a case. You will notice that many writers of arguments offer as evidence what they themselves have seen, heard, and done. Such experiences may be from the past. For example, Sidney Hook's account of his own suffering after a nearly fatal stroke, told in sharp detail (see pages 64–66), makes a compelling case for euthanasia.

Alternatively, you may seek out a specific personal experience as you inquire into your topic. For example, one student writing about the homeless in Dallas decided to visit a shelter. She called ahead to receive permission and schedule the visit. Her paper was memorable because she was able to include the stories and physical descriptions of several homeless women, with details of their conversations.

Questionnaires and Surveys

You may be able to get information on some topics, especially if they are campus related, by doing surveys or questionnaires. Be forewarned, however, that it is very difficult to conduct a reliable survey.

First, there is the problem of designing a clear and unbiased instrument. If you have ever filled out an evaluation form for an instructor or a course, you will know what we mean about the problem of clarity: one evaluation might ask whether an instructor returns papers "in a reasonable length of time"; however, what is "reasonable" to some students may be far too long for other students. As for bias, consider the question, "Have you ever had trouble getting assistance from the library's reference desk?" To get a fair response, this questionnaire had better also ask how many requests for help were handled promptly and well. If you do decide to draft a questionnaire, we suggest you do it as a class project, so that students on all sides of the issue can contribute and troubleshoot for areas of ambiguity.

Second is the problem of getting a representative response. For the same reasons we doubt the results of certain magazine-sponsored surveys of people's sex lives, we need to doubt the statistical accuracy of surveys targeting a group that may not be representative of the whole. For example, it might be difficult to generalize about all first-year college students in the United States based on a survey of just your English class—or even the entire first-year class at your college. Consider too that those who respond to a survey often have an ax to grind on the topic.

We don't rule out the value of surveys here, but we caution you to consider the difficulties of designing, administering, and interpreting such research tools.

Interviews

You can get a great deal of current information about an issue as well as informed opinions by talking to experts. As with any kind of research, the first step in conducting an interview is to decide exactly what you want to find out. Write down your questions, whether you plan to conduct the interview over the telephone or in person.

The next step, which can take some effort and imagination, is to find the right person to interview. As you read about an issue, note the names (and the possible biases) of any organizations mentioned; these may have local offices, whose telephone numbers you could find in the directory. In addition, institutions such as hospitals, universities, and large corporations have information and public relations offices whose staff are responsible for providing information to those who seek it. An excellent source of over 30,000 names and phone numbers of experts in almost any field is a book by Matthew Lesko, *Lesko's Info-Power.* Finally, do not overlook the expertise available from faculty members at your own school.

Once you have determined possible sources for interviews, you must begin a patient and courteous round of telephone calls until you are connected with the right person; according to Lesko, this may take up to seven calls. Remain cheerful and clear in your pursuit.

Whether your interview is face-to-face or over the telephone, begin by being sociable but also by acknowledging that the interviewee's time is valuable. Tell the person something about the project you are working on, but withhold your own position on any controversial matters. Try to sound neutral, and be specific about what you want to know. Take notes, and include the title and background of the person being interviewed as well as the date of the interview, which you will need when citing this source in the finished paper. If you want to tape the interview, be sure to ask permission. Finally, if you have the individual's mailing address, it is thoughtful to send a follow-up note thanking him or her for the assistance.

If everyone in your class is researching a single topic and it is likely that more than one person would contact a particular expert on campus or in your community, avoid flooding that person with requests for his or her time. Perhaps one or two students could be designated to interview the subject and report to the class, or, if convenient, the expert could be invited to visit the class.

Library Research

University libraries are vast repositories of information. To use them most efficiently, consult with professional librarians. Do not hesitate to ask for help. Even college faculty can discover new sources of information by talking with librarians about current research projects.

Library of Congress Subject Headings

Finding sources will involve using your library's card or computerized catalog, reference books, and indexes to periodicals. Before using these, however, it makes sense to look first through a set of books every library locates near its catalog—the *Library of Congress Subject Headings.* This multivolume set will help you know what terms to look under when you move on to catalogs and indexes. Consulting these subject headings first will save you time in the long run: it will help you narrow your search and keep you from overlooking potentially good sources because it also suggests related terms to look under. For example, if you look under the term "mercy killing," you will be directed to "euthanasia," where you can find the following helpful information:

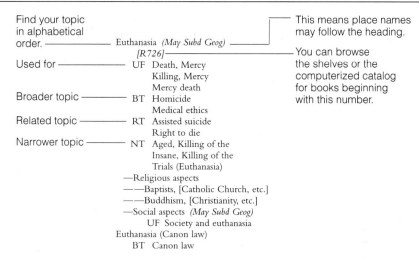

Find your topic in alphabetical order. ——— Euthanasia *(May Subd Geog)*

This means place names may follow the heading.

[R726]

You can browse the shelves or the computerized catalog for books beginning with this number.

Used for ——————— UF Death, Mercy
Killing, Mercy
Mercy death

Broader topic ——— BT Homicide
Medical ethics

Related topic ——— RT Assisted suicide
Right to die

Narrower topic ——— NT Aged, Killing of the
Insane, Killing of the
Trials (Euthanasia)
—Religious aspects
——Baptists, [Catholic Church, etc.]
——Buddhism, [Christianity, etc.]
—Social aspects *(May Subd Geog)*
UF Society and euthanasia
Euthanasia (Canon law)
BT Canon law

The Card or Computerized Catalog

Use your library's catalog primarily to find books or government documents. (For arguments and information on very current issues, however, keep in mind that the card or computer catalog is not the best source; because books take years to write and publish, they quickly become outdated.) Library catalogs list all holdings and are referenced according to author, title, and subject. With a computerized catalog, it is also possible to find works according to key words and by Library of Congress number. Look under the subject headings you find in the *Library of Congress Subject Headings.* Moreover, because the Library of Congress system groups books according to subject matter, you may want to browse in the catalog (or on the shelves) for other books in the same range of call numbers.

Typically, the library's catalog card or screen will appear as illustrated below.

```
Search Request: A=FALUDI SUSAN
BOOK - Record 2 of 3 Entries Found                        Brief View
-------------------------- Screen 1 of 1 ----------------------------
        TITLE:  Backlash : the undeclared war against American women
      EDITION:  1st ed.
       AUTHOR:  Faludi, Susan.

    PUBLISHER:  New York : Crown, c1991.
  DESCRIPTION:  xxiii, 552 p. : 25 cm.

     SUBJECTS:  Feminism--United States.
               Women--United States--Social conditions.
               Women--Psychology.
--------------------------------------------------------------------
    LOCATION:            CALL NUMBER:                  STATUS:
1. Fondren Browsing       HQ1426 .F35 1991        Charged, Due: 04/02/93
   Coll.


--------------------------------------------------------------------
 COMMANDS:           LO  Long View         I  Index
                     N   Next Record        H  Help
 O  Other Options    P   Previous Record

NEXT COMMAND:
```

Indexes to Periodicals

Good libraries contain many indexes that list articles in newspapers, magazines, and journals. Some of these are printed and bound; others are computerized on CD-ROM. Once again, the *Library of Congress Subject Headings* can help you determine the best words to search in these indexes.

Newspaper Indexes The *New York Times Index* is printed and bound in volumes. Each volume indexes articles for one year, grouped according to subject and listed according to the month and day of publication. The subject headings in the *New York Times Index* tend to be very general. For example, we could not find the heading "euthanasia," the term for mercy killing used in the *Library of Congress Subject Headings*. We had to think of a more general term, so we tried "medicine." There, we found the following:

MEDICINE AND HEALTH. See also
Abortion
Accidents and Safety
Acupuncture
Aged
Anatomy and Physiology
Anesthesia and Anesthetics
Antibiotics
Autopsies
Bacteria
Birth Control and Family Planning
Birth Defects
Blood
Death ———————————————————————— The subject
Environment   heading most
Epidemics   likely to lead
Exercise   to articles on
Faith Healers   euthanasia
First Aid
Food Contamination and Poisoning
Handicapped
Hormones
Immunization and Immunity
Implants
Industrial and Occupational Hazards
Malpractice Insurance
Mental Health and Disorders
Nursing Homes
Pesticides and Pests
Population
Radiation
Smoking
Spas
Surgery and Surgeons
Teeth and Dentistry
Transplants
Vaccination and Vaccines
Veterinary Medicine
Viruses
Vitamins
Water Pollution
Workmen's Compensation Insurance
X-Rays

We decided the term "death" on this list seemed most likely to lead us to articles on euthanasia, and we were correct. Following is a small selection of what we found.

Topic headings are listed in alphabetical order.

DEATH. See also
Deaths

Several laws enacted in New York State in 1990 are set to take effect, including measure that will allow New Yorkers to designate another person to make health-care decisions on their behalf if they become unable to do so (M). Ja 1.1. 32:1

Articles are listed in chronological order.

Another right-to-die case emerges in Missouri, where Christine Busalacchi has been in persistent vegetative state as result of auto accident on May 29, 1987, when she was 17-year-old high school junior: her father, Pete Busalacchi, who has been seeking unsuccessfully to have his daughter transferred to Minnesota, where feeding tube may possibly be removed, says that Christine never discussed matters of life or death; Nancy Cruzan case recalled; photo (M). Ja 2. A.12:1

Each entry contains an abstract.

Missouri state court dismisses order preventing Pete Busalacchi from moving his comatose daughter Christine to another state where less strict rules might allow removal of feeding tube (S). Ja S.A.16:1

(S), (M), or (L) before date indicates whether an article is short, medium, or long.

In a case that medical ethicists and legal experts say is apparently a first, Minneapolis-based Hennapin County Medical Center plans to go to court for permission to turn off 37-year-old Helga Wanglie's life support system against her family's wishes; photos (L). Ja 10.A.1:1

Probate Judge Louis Kohn of St. Louis County rules that Pete Busalacchi may move his daughter, Christine, from Missouri hospital where she has lain for more than three years with severe brain damage and take her to Minnesota where law might allow removal of her feeding tube (S). Ja 17.3.5:1

Each entry concludes with the month, day, section, page, and column.

People wishing to avoid heroic medical treatment in event they become hopelessly ill and unable to speak for themselves are often poorly served by so-called "living wills" to achieve that end: many health care experts recommend a newer document, health care proxy, in which patients designate surrogate who has legal authority to make medical decisions if they are too sick to offer an opinion; others recommend combining living will with health care proxy; drawing (M). Ja 17.3.9:1

Missouri Judge Louis Kohn rules Pete Busalacchi has right to determine medical care of his daughter Christine, who has been severely brain-damaged for more than three years; gives him authority to have feeding tube removed (S). Ja 18.A.16:4

Missouri appeals court bars Pete Busalacchi from moving his comatose 20-year-old daughter Christine to Minnesota where laws governing removal of life-support systems are less restrictive (S). Ja 19.1.17:2

Editorial Notebook commentary by Fred M. Hechinger says his 94-year-old mother's last days were filled with needless suffering and fear because doctors ignored her, and her family's wish that no heroic efforts be taken to prolong her life; says inhumane legal restrictions have made doctors accomplices in torture, and medical profession has shown little courage in fighting them (M). Ja 24.A.22:1

As mentioned, you will also find a limited number of *New York Times* articles listed in the computerized periodicals index known as *InfoTrac.*

Other printed and bound newspaper indexes carried by most libraries are the *Christian Science Monitor Index,* the *Times Index* (to the London *Times,* a good source for international issues), the *Wall Street Journal Index,* and the *Washington Post Index* (good for federal government issues).

Newsbank offers computerized indexes for hundreds of local and state newspapers. Your library is likely to subscribe to *Newsbank* for indexes of only one or two regional papers in your area. *Newsbank*'s CD-ROMs contain the entire text of each article indexed.

Indexes to Magazines, Journals, and Other Materials Many libraries have CD-ROM databases indexing journals in business and academic fields. *InfoTrac,* one such database, indexes current articles from the *New York Times* and many other periodicals, so you may want to begin your search here rather than with the printed and bound indexes discussed previously. Be aware, however, that *InfoTrac* is a very selective index, far less comprehensive than the printed and bound indexes, which also go back much further in time. In addition, *InfoTrac* will not include many articles that can be found in the specialized indexes that follow. *InfoTrac* is, however, constantly being upgraded, so check with your reference librarian to see how this database can help you research your issue.

1. General interest indexes

   Readers' Guide to Periodical Literature
   Public Affairs Information Service (PAIS)
   Essay and General Literature Index
   Speech Index

2. Arts and humanities indexes

   Art Index
   Film Literature Index
   Humanities Index
   Music Index
   Philosopher's Index
   Popular Music Periodical Index

3. Social science, business, and law indexes

   Business Periodicals Index
   Criminology Index
   Education Index
   Index to Legal Periodicals
   Psychological Abstracts
   Social Sciences Index
   Sociological Abstracts
   Women's Studies Abstracts

4. Science and engineering indexes

> *Applied Science and Technology Index*
> *Biological and Agricultural Index*
> *Current Contents*
> *Environmental Index*
> *General Science Index*

Reference Books

Students tend to overlook many helpful reference books, often because they are unaware of their existence. You may find reference books useful early in the process of inquiring into your issue, but they are also useful for locating supporting evidence as you develop your own argument.

> *First Stop: The Master Index to Subject Encyclopedias* (a subject index to 430 specialized encyclopedias—a good source of general background information)
> *Demographic Yearbook*
> *Facts on File*
> *Guide to American Law* (a reference work that explains legal principles and concepts in plain English)
> *Statistical Abstract of the United States*
> *World Almanac and Book of Facts*

Bibliographies

Books and articles sometimes include a works-cited list or bibliography, which can reveal numerous additional sources. Library catalog entries and many indexes indicate whether a book or article contains a bibliography.

Internet Research

The Internet is a network that links computers, and the files stored on them, to each other. It is a valuable research tool because it provides access to information in the computers of educational institutions, businesses, government bureaus, and nonprofit organizations all over the world. The Internet also provides the connections for E-mail and real-time communications, such as ongoing discussions among groups with common areas of interest; the communication functions of the Internet can also be useful for researching a topic. Because nearly all college computer networks are linked to the Internet, as a student you will have access to it. Most schools have a department of computer and educational technology that can tell you where and how to get connected.

Just as we advise you to seek help from a librarian when beginning your library research, so we also suggest that you begin electronic, or on-line, research by consulting one of the librarians at your school who has specialized training in navigating the information superhighway. Because the Internet is so large, complex, and—like most real highways—always "under construction," we will offer only general advice about what Internet resources would be most useful for undergraduate research on comtemporary public issues. One of the best on-line sources for help with the Internet is the Library of Congress Resource Page <http://lcweb.loc.gov/global/search.html>. Once you are connected to this page, you can link to any number of the following resources.

The World Wide Web

Of all the networks on the Internet, the World Wide Web is the friendliest and the most fun because it links files from various "host" computers around the world; from one site on the Web, you can click on highlighted words that will take you to other sites on the Web where related information is stored. For example, an on-line article on euthanasia may highlight the words "Hippocratic oath"; clicking on the highlighted words will allow you to see a copy of the oath and learn a little more about it. "Hypertext" is the term for these intertextual connections.

Unfortunately, finding useful sites on the Web is not as easy as finding books and articles in the library, because as material is posted, there is no system that neatly catalogues all the information. However, technology to help navigate the Internet is constantly improving. The Web does support a number of "search engines," which index existing and newly posted information, usually through the use of key words. Once your screen is connected to your school's Internet browser (such as Netscape or Mosaic), you can type in the address of one of these engines, or you may be able to load the engine by simply clicking on an icon. Addresses on the Internet are known as URLs (Uniform Resource Locators). Below are the URLs for popular search engines. Note that World Wide Web URLs begin with http, which stands for hypertext transfer protocol.

> AltaVista <http://altavista.digital.com>
> Infoseek <http://www.infoseek.com>
> Lycos <http://lycos:cs.cmu.edu>
> Webcrawler <http://webcrawler.com.html>
> Yahoo! <http://www.yahoo.com>   (Yahoo searches by subject, not by a key word.)
> Metacrawler <http://www2.metacrawler.com>

Once you access the search engine, enter key words describing the information you want. For example, by typing in "search engine" you can find the addresses of other search engines. We recommend that you try this, because new search engines are being created all the time. In fact, that is how we discovered Metacrawler, which as its name suggests, searches all the other search engines.

We want to caution you that surfing the Web is not a quick and easy way to do research. Be prepared to spend some time and to try a variety of search engines. Web searches can often take more time than library research because you will encounter so much irrelevant information. You will also find much information that is not suitable for use in academic writing. Because anyone can post a document on the Web, you need to check the author's credentials carefully. (The section "Evaluating Sources" will discuss this further.)

GopherSpace

Gopher, named for the Golden Gopher mascot at the University of Minnesota, where this software was developed, is an older system than the World Wide Web. Many documents are stored in GopherSpace; once Gopher has retrieved a document for you, you can read it on your screen, save it on a disk, or even print out a copy of it. Instead of hypertext links, Gopher organizes hierarchical menus based on topic areas. For example, you may open a menu that lists major subject areas such as "government and politics." If you select this category, you will get another menu that may have the item "Supreme Court cases." Selecting that, you will find another list, and so on. Many of the Web search engines previously described include GopherSpace in their searches, so you may happen to find Gopher documents while you are searching the World Wide Web. However, you should know about some of the Gopher servers that will allow you to search GopherSpace through a mechanism known as Veronica, which uses key words. These servers are located at universities throughout the world. You can find them at <gopher://minerva.acc.Virginia.EDU:70/11/internet/othergophers/Veronica>. You may also search a group of excellent Gopher sites known as Gopher Jewels, which are maintained at the University of Southern California at <gopher://cwis.usc.edu:3456/7>. Note that GopherSpace addresses begin with gopher.

Listservs and Usenet Newsgroups

The Internet allows groups of people to communicate with each other on topics of common interest; observing and participating in such groups is another way to learn about a topic and find out what issues are being debated. Listservs are like electronic bulletin boards, where people with a shared interest can post information, ask for information, and simply converse about a topic. Listservs are supported by E-mail, so if you have an E-mail account, it will cost you nothing to join a group. You may find an appropriate Listserv group by E-mailing <listserv@listserve.net> with a message specifying your area of interest, such as "list environmentalism" or "list euthanasia." You can also find listserv groups on the World Wide Web at <http://tile.net/lists/>. Usenet newsgroups also act like electronic bulletin boards, which your college's system administrator may or may not make available on your school's server. To find lists of active newsgroups, type in "newsgroups" as a search term in one of the Web search engines, such as Yahoo! Newsgroups and listservs are often composed of highly specialized professionals who expect other participants to have followed their discussions for weeks and months before participating. They even post lists of frequently asked questions (FAQs) to avoid having to cover the same topics repeatedly. Finding the exact information you need in the transcripts of their discussions is like looking for a needle in a haystack, so Usenet is not likely to be as useful as the Web as a general research tool.

However, while searching the Web, you may encounter links to some discussions relevant to your topic that have been archived on the Web. You may want to cite information gathered from these groups, but you need to be very careful about what you choose to use as a source because anyone can join in, regardless of his or her credentials and expertise. Most correspondents who have professional affiliations list them along with their name and "snail mail" (U.S. postal service) address. In addition to credentials, be sure to note the name of the group, the name of the individual posting the message, the date and time it was posted, as well as the URL if you have found it on the Web. (See the section "Creating a Works-Cited or Reference List" for more information on citing electronic sources.)

EVALUATING SOURCES

Before you begin to read and evaluate your sources, you may need to re-evaluate your issue. If you have been unable to find many sources that address the question you are raising, step back and consider changing the focus of your argument or at least expanding its focus.

For example, one student had the choice of any issue under the broad category of the relationship between humans and other animals. Michelle decided to focus on the mistreatment of circus animals, based on claims made in leaflets handed out at the circus by animal rights protestors. Even with a librarian's help, however, Michelle could find no subject headings that led to even one source in her university's library. She then called and visited animal rights activists in her city, who provided her with more materials written and published by the animal rights movement. She realized, however, that re-searching the truth of their claims was more than she could undertake, so she had to acknowledge that her entire argument was based on inadequate inquiry and heavily biased sources.

Once you have reevaluated your topic, use the following method to record and evaluate sources.

Eliminate Inappropriate Sources

If you are a first-year college student, you may find that some books and articles are intended for audiences with more specialized knowledge of the subject than you have. If you have trouble using a source—if it confuses you or shakes your confidence in your reading comprehension—put it aside, at least temporarily.

Also, carefully review any electronic sources you are using. Unlike printed books and articles, on-line documents often have met no professional standards for scholarship. Material can be "published" electronically without the rigorous review by experts, scholars, and editors that must occur in traditional publishing. Nevertheless, you will find legitimate scholarship on the Internet—many news services, encyclopedias, government documents, and even scholarly journals appear on-line. While the freedom of electronic publishing creates an exciting and democratic arena for discussion, it also puts a much heavier burden on students to ensure that the sources they use are worthy of readers' respect.

Carefully Record Complete Bibliographic Information

For every source you are even considering using, be sure to record full bibliographic information. You should take this information from the source itself, not from an index, which may be incomplete or even inaccurate. If you make a record of this information immediately, you will not have to go back later to fill in careless omissions. We recommend that you use a separate index card for each source, but whatever you write on, you must record the following:

1. For a book:

> Author's full name (or names)
> Title of book
> City where published
> Name of publisher
> Year published

For an article or essay in a book, record all of the information for the book, including the names of the book's author or editor as well as the title and the author(s) of the article; also record the inclusive page numbers of the article or chapter (for example, "pp. 100–150").

2. For a periodical:

> Author's full name (or names)
> Title of the article
> Title of the periodical
> Date of the issue
> Volume number, if given
> Inclusive page numbers

3. For a document found on the World Wide Web:

> Author's full name (or names)
> Title of the work
> Original print publication data, if applicable
> Title of the database
> Full http address
> Date you accessed the document

4. For a document found through Gopher:

> Author's full name (or names)
> Title of the work

Original print publication data, if applicable
Title of the database
Full Gopher search path that accessed the document
Date you accessed the document

5. For material found through listservs and Usenet News groups:

Author's full name (or names)
Author's E-mail address
Subject line from the posting
Date of the posting
Address of the listserv or newsgroups
Date you accessed the document

Read the Source Critically

As discussed in Chapter 3, critical reading depends on having some prior knowledge of the subject and the ability to see a text in its rhetorical context. As you research a topic, your prior knowledge naturally becomes deeper with each article you read. But your sources are not simply windows onto your topic, giving you a clear view; whether argumentative or informative, they present a bias. Before looking through them, you must look *at* them. Therefore, it is essential that you devote conscious attention to the rhetorical context of the sources you find. As you read, keep these questions in mind.

Who Is the Writer and What Is His or Her Bias?

Is there a note that tells you anything about the writer's professional title or university or institutional affiliation? If not, a quick look in the *Dictionary of American Biographies* might help; or you can consult the *Biography and Genealogy Master Index*, which will send you to numerous specialized biographical sketches. If you are going to cite the writer as an authority in your argument, you need to be able to convince your audience of his or her credibility.

Again, checking for credibility is particularly important when you are working with electronic sources. For example, one student found two sites on the World Wide Web, both through a key-word search on "euthanasia." One, entitled "Stop the Epidemic of Assisted Suicide," was posted by a person identified only by name, the letters MD, and the affiliation "Association for Control of Assisted Suicide." There was no biographical information, and the "snail mail" address was a post office box. The other Web site, entitled "Ethics Update: Euthanasia," was posted by a professor of philosophy at the University of San Diego whose home page included a complete professional biography detailing his educational background and the titles and publishers of his many other books and articles. The author gave his address at USD in the Department of Philosophy. The student decided that while the first source had some interesting information—including examples of individual patients who were living with pain rather than choosing suicide—it was not a source that skeptical readers would find credible. Search engines often land you deep within a

Web site, and you will have to visit the site's home page to get any background information about the source and its author.

When Was This Source Written?

If you are researching a very current issue, you need to decide what sources may be too dated. Keep in mind, though, that arguments on current issues often benefit from earlier perspectives.

Where Did This Source Appear?

If you are using an article from a periodical, be aware of the periodical's readership and any editorial bias. For example, *National Review* has a conservative bent, while *The Nation* is liberal; an article in the *Journal of the American Medical Association* will usually defend the medical profession. Looking at the table of contents and scanning any editorial statements will help give you a feel for the periodical's political leanings. Also look at the page that lists the publisher and the editorial board. You would find, for example, that *New American* is published by the ultra-right-wing John Birch Society. If you need help determining political bias, ask a librarian. A reference book that lists periodicals by subject matter and explains their bias is *Magazines for Libraries*.

Why Was the Book or Article Written?

While some articles are occasioned by events in the news, most books and arguments are written as part of an ongoing debate or conversation among scholars or journalists. Being aware of the issues and the participants in this conversation is essential, as you will be joining it with your own researched argument. You can check *Book Review Index* to find where a book has been reviewed and then consult some reviews to see how the book was received.

What Is the Author's Aim?

Be aware, first, whether the source is intended to inform or whether it is an argument with a claim to support. Both informative and argumentative sources are useful, and even informative works will have some bias. When your source is an argument, note whether it aims primarily to inquire, to convince, to persuade, or to mediate.

How Is the Source Organized?

If the writer does not employ subheadings or chapter titles, try to break the text into its various parts, and note what function each part plays in the whole.

Inquire into the Source

Because we devote so much attention to inquiry in Chapters 4 and 5, we will not go into detail about this process here. However, you should identify any author's claim and evaluate the support offered for it. Look especially hard at arguments that support your own position; seeing weaknesses in such "friendly" arguments has caused many students to experience an epiphany, or a moment of enlightenment, in which they change their whole stance on an issue.

Consider How You Might Use the Source

If you are fortunate, your research will uncover many authoritative and well-crafted arguments on your issue. The challenge you now face is to work out a way to use them in an argument of your own, with your own structure and strategy and suited to your own aim and audience.

A good argument results from synthesizing, or blending together, the results of your research. Your sources should help you come up with strong reasons and evidence, as well as ideas about opposing views. But it is unlikely that all your reasons will come from one source, or that each part of your argument will draw primarily upon a single source, and you don't want to create an argument that reads like a patchwork of other people's ideas. Thus, you must organize your sources according to your own argumentative strategy and integrate material from a variety of sources into each part of your argument.

We suggest that you review Chapter 6, where we discuss developing and refining a thesis (or claim) and constructing a brief of your argument. As you make your brief, identify those sources that will help you offer reasons or support, such as expert opinion or specific data.

USING SOURCES

How you use a source depends on what you need it for. After you have drafted an argument, you may simply need to consult an almanac for some additional evidence or, say, look up John F. Kennedy's inaugural address to find a stirring quotation. But at earlier stages of the writing process, you may be unsure of your own position and even in need of general background information on the issue. What follows is some advice for those early stages, when you will be encountering a great deal of information and opposing viewpoints. As you research, remember to write down all of the bibliographical information for every source you might use.

Taking Notes

Just as you can check out books from the library for your own use at home or in your dormitory, so you can photocopy entire articles for your personal use away from the library. Likewise, if you are working with electronic sources, you can print out the entire text of many on-line documents. These various methods of gathering materials are helpful for doing research, but when it comes time to use the sources in a paper of your own, the traditional writing skills of note-taking, paraphrasing, and summarizing will help you work efficiently and avoid plagiarism.

Whether you are working with a book, a photocopied article, or a document printed off of the Internet, you will save time in the long run if you write down—preferably on a large notecard—anything that strikes you as important or useful. By taking notes, you will avoid having to sort through the entire text of your research materials to find the idea you thought would work in your paper two weeks ago.

SUGGESTIONS FOR TAKING NOTES

1. Note your source. Use the author's last name or an abbreviated title, or devise a code, such as "A," "B," "C," and so forth.
2. Note the exact page or pages where the information or quotation appears.
3. When you quote, be exact and put quotation marks around the writer's words, to avoid plagiarism if you use them later in your paper.
4. Paraphrase and summarize whenever possible; reserve quotations for passages where the writer's words are strongly opinionated or especially memorable.

Paraphrasing

Paraphrasing, which means restating a passage in your own words, improves reading comprehension. When you put an idea, especially a complex one, into your own words, you are actually explaining the idea to yourself. When you have a firm grasp of an idea, you can write more confidently, with a sense of owning the idea rather than just borrowing it.

SUGGESTIONS FOR PARAPHRASING

1. Use a dictionary if any words in the original are not completely familiar to you.
2. Work with whole ideas—that is, paraphrasing involves more than keeping the original word order and just plugging in synonyms. Don't be afraid to make your paraphrase longer than the original. Try to break a complex sentence into several simpler ones of your own; take apart a difficult idea and rebuild it, step-by-step. Don't just echo the original passage thoughtlessly.
3. Don't be a slave to the original—or to the thesaurus. Read the passage until you think you understand it, or a part of it. Then write your version, without looking back at the original. Rearrange the order of ideas if doing so makes the passage more accessible.
4. Don't strain to find substitutes for words that are essential to the meaning of a passage.

We will illustrate paraphrasing with an excerpt from a source selected by one student, Patrick Pugh, who was researching the topic of euthanasia and planning to defend active euthanasia, or assisted suicide. In the university library Patrick found a book entitled *Suicide and Euthanasia: The Rights of Personhood,* a collection of essays written by doctors, philosophers, theologians, and legal experts. Published in 1981, the book was somewhat dated in 1991, when Patrick was doing his research, but he felt the question of whether suicide is moral or immoral was a timeless one. He read an essay entitled "In Defense of Suicide" by Joseph Fletcher, a former professor at the Episcopal Divinity School and president of the Society for the Right to Die. Before taking notes on Fletcher's essay, Patrick made a bibliography card recording all the necessary information about this source, as follows:

Fletcher, Joseph. "In Defense of Suicide."
In Suicide and Euthanasia : The
Rights of Personhood. Eds. Samuel E.
Wallace and Albin Eser. Knoxville : U of
Tennessee P 1981

Fletcher's article : pp. 38–50.

The following passage from Fletcher's essay offers a crucial definition; it is the kind of passage that a researcher should paraphrase on a notecard rather than quote, so that the idea becomes part of one's own store of knowledge.

> We must begin with the postulate that no action is intrinsically right or wrong, that nothing is inherently good or evil. Right and wrong, good and evil, desirable and undesirable—all are ethical terms and all are predicates, not properties. The moral "value" of any human act is always contingent, depending on the shape of the action in the situation. . . . The variables and factors in each set of circumstances are the determinants of what ought to be done—not prefabricated generalizations or prescriptive rules. . . . No "law" of conduct is always obliging; what we ought to do is whatever maximizes human well-being.

—JOSEPH FLETCHER, "In Defense of Suicide"

Patrick paraphrased this passage on the following notecard. Note that he names the author of the essay as well as the editors of the book and the exact pages on which the idea was found.

Fletcher's definition of ethical action:

The ethical value of any human action is not a quality inherent in the act itself. It is a judgment that we make about the act after examining the entire situation in which it takes place. Rather than relying on general rules about what is moral and immoral, we should make our decision on the basis of what is best for human well-being in any given set of circumstances.

Fletcher, pp. 38-39, in Wallace/Eser.

Following Through

From your own research, select a passage of approximately one paragraph that presents a complicated idea. Write a paraphrase of the passage.

Alternatively, you may write a paraphrase of the following paragraph, also from Joseph Fletcher's "In Defense of Suicide":

> What is called positive euthanasia—doing something to shorten or end life deliberately—is the form [of euthanasia] in which suicide is the question, as a voluntary, direct choice of death. For a long time the Christian moralists have distinguished between negative or indirectly willed suicide, like not taking a place in one of the *Titanic's* lifeboats, and positive or directly willed suicide, like jumping out of a lifeboat to make room for a fellow victim of a shipwreck. The moralists mean that we may choose to allow an evil by acts of omission but not to do an evil by acts of comission. The moralists contend that since all suicide is evil, we may only "allow" it; we may not "do" it. (47)

Your instructor may ask you to compare your paraphrase with that of a classmate before revising it and handing it in.

Summarizing

While a paraphrase may be longer or shorter than the original passage, a summary is always considerably shorter. It ought to be at least one-third the length of the original and is often considerably less: you may, for example, reduce an entire article to one or two paragraphs.

A summary of an argument must contain the main idea or claim and the main points of support or development. The amount of evidence and detail you include depends on your purpose for summarizing: if you just want to give your audience (or remind yourself of) the gist of the original, a bare-bones summary is enough; but if you plan to use the summary as part of making your case, you had better include the original's evidence as well.

For an example of using a summary as part of an argument, we return to Patrick Pugh's investigation of euthanasia. In another book, *The End of Life: Euthanasia and Morality* by James Rachels, Patrick found what Rachels describes as the chief religious objections to euthanasia, with Rachels's rebuttals for each. Patrick decided to include this material, in summary, in his paper. First read the passage from Rachels's book; then read Patrick's summarized version that follows immediately after.

SUGGESTIONS FOR SUMMARIZING

1. Read and reread the original text until you have identified the thesis and main points. You ought to be able to state these in your own words without looking back at the source.
2. Make it clear at the start whose ideas you are summarizing. Refer to the writer again only as necessary for clarity.
3. If you are summarizing a long passage, break it down into subsections and work on summarizing each one at a time.
4. As with paraphrasing, work as independently as you can—from memory—as you attack each part. Then go back to the text to check your version for accuracy.
5. Try to maintain the original order of points, with this exception: if the author delayed presenting the thesis, you may want to refer to it earlier in your summary.
6. Use your own words as much as possible.
7. Avoid quoting entire sentences. If you want to quote key words and phrases, try to incorporate them into sentences of your own, using quotation marks around just the borrowed words.
8. Write a draft summary; then summarize your draft.
9. Revise for conciseness and coherence; look for ways to combine sentences, using connecting words to show how ideas relate. See the section in Appendix B entitled "Use Transitions to Show Relationships between Ideas."

JAMES RACHELS

from *The End of Life*

RELIGIOUS ARGUMENTS

SOCIAL OBSERVERS are fond of remarking that we live in a secular   *1*
age, and there is surely something in this. The power of religious conceptions
was due, in some considerable measure, to their usefulness in explaining things.
In earlier times, religious ideas were used to explain everything from the
origins of the universe to the nature of human beings. So long as we had no
other way of understanding the world, the hold of religion on us was powerful
indeed. Now, however, these explanatory functions have largely been taken
over by the sciences: physics, chemistry, and their allies explain physical nature,
while evolutionary biology and psychology combine to tell us about ourselves.
As there is less and less work for religious hypotheses to do, the grip of
religious ideas on us weakens, and appeals to theological conceptions are heard
only on Sunday mornings. Hence, the "secular age."

However, most people continue to hold religious beliefs, and they especially appeal to those beliefs when morality is at issue. Any discussion of
mercy-killing quickly leads to objections based on theological grounds, and
"secular" arguments for euthanasia are rejected because they leave out the
crucial element of God's directions on the matter.

Considering the traditional religious opposition to euthanasia, it is
tempting to say: If one is not a Christian (or if one does not have some similar
religious orientation), then perhaps euthanasia is an option; but for people
who do have such a religious orientation, euthanasia cannot be acceptable.
And the discussion might be ended there. But this is too quick a conclusion;
for it is possible that the religious arguments against euthanasia are not valid
even for religious people. Perhaps a religious perspective, even a conventional
Christian one, does *not* lead automatically to the rejection of mercy-killing.
With this possibility in mind, let us examine three variations of the religious
objection.

What God Commands

It is sometimes said that euthanasia is not permissible simply because
God forbids it, and we know that God forbids it by the authority of either
scripture or Church tradition. Thus, one eighteenth-century minister, Hum-
phrey Primatt, wrote ironically that, in the case of aged and infirm animals,

> God, the Father of Mercies, hath ordained Beasts and Birds of Prey
> to do that distressed creature the kindness to relieve him his misery,
> by putting him to death. A kindness which *We* dare not show to our
> own species. If thy father, thy brother, or thy child should suffer the
> utmost pains of a long and agonizing sickness, though his groans
> should pierce through thy heart, and with strong crying and tears he

should beg thy relief, yet thou must be deaf unto him; he must wait his appointed time till his charge cometh, till he sinks and is crushed with the weight of his own misery.

When this argument is advanced, it is usually advanced with great con- 5 fidence, as though it were *obvious* what God requires. Yet we may well wonder whether such confidence is justified. The sixth commandment does not say, literally, "Thou shalt not *kill*"—that is a bad translation. A better translation is "Thou shalt not commit *murder*," which is different, and which does not obviously prohibit mercy-killing. Murder is by definition *wrongful* killing; so, if you do not think that a given kind of killing is wrong, you will not call it murder. That is why the sixth commandment is not normally taken to forbid killing in a just war; since such killing is (allegedly) justified, it is not called murder. Similarly, if euthanasia is justified, it is not murder, and so it is not prohibited by the commandment. At the very least, it is clear that we cannot infer that euthanasia is wrong *because* it is prohibited by the commandment.

If we look elsewhere in the Christian Bible for a condemnation of euthanasia, we cannot find it. These scriptures are silent on the question. We do find numerous affirmations of the sanctity of human life and the fatherhood of God, and some theologians have tried to infer a prohibition on euthanasia from these general precepts. (The persistence of the attempts, in the face of logical difficulties, is a reminder that people insist on reading their moral prejudices *into* religious texts much more often than they derive their moral views *from* the texts.) But we also find exhortations to kindness and mercy, and the Golden Rule proclaimed as the sum of all morality; and these principles, as we have seen, support euthanasia rather than condemn it.

We *do* find a clear condemnation of euthanasia in Church tradition. Regardless of whether there is scriptural authority for it, the Church has historically opposed mercy-killing. It should be emphasized, however, that this is a matter of history. Today, many religious leaders favour euthanasia and think the historical position of the Church has been mistaken. It was an Episcopal minister, Joseph Fletcher, who in his book *Morals and Medicine* formulated the classic modern defence of euthanasia. Fletcher does not stand alone among his fellow churchmen. The Euthanasia Society of America, which he heads, includes many other religious leaders; and the recent "Plea for Beneficent Euthanasia," sponsored by the American Humanist Association, was signed by more religious leaders than people in any other category. So it certainly cannot be claimed that *contemporary* religious forces stand uniformly opposed to euthanasia.

It is noteworthy that even Roman Catholic thinkers are today reassessing the Church's traditional ban on mercy-killing. The Catholic philosopher Daniel Maguire has written one of the best books on the subject, *Death By Choice*. Maguire maintains that "it may be moral and should be legal to accelerate the death process by taking direct action, such as overdosing with morphine or injecting potassium"; and moreover, he proposes to demonstrate that this view is "*compatible with historical Catholic ethical theory,*" contrary to what most opponents of euthanasia assume. Historical Catholic ethical theory, he says, grants individuals permission to act on views that are supported by "good and serious reasons," even when a different view is supported by a majority of authorities. Since the morality of euthanasia *is* supported by "good and serious reasons," Maguire concludes that Catholics are permitted to accept that morality and act on it.

Thus, the positions of both scripture and Church authorities are (at least) ambiguous enough so that the believer is not bound, on these grounds, to reject mercy-killing. The argument from "what God commands" should be inconclusive, even for the staunchest believer.

The Idea of God's Dominion

Our second theological argument starts from the principle that "The life of man is solely under the dominion of God." It is for God alone to decide when a person shall live and when he shall die; we have no right to "play God" and arrogate this decision unto ourselves. So euthanasia is forbidden. 10

This is perhaps the most familiar of all the theological objections to euthanasia; one hears it constantly when the matter is discussed. However, it is remarkable that people still advance this argument today, considering that it was decisively refuted over 200 years ago, when Hume made the simple but devastating point that *if it is for God alone to decide when we shall live and when we shall die, then we "play God" just as much when we cure people as when we kill them.* Suppose a person is sick and we have the means to cure him or her. If we do so, then we are interfering with God's "right to decide" how long the life shall last! Hume put it this way:

> Were the disposal of human life so much reserved as the peculiar providence of the Almighty that it were an encroachment on his right, for men to dispose of their own lives; it would be equally criminal to act for the preservation of life as for its destruction. If I turn aside a stone which is falling upon my head, I disturb this course of nature, and I invade the peculiar providence of the Almighty by lengthening out my life beyond the period which by the general laws of matter and motion he had assigned it.

We alter the length of a person's life when we save it just as much as when we take it. Therefore, if the taking of life is to be forbidden on the grounds that only God has the right to determine how long a person shall live, then the saving of life should be prohibited on the same grounds. We would then have to abolish the practice of medicine. But everyone (except, perhaps, Christian Scientists) concedes that this would be absurd. Therefore, we may *not* prohibit euthanasia on the grounds that only God has the right to determine how long a life shall last. This seems to be a complete refutation of this argument, and if refuted arguments were decently discarded, as they should be, we would hear no more of it.

Suffering and God's Plan

The last religious argument we shall consider is based on the idea that suffering is a part of God's plan for us. God has ordained that people should suffer; he never intended that life should be continually pleasurable. (If he had intended this, presumably he would have created a very different world.) Therefore, if we were to kill people to "put them out of their misery," we would be interfering with God's plan. Bishop Joseph Sullivan, a prominent Catholic opponent of euthanasia, expresses the argument in a passage from his essay "The Immorality of Euthanasia":

> If the suffering patient is of sound mind and capable of making an act of divine resignation, then his sufferings become a great means of merit whereby he can gain reward for himself and also win great favors for the souls in Purgatory, perhaps even release them from their suffering. Likewise the sufferer may give good example to his family and friends and teach them how to bear a heavy cross in a Christlike manner.
>
> As regard those that must live in the same house with the incurable sufferer, they have a great opportunity to practice Christian charity. They can learn to see Christ in the sufferer and win the reward promised in the Beatitudes. This opportunity for charity would hold true even when the incurable sufferer is deprived of the use of reason. It may well be that the incurable sufferer in a particular case may be of greater value to society than when he was of some material value to himself and his community.

This argument may strike some readers as simply grotesque. Can we imagine this being said, seriously, in the presence of suffering such as that experienced by Stewart Alsop's roommate? "We know it hurts, Jack, and that your wife is being torn apart just having to watch it, but think what a good opportunity this is for you to set an example. You can give us a lesson in how to bear it." In addition, some might think that euthanasia is exactly what *is* required by the "charity" that bystanders have the opportunity to practise.

But, these reactions aside, there is a more fundamental difficulty with the argument. For if the argument were sound, it would lead not only to the condemnation of euthanasia but of *any* measures to reduce suffering. If God decrees that we suffer, why aren't we obstructing God's plan when we give drugs to relieve pain? A girl breaks her arm; if only God knows how much pain is right for her, who are we to mend it? The point is similar to Hume's refutation of the previous argument. This argument, like the previous one, cannot be right because it leads to consequences that no one, not even the most conservative religious thinker, is willing to accept.

We have now looked at three arguments that depend on religious as- ¹⁵ sumptions. They are all unsound, but I have *not* criticized them simply by rejecting their religious presuppositions. Instead, I have criticized them on their own terms, showing that these arguments should not be accepted even by religious people. As Daniel Maguire emphasizes, the ethics of theists, like the ethics of all responsible people, should be determined by "good and serious reasons," and these arguments are not good no matter what world-view one has.

The upshot is that religious people are in the same position as everyone else. There is nothing in religious belief in general, or in Christian belief in particular, to preclude the acceptance of mercy-killing as a humane response to some awful situations. So, as far as these arguments are concerned, it appears that Christians may be free, after all, to accept the Golden Rule.

PATRICK PUGH

Summary of Excerpt from The End of Life

(The numbers in parentheses indicate the original pages where material appeared. We will explain this method of documentation later in this chapter.)

ACCORDING TO James Rachels, in spite of the fact that we live in a secular age, many objections to active euthanasia focus on religion, and particularly Christianity. However, even religious people ought to be able see that these arguments may not be valid. For example, one of the most often-stated objections is that, in the Ten Commandments, God forbids killing. Rachels counters by pointing out that the Sixth Commandment is more accurately translated as "Thou shalt not commit murder." Since we define murder as "wrongful killing," we will not call some killing murder if we do not see it as wrong. Thus, the Sixth Commandment "is not normally taken to forbid killing in a just war . . . since such killing is (allegedly) justified" (161–62). Rachels points out that while the scriptures do not mention euthanasia, and in fact affirm the "sanctity of human life," one also finds "exhortations to kindness and mercy" for fellow humans, principles which "support active euthanasia rather than condemn it" (162).

To those who claim that "[i]t is for God alone to decide when a person shall live and when he shall die," Rachels responds that "if it is for God alone to decide when we shall live and when we shall die, then we 'play God' just as much when we cure people as when we kill them" (163). He notes that philosopher David Hume made this argument over two hundred years ago.

A third common Christian argument is that since suffering is a part of God's plan for humans, we should not interrupt it by euthanasia. Rachels responds to this with the question, How can we then justify the use of any pain-relieving drugs and procedures? (165). He concludes that "[t]here is nothing in religious belief in general, or in Christian belief in particular, to preclude the acceptance of mercy-killing as a humane response to some awful situations" (165).

Following Through

Write a summary of the argument opposing euthanasia entitled "Rising to the Occasion of Our Death" by William F. May, on pages 62–63. Or summarize any other argument that you are considering using as a source for a project you are currently working on.

Creating an Annotated Bibliography

To get an overview of the sources they have compiled, many writers find it useful to create an annotated bibliography. A bibliography is simply a list of works on a particular topic; it can include any kind of source—from newspaper articles to books to government documents. The basic information of a bibliography is identical to that of a works-cited list: author, title, publisher, date, and, in the case of articles, periodical name, volume, and page numbers. (See the section "Creating a Works-Cited or Reference List" for examples.) Like a works-cited list, a bibliography is arranged in alphabetical order, based on each author's last name.

To annotate a bibliography means to include critical commentary about each work on the list, usually in the form of one or two short paragraphs. Each annotation should contain the following:

> A sentence or two about the rhetorical context of the source. Is it an informative news article, an opinion column, a scholarly essay? Is it intended for lawyers, the public, students, the elderly? What is the bias?
> A capsule summary of the content.
> A note about why this source seems valuable and how you might use it.

Sample Annotated Bibliography Entry

Ames, Katrine. "Last Rights." *Newsweek* 26 Aug. 1991:
40-41. This is a news article for the general public about the popularity of a book called *Final Exit*, on how to commit suicide. Ames explains the interest in the book as resulting from people's perception that doctors, technology, and hospital bureaucrats are making it harder and harder to die with dignity in this country. The article docu-

ments with statistics the direction of public
opinion on this topic and also outlines some options, beside suicide, that are becoming available
to ensure people of the right to die. Ames shows a
bias against prolonging life through technology,
but she includes quotations from authorities on
both sides. This is a good source of evidence
about public and professional opinion.

Following Through

Write an annotated bibliography of the sources you are using for a researched argument of your own.

INCORPORATING AND DOCUMENTING SOURCE MATERIAL IN THE TEXT OF YOUR ARGUMENT

We turn now to the more technical matter of how to incorporate source
material into your own writing and how to document the material you include. You incorporate material through direct quotation or through summary
or paraphrase; you document material by naming the writer and providing full
publication details of the source—a two-step process. In academic writing,
documenting sources is essential, even for indirect references, with one exception: you do not need to document your source for factual information that
could easily be found in many readily available sources, such as the current
number of women in the U.S. Senate or a Supreme Court decision.

Different Styles of Documentation

Different disciplines have specific formal conventions for documenting
sources in scholarly writing. In the humanities, the most common style is that
of the Modern Language Association (MLA). In the physical, natural, and
social sciences, the American Psychological Association (APA) style is most
often used. We will illustrate both in the examples that follow. Unlike the
footnote style of documentation, MLA and APA use parenthetical citations in
the text and simple, alphabetical bibliographies at the end of the text, making
revision and typing much easier. (For a detailed explanation of these two styles,
refer to the following manuals: *MLA Handbook for Writers of Research Papers.*
4th ed. New York: MLA, 1995; and *Publication Manual of the American Psychological Association.* 4th ed. Washington, DC: APA, 1994.)

In both MLA and APA formats, you provide some information in the body of your paper and the rest of the information under the heading *Works Cited* (MLA) or *References* (APA) at the end of your paper.

MLA Style

1. In parentheses at the end of both direct and indirect quotations, supply the last name of the author of the source and the exact page number(s) where the quoted or paraphrased words appear. If the name of the author appears in your sentence that leads into the quotation, you can omit it in the parentheses.

```
A San Jose State University professor who is black ar-

gues that affirmative action "does not teach skills,

or educate, or instill motivation" (Steele 121).


Shelby Steele, a black professor of English at San

Jose State University, argues that the disadvantages

of affirmative action for blacks are greater than the

advantages (117).
```

2. In a works-cited list at the end of the paper, provide complete bibliographical information in MLA style, as explained and illustrated later in this appendix.

APA Style

1. In parentheses at the end of the directly or indirectly quoted material, place the author's last name, the date of the cited source, and the exact page number(s) where the material appears. If the author's name appears in the sentence, the date of publication should follow the name directly, in parentheses; the page number still comes in parentheses at the end of the sentence. Unlike MLA, the APA style uses commas between the parts of the citation, and *p.* or *pp.* before the page numbers.

```
A San Jose State University professor who is black ar-

gues that affirmative action "does not teach skills,

or educate, or instill motivation" (Steele, 1990,

p. 121).


Shelby Steele (1990), a black professor of English at

San Jose State University, argues that the disadvan-
```

```
tages of affirmative action for blacks are greater
than the advantages (p. 117).
```

2. In a reference list at the end of the paper, provide complete bibliographical information in APA style, as explained and illustrated later in this appendix.

GUIDELINES FOR USING MLA AND APA STYLE

Avoid plagiarism by being conscious of whether you are quoting or paraphrasing. Any time that you take exact words from a source, even if it is only a phrase or a significant word that expresses an author's opinion, you are quoting. You must use quotation marks in addition to documenting your source. If you make any change at all in the wording of a quotation, you must indicate the change with ellipses or brackets. Even if you use your own words to summarize or paraphrase any portions of a source, you must still name that source in your text and document it fully. Be careful about using your own words when paraphrasing and summarizing.

1. At the very least, use an attributive tag such as "According to . . ." to introduce quotations, both direct and indirect. Don't just drop them in to stand on their own.
2. Name the person whose words or idea you are using. Give the person's full name on first mention.
3. Identify the author(s) of your source by profession or affiliation so readers will understand the significance of what he or she has to say. Omit this if the speaker is someone readers would recognize without your help.
4. Transitions into and out of quotations should link the ideas they express to whatever point you are making—that is, to the context of your essay.
5. If your lead-in to a quotation is a simple phrase, follow it with a comma. But if your lead-in can stand alone as a sentence, follow it with a colon.
6. The period at the end of a quotation or paraphrase comes after the parenthetical citation, except with block quotations.

Direct Quotations

Direct quotations are exact words taken from a source. The simplest direct quotations are whole sentences, worked into your text, as illustrated in the following excerpt from a student essay.

MLA Style

> In a passage that echos Seneca, *Newsweek* writer Ka-
> trine Ames describes the modern viewpoint: "Most of us
> have some choices in how we live, certainly in how we
> conduct our lives" (40).

This source is listed in the works-cited list as follows:

> Ames, Katrine. "Last Rights." *Newsweek* 26 Aug. 1991:
> 40-41.

APA Style

> In a passage that echos Seneca, *Newsweek* writer Ka-
> trine Ames (1991) describes the modern viewpoint:
> "Most of us have some choices in how we live, cer-
> tainly in how we conduct our lives" (p. 40).

This source is listed in the reference list as follows:

> Ames, K. (1991, August 26). Last rights. *News-*
> *week*, pp. 40-41.

Altering Direct Quotations with Ellipses and Brackets

While there is nothing wrong with quoting whole sentences, it is often more economical to quote selectively, working some words or parts of sentences from the original into sentences of your own. When you do this, use ellipses (three evenly spaced periods) to signify the omission of words from the original; use brackets to substitute words, to add words for purposes of clarification, and to change the wording of a quotation so that it fits gracefully into your own sentence.

The following passage from a student paper illustrates quoted words integrated into the student's own sentence, using both ellipses and brackets. The citation is in MLA style.

> Robert Wennberg, a philosopher and Presbyterian min-
> ister, explains that "euthanasia is not an exclu-
> sively modern development, for it was widely endorsed
> in the ancient world. [It was] approved by such re-
> spected ancients as . . . Plato, Sophocles, . . . and
> Cicero" (1).

The source appears in the works-cited list as follows:

Wennberg, Robert N. *Terminal Choices: Euthanasia,*

    Suicide, and the Right to Die. Grand Rapids, MI:

    Eerdmans, 1989.

Using Block Quotations

    If a quoted passage takes up more than four lines of text in your essay, you should indent it one inch (or ten spaces if typewritten) from the left margin, double-space it as you do the whole paper, and omit quotation marks. In block quotations, a period is placed at the end of the final sentence, followed by one space and the parenthetical citation.

> The idea of death as release from suffering was expressed by Seneca, a Stoic philosopher of Rome, who lived during the first century C.E.:
>
> > Against all the injuries of life, I have the refuge of death. If I can choose between a death of torture and one that is simple and easy, why should I not select the latter? As I chose the ship in which I sail and the house which I inhabit, so will I choose the death by which I leave life. . . . Why should I endure the agonies of disease . . . when I can emancipate myself from all my torments? (qtd. in Wennberg 42-43)

Note that the source of the Seneca quotation is the book by Wennberg. In the parenthetical citation, *qtd.* is an abbreviation for *quoted.* The entry on the works-cited page would be the same as for the previous example.

Indirect Quotations

    Indirect quotations are paraphrases or summaries of material, either fact or opinion, taken from a source. Following is an example of a direct quotation on a student notecard.

> *Expert's opinion — pro:*
>
> *"It is time to rethink many of our attitudes toward death and dying.... I feel that society is ready to take a giant step toward a better understanding of the dignity of death, and in the attainment of that dignity, if necessary, through the acceptance of euthanasia."*
>
> *— Barnard in Barnard, p.8*

Here is how this quotation might be incorporated into a paper as an indirect quotation. Note that the author of the book is the same as the person indirectly quoted, so it is not necessary to repeat his name in parentheses.

MLA Style

```
One cannot help but agree with pioneer heart-
transplant surgeon Christiaan Barnard that death
should involve dignity, and that society may have to
accept the practice of euthanasia as a means to death
with dignity (8).
```

The entry on the works-cited list would appear as follows:

```
Barnard, Christiaan. Good Life, Good Death. Englewood
     Cliffs: Prentice, 1980.
```

APA Style

```
One cannot help but agree with pioneer heart-
transplant surgeon Christiaan Barnard (1980) that
death should involve dignity, and that society may
have to accept the practice of euthanasia as a means
to death with dignity (p. 8).
```

The entry in the reference list would appear as follows:

```
        Barnard, C. (1980). Good life, good death. Engle-
   wood Cliffs, NJ: Prentice-Hall.
```

In-Text References to Electronic Sources

Obviously, the conventions described above apply to print sources, but you should adapt the examples given, being as specific as you can, when you are using sources drawn from the Internet and other electronic communications. As you will be including the electronic sources in your works-cited or reference list at the end of your paper, your in-text citations should help your reader make the connection between the material you are quoting or paraphrasing in your text and the matching citation on the list. Therefore, your in-text citation, whether parenthetical or not, should begin with the author's name or, in the absence of an author, the title of the work or posting. The APA format would require that you also include the date of the posting.

CREATING A WORKS-CITED OR REFERENCE LIST

At the end of your paper, include a bibliography of all sources that you quoted, paraphrased, or summarized. If you are using MLA style, your heading for this list will read *Works Cited;* if you are using APA style, your heading will read *References.* In either case, the list is in alphabetical order based on either the author's (or editor's) last name or—in the case of anonymously written works—the first word of the title, not counting articles (*a, an, the*). The entire list is double-spaced, both within and between entries. See the works-cited page of the sample student paper at the end of this appendix for the correct indentation and spacing.

The following examples illustrate the correct form for the types of sources you will most commonly use.

Books

Book by One Author

MLA: Crusius, Timothy W. *Discourse: A Critique &*

                     Synthesis of Major Theories. New York: MLA,

                     1989.

APA: Crusius, T. W. (1989). *Discourse: A critique*

           & synthesis of major theories. New York: Modern

           Language Association.

(Note that APA uses initials rather than the author's first names and capitalizes only the first word and proper nouns in the titles and subtitles of books and articles.)

Two or More Works by the Same Author

MLA: Crusius, Timothy W. *Discourse: A Critique & Syn-*

thesis of Major Theories. New York: MLA, 1989.

---. *A Teacher's Introduction to Philosophical*

Hermeneutics. Urbana, IL: NCTE, 1991.

(Note that MLA arranges works alphabetically by title and uses three hyphens to show that the name is the same as the one directly above.)

APA: Crusius, T. W. (1989). *Discourse: A critique*

& synthesis of major theories. New York: Modern

Language Association.

Crusius, T. W. (1991). *A teacher's*

introduction to philosophical hermeneutics.

Urbana, IL: National Council of Teachers of

English.

(Note that APA repeats the author's name and arranges works in chronological order.)

Book by Two or Three Authors

MLA: Deleuze, Gilles, and Felix Guattari. *Anti-Oedipus:*

Capitalism and Schizophrenia. New York:

Viking, 1977.

APA: Deleuze, G., & Guattari, F. (1977). *Anti-*

Oedipus: Capitalism and schizophrenia. New York:

Viking.

(Note that MLA style inverts only the first author's name. APA style, however, inverts both authors' names and uses an ampersand (&) instead of the word "and.")

Book by Four or More Authors

MLA: Bellah, Robert N., et al. *Habits of the*

Heart: Individualism and Commitment

in American Life. New York: Harper,

1985.

(Note that the Latin abbreviation *et al.,* meaning "and others," stands in for all subsequent authors' names. MLA style also accepts spelling out all authors' names instead of using *et al.*)

APA: Bellah, R., Madsen, R., Sullivan, W., Swidler,

A., & Tipton, S. (1985). *Habits of the heart:*

Individualism and commitment in American

life. New York: Harper & Row.

(Note that APA does not use *et al.,* regardless of the number of authors.)

Book Prepared by an Editor or Editors

MLA: Connors, Robert J., ed. *Selected Essays of Edward*

P.J. Corbett. Dallas: Southern Methodist UP,

1989.

APA: Connors, R. J. (Ed.). (1989). *Selected*

essays of Edward P.J. Corbett. Dallas: Southern

Methodist University Press.

Work in an Edited Collection

MLA: Jackson, Jesse. "Common Ground: Speech to the

Democratic National Convention." *The*

American Reader. Ed. Diane Ravitch. New York:

Harper, 1991. 367-71.

APA: Jackson, J. (1991). Common ground: Speech to

the Democratic National Convention. In D. Ravitch

(Ed.), *The American reader* (pp. 367-371). New

York: HarperCollins.

Translated Book

MLA: Vattimo, Gianni. *The End of Modernity: Nihilism*

and Hermeneutics in Postmodern Culture.

Trans. Jon R. Snyder. Baltimore: Johns

Hopkins UP, 1988.

APA:　　　　　　Vattimo, G. (1988). *The end of modernity:*

Nihilism and hermeneutics in postmodern culture.

(J. R. Snyder, Trans.). Baltimore: Johns Hopkins

University Press.

Periodicals

Article in a Journal with Continuous Pagination

MLA:　　　　　Herron, Jerry. "Writing for My Father." *College*

English 54 (1992): 928-37.

APA:　　　　　　Herron, J. (1992). Writing for my father.

College English, 54, 928-937.

(Note that in APA style the article title is not fully capitalized, but the journal title is. Note also that the volume number is italicized in APA style.)

Article in a Journal Paginated by Issue

MLA:　　　　　McConnell, Margaret Liu. "Living with *Roe v.*

Wade." *Commentary* 90.5 (1990): 34-38.

APA:　　　　　McConnell, M. L. (1990). Living with *Roe v.*

Wade. Commentary, 90(5), 34-38.

(In both these examples, *90* is the volume number, and *5* is the number of the issue.)

Article in a Magazine

MLA:　　　　　D'Souza, Dinesh. "Illiberal Education." *Atlantic*

Mar. 1990: 51+.

(Note that the plus sign indicates the article runs on nonconsecutive pages.)

APA:　　　　　D'Souza, D. (1990, March). Illiberal education.

Atlantic, pp. 51-58, 62-65, 67, 70-74, 76,

78-79.

(Note that APA requires all page numbers to be listed.)

Anonymous Article in a Newspaper

MLA:　　　　　"Clinton Warns of Sacrifice." *Dallas Morning News*

7 Feb. 1993: A4.

APA: Clinton warns of sacrifice. (1993, February 7).

                       The Dallas Morning News, p. A4.

(In both these examples the *A* refers to the newspaper section in which the article appeared.)

Editorial in a Newspaper

MLA: Lewis, Flora. "Civil Society, the Police and

                       Abortion." Editorial. *New York Times* 12

                       Sept. 1992: A14.

APA: Lewis, F. (1992, September 12). Civil

                       society, the police and abortion [Editorial]. *The*

                       New York Times, p. A14.

Nonprint Sources

Interview

MLA: May, William. Personal interview. 24 Apr. 1990.

(Note that APA style documents personal interviews only parenthetically within the text: "According to W. May (personal interview, April 24, 1990), . . ." Personal interviews are not included on the reference list.)

Sound Recording

MLA: Glass, Philip. *Glassworks.* CBS Sony, MK 37265,

                       1982.

APA: Glass, P. (1982). *Glassworks* [CD Recording

                       No. MK 37265]. Tokyo: CBS Sony.

Film

MLA: Scott, Ridley, dir. *Thelma and Louise.* Perf.

                       Susan Sarandon, Geena Davis, and Harvey

                       Keitel. MGM/UA Home Video, 1991.

APA: Scott, R. (Director). (1991). *Thelma and*

                       Louise [Film]. Culver City, CA: MGM/UA Home

                       Video.

(Note that with nonprint media, APA asks you to identify the medium—CD, cassette, film, and so forth. MLA includes the principal actors, but APA does not. APA specifies the place of production, but MLA does not.)

Electronic Sources

Whether you are using APA or MLA citation form, provide the following information: the author's name, if available; the title of the work; the complete work it appears in, if applicable; the edition of the work, if relevant; the date of issue, if available (in the case of news articles, journal articles, encyclopedia entries, books, and other documents); the medium in which the work appears (CD-ROM, on-line, electronic data bank—by name, such as ERIC); the URL, if applicable; and, in parentheses, the date you accessed the material. For E-mail, listserv, and newsgroup postings, in place of a title, use the subject line from the posting. Give the E-mail address of the listserv or newsgroup, or the author's E-mail address, except in the case of personal E-mail messages. The following section provides examples of the more common types of electronic-source citations used in undergraduate papers.

An Entire Work

MLA: Strunk, William. *The Elements of Style.* 1st ed.

                Geneva, NY: Humphrey, 1918. On-line.

                Columbia U, Academic Information Systems,

                Bartleby Lib. Internet. 7 Jan. 1997.

                Available: http://www.Columbia.edu/acis/

                bartleby/strunk/strunk100.html.

APA: Strunk, W. (1918). The elements of style

                (1st ed.) [On-line]. Available: http://

                www.Columbia.edu/acis/bartleby/strunk/

                strunk100.html.

Note that MLA requires that the original publication data be included if it is available for works that originally appeared in print. The APA, however requires only an on-line availability statement.

World Wide Web Site

MLA: Hinman, Lawrence. "Euthanasia." *Ethics Updates.*

                On-line. Internet. 7 Jan. 1997. Available:

                http://pwa.acusd.edu/~hinman/euthanasia.html.

APA: Hinman, L. Euthanasia. (1997, January 7).

                Ethics Updates [On-line]. Available: http://

                pwa.acusd.edu/~hinman/euthanasia.html.

Article in an Electronic Journal

MLA: Harnack, Andrew, and Gene Kleppinger. "Beyond the

MLA Handbook: Documenting Sources on the

Internet." *Kairos*. 1.2 (Summer 1996). On-

line. Internet. 7 Jan. 1997. Available: http:

//english.ttu.edu/Kairos/1.2/index.html.

APA: Harnack, A., & Kleppinger, G. (1996). Beyond

the *MLA Handbook:* Documenting sources on the

Internet. *Kairos* [On-line], *1*(2). Available: http:

//english.ttu.edu/Kairos/1.2/index.html.

Encyclopedia Article on CD-ROM

MLA: Duckworth, George. "Rhetoric." *Microsoft Encarta*

'95. CD-ROM. Redmond: Microsoft, 1995.

APA: Duckworth. G. (1995). Rhetoric. In *Microsoft*

encarta '95 [CD-ROM]. Redmond, WA: Microsoft.

Encyclopedia Article On-Line
      If you access an on-line encyclopedia through a commercial service such
as America Online, you should include the name of that service in your
citation. Place it immediately before the date of access.

MLA: "Rhetoric: The Nature of the New Rhetoric."

Britannica Online. (1997). On-line.

Internet. 20 Jan. 1997.

APA: Rhetoric: The nature of the new rhetoric.

(1997). In *Britannica Online* [On-line].

E-Mail, Listserv, and Newsgroup Citations
      For MLA give, in this order, the author's name, the author's E-mail
address in angled brackets, the subject line from the posting, the date it was
posted, the E-mail address of the listserv (in angled brackets) or name of the
newsgroup, and the date of access in parentheses.

MLA: Stockwell, Stephen. <S. Stockwell@eda.gu.edu.au>

"Rhetoric and Democracy." 13 Jan. 1997. On-

```
line posting. <H-Rhetor@msu.edu.> (Internet.)
(22 Jan. 1997.)
```

For APA, the custom is to not include E-mail, listservs, and newsgroups in a reference list but rather to give a detailed in-text citation as follows: (S. Stockwell, posting to H-Rhetor@msu.edu, January 13, 1997).

A STUDENT RESEARCH PAPER (MLA STYLE)

Following is student Patrick Pugh's research paper in MLA style.

Patrick Pugh

English 1302

October 21, 1992

Professor Smith

Legalizing Euthanasia: A Means
to a More Comfortable Dying Process

All people are linked by one indisputable fact:
Every human being dies. For some, death comes early,
seeming to cut off life before many of its mysteries
have even begun to unfold. For others, death
is the conclusion to a lengthy and experience-
filled existence. Death is life's one absolute
certainty.

At issue, however, is the desire by some men
and women, many of the most vocal of whom are in
the medical profession, to intervene in what they
describe as a heartless extension of the dying
process. The term "euthanasia," a Greek word whose
literal translation is "good death," has been adopted
by those who advocate legalizing certain measures to
ensure a transition from life to death which is as
comfortable and dignified as possible. One cannot
help but agree with pioneer heart-transplant surgeon
Dr. Christiaan Barnard that death should involve
dignity, and that society may have to accept the
practice of euthanasia as a means to death with
dignity (8).

To me, having watched both my grandfather and my
aunt spend months dying slow, torturous deaths from
incurable lung cancer, there can be little doubt that
euthanasia would have provided a far more humane
close to their lives than the painful and prolonged
dying that the ultimately futile regimens of chemo-
therapy and radiation caused them to suffer. My
family members' experiences were far too common,
for "80 percent of Americans who die in hospitals
are likely to meet their end . . . in a sedated or
comatose state; betubed nasally, abdominally, and
intravenously, far more like manipulated objects
than moral subjects" (Minow 124).

Advocates of euthanasia can turn to history for
support of their arguments. Robert Wennberg, a
philosopher and Presbyterian minister, explains that
"euthanasia is not an exclusively modern development,
for it was widely endorsed in the ancient world. [It
was] approved by such respected ancients as . . .
Plato, Sophocles, . . . and Cicero" (1). The idea
that we have a right to choose death was expressed by
Seneca, a Stoic philosopher of Rome, who lived in the
first century C.E.:

> Against all the injuries of life, I have
> the refuge of death. If I can choose
> between a death of torture and one that is
> simple and easy, why should I not select

Pugh 3

> the latter? As I chose the ship in
> which I sail and the house which I in-
> habit, so will I choose the death by which
> I leave life. In no matter more than death
> should we act according to our desire. . . .
> Why should I endure the agonies of dis-
> ease . . . when I can emancipate myself
> from all my torments? (qtd. in Wennberg
> 42-43)

In a passage that echos Seneca, *Newsweek* writer
Katrine Ames describes the modern viewpoint: "Most
of us have some choices in how we live, certainly in
how we conduct our lives. How we die is an equally
profound choice, and, in the exhilarating and
terrifying new world of medical technology, perhaps
almost as important" (40).

Regardless of historical precedents and humane
implications, euthanasia in both of its forms remains
a controversial issue for many. In the first kind,
known as passive, or indirect, euthanasia, death
results from such measures as withholding or
withdrawing life-support systems or life-sustaining
medications. Passive euthanasia is often equated
with simply "letting someone die," in contrast to the
far more controversial active, or direct, euthanasia
in which life is ended by direct intervention, such as

giving a patient a lethal dose of a drug or assisting
a patient in his or her suicide.

During the past two decades, the so-called
Right to Die movement has made great strides in the
promotion of passive euthanasia as an acceptable
alternative to the extension of impending death.

> There seems to be a clear consensus that
> the competent adult has the right to refuse
> treatments. . . . This legal recognition
> of the right to reject medical treatment
> is grounded in a respect for the bodily
> integrity of the individual, for the
> right of each person to determine when
> bodily invasions will take place.
> (Wennberg 116)

Passive euthanasia, as an extension of the stated
wishes of the dying patient, has become a widely
accepted practice, a fact confirmed by medical
ethicist and theologian Joseph Fletcher:

> What is called passive euthanasia, letting
> the patient die . . . , is a daily event in
> hospitals. Hundreds of thousands of Living
> Wills have been recorded, appealing to
> doctors, families, pastors, and lawyers
> to stop treatment at some balance point
> of the pro-life, pro-death assess-
> ment. (47)

The case for passive euthanasia has withstood, for
the most part, the arguments of those who claim that
life must be preserved and extended at all costs.

The euthanasia debate that is currently being
waged focuses on active, or direct, euthanasia, where
another person, notably a physician, assists a
terminally ill patient in dying by lethal injection
or provides the dying patient with the means to
commit suicide. The case for active euthanasia is
strong. For example, active euthanasia is preferable
to passive euthanasia in cases of chronic and
incurable diseases which promise the patient pain and
suffering for the duration of his or her life. As
Robert K. Landers explains, with the advance of AIDS
and diseases such as Alzheimer's affecting our aging
population, Americans are paying more attention to
the idea of "giving death a hand" (555). Surely,
many terminally ill patients, whose only hope for
release from agonizing pain or humiliating
helplessness is death, would welcome the more
comfortable and dignified death that physician-
assisted suicide can bring.

Still, there are those who argue that while
passive euthanasia is moral, the active type is
not. Ethically, is there a difference between passive and active euthanasia? Christiaan Barnard
thinks not:

Pugh 6

Passive euthanasia is accepted in general by
the medical profession, the major religions,
and society at large. Therefore, when it is
permissible for treatment to be stopped or
not instituted in order to allow the patient
to die, it makes for small mercy and less
sense when the logical step of actively
terminating life, and hence suffering, is
not taken. Why, at that point, can life not
be brought to an end, instead of extending
the suffering of the patient by hours or
days, or even weeks? . . . Procedurally,
there is a difference between direct and
indirect euthanasia, but ethically, they are
the same. (68-69)

Barnard's ethics are supported by Joseph Fletcher's
definition of ethical action, which holds that the
ethical value of any human action is not a quality
inherent in the act itself, but rather a judgment
that we make about the act after examining the entire
situation in which it takes place. We should decide
what is moral and immoral on the basis of what is
best for human well-being in any given set of
circumstances (38-39).

While Fletcher is an Episcopal theologian, many
other Christians do make arguments against active

euthanasia on religious grounds. However, according
to ethicist James Rachels, even religious people
ought to be able to see that these arguments may not
be valid. For example, one of the most often-stated
objections is that, in the Ten Commandments, God
forbids killing. Rachels counters by pointing out
that the Sixth Commandment is more accurately
translated as "Thou shalt not commit murder." Since
we define murder as "wrongful killing," we will not
call some killing murder if we do not see it as
wrong. Thus, the Sixth Commandment "is not normally
taken to forbid killing in a just war . . . since
such killing is (allegedly) justified" (161-162).
Rachels points out that while the scriptures do not
mention euthanasia, and in fact affirm the "sanctity
of human life," one also finds "exhortations to
kindness and mercy" for fellow humans, principles
which "support active euthanasia rather than condemn
it" (162).

To those who claim that "[i]t is for God alone
to decide when a person shall live and when he shall
die," Rachels responds that "if it is for God alone
to decide when we shall live and when we shall die,
then we 'play God' just as much when we cure people
as when we kill them" (163). He notes that
philosopher David Hume made this argument over
two hundred years ago.

A third common Christian argument is that since
suffering is a part of God's plan for humans, we
should not interrupt it by euthanasia. Rachels
responds to this with the question, How can we then
justify the use of any pain-relieving drugs and procedures? (165). He concludes that "[t]here is
nothing in religious belief in general, or in
Christian belief in particular, to preclude the
acceptance of mercy-killing as a humane response to
some awful situations" (165).

In fact, there is increasing support for the
legalization of active euthanasia, specifically
physician-assisted euthanasia, as an alternative
to a lingering death for terminal patients. Landers
reports that a July 1990 poll showed half the
respondents believed someone suffering from incurable
disease had a "moral right to commit suicide" (560).
In October 1991, a poll sponsored by the Boston Globe
and the Harvard School of Public Health found that 64
percent of Americans sampled favor the legalization
of physician-assisted suicide, and 52 percent think
they would actually consider it themselves. The
public interest in suicide as a way out of suffering
is also evident in the popularity of *Final Exit*, a
detailed guide on how to commit suicide, published in
March 1991. By August, that book was at the top of
the *New York Times'* best-seller list in the category
of how-to books.

Some states have put the question of legalizing active euthanasia before their voters. For example, the issue was placed on the Washington state ballot, as Initiative 119, in November of 1991 after 223,000 people signed petitions to place it there. The most controversial section of Initiative 119 stated that a conscious adult patient, who had been diagnosed with a terminal disease and who was deemed to have no more than six months to live, could ask a doctor to hasten death. The doctor had no obligation to comply, nor must the hospital allow it. But if the doctor and/or the hospital refused the patient's request, the patient had the right to be referred to a doctor or a hospital which would honor the request. Although voters in Washington rejected Initiative 119 by a 54 to 46 percent margin, the issue is far from decided. Citizens in Oregon, Florida, California, and Washington, D.C., will soon vote on similar initiatives.

At this point, there is no way to predict whether active euthanasia will be legalized in the near future. One thing is reasonably certain, however. Any compassionate person, who has sat helplessly by as a fellow human being has spent his or her final days thrashing around on a sweat-soaked bed, or who has observed a once-alert mind that has become darkened by the agony of inescapable pain,

will give consideration to the eventual fate that
awaits him or her. In times like these, frightened
humans are united in the universal prayer, "God,
spare me from this when my time comes," and even the
most stubborn anti-euthanasia minds are opened to the
option of an easier journey between life and death,
an option that can be made a reality by the
legalization of physician-assisted euthanasia.

Pugh 11

Works Cited

Ames, Katrine. "Last Rights." *Newsweek* 26 Aug. 1991:
    40-41.

Barnard, Christiaan. *Good Life, Good Death.*
    Englewood Cliffs: Prentice, 1980.

Fletcher, Joseph. "In Defense of Suicide." *Suicide*
    and Euthanasia: The Rights of Personhood. Ed.
    Samuel E. Wallace and Albin Eser. Knoxville: U
    of Tennessee P, 1981. 38-50.

Landers, Robert. "Right to Die: Medical, Legal, and
    Moral Issues." *Editorial Research Reports* 1.36
    (1990): 554-64.

Minow, Newton. "Communications in Medicine." *Vital*
    Speeches of the Day. 1 Dec. 1990: 121-25.

Rachels, James. *The End of Life.* Oxford: Oxford UP,
    1987.

Wennberg, Robert N. *Terminal Choices: Euthanasia,*
    Suicide, and the Right to Die. Grand Rapids, MI:
    Eerdmans, 1989.

Editing and
Proofreading

Editing and proofreading are the final steps in creating a finished piece of writing. Too often, however, these steps are rushed, as writers race to meet a deadline. Ideally, you should distinguish between the acts of revising, editing, and proofreading. Because each step requires that you pay attention to something different, you cannot reasonably expect to do them well if you try to do them all at once.

Our suggestions for revising appear in each of Chapters 5–8 on the aims of argument. Revising means shaping and developing the whole argument, with an eye to audience and purpose; when you revise, you are ensuring that you have accomplished your aim. Editing, on the other hand, means making smaller changes within paragraphs and sentences. When you edit, you are thinking about whether your prose will be a pleasure to read. Editing improves the sound and rhythm of your voice. It makes complicated ideas more accessible to readers and usually makes your writing more concise. Finally, proofreading means eliminating errors. When you proofread, you correct everything you find that will annoy readers, such as misspellings, punctuation mistakes, and faulty grammar.

In this appendix, we offer some basic advice on what to look for when editing and proofreading. For more detailed help, consult a handbook on grammar and punctuation and a good book on style, such as Joseph Williams's *Ten Lessons in Clarity and Grace* or Richard Lanham's *Revising Prose*. Both of these texts guided our thinking in the advice that follows.

EDITING

Most ideas can be phrased in a number of ways, each of which gives the idea a slightly distinctive twist.

In New York City, about 74,000 people die each year.

In New York City, death comes to one in a hundred people each year.

Death comes to one in a hundred New Yorkers each year.

To begin an article on what becomes of the unknown and unclaimed dead in New York, Edward Conlon wrote the final of these three sentences. We can only speculate about the possible variations he considered, but because openings are so crucial, he almost certainly cast these words quite deliberately.

For most writers, such deliberation over matters of style occurs during editing. In this late stage of the writing process, writers examine choices made earlier, perhaps unconsciously, while drafting and revising. They listen to how sentences sound, to patterns of rhythm both within and among sentences. Editing is like an art or craft; it can provide you the satisfaction of knowing you've said something gracefully and effectively. To focus on language this closely, you will need to set aside enough time following the revision step.

In the following section, we list some things to look for when editing your own writing. Don't forget, though, that editing does not always mean looking for weaknesses. You should also recognize passages that work well just as you wrote them, that you can leave alone or play up more by editing passages that surround them.

Editing for Clarity and Conciseness

Even drafts revised several times may have wordy and awkward passages; these are often places where a writer struggled with uncertainty or felt less than confident about the point being made. Introductions often contain such passages. In editing, you have the opportunity to take one more stab at clarifying and sharpening your ideas.

Express Main Ideas Forcefully

Emphasize the main idea of a sentence by stating it as directly as possible, using the two key sentence parts (*subject* and *verb*) to convey the two key parts of the idea (*agent* and *act*).

As you edit, first look for sentences that state ideas indirectly rather than directly; such sentences may include (1) overuse of the verb *to be* in its various forms (*is, was, will have been,* and so forth); (2) the opening words "There is . . ." or "It is . . ."; (3) strings of prepositional phrases; (4) many vague nouns. Then ask, "What is my true subject here, and what is that subject's action?" Here is an example of a weak, indirect sentence:

> It is a fact that the effects of pollution are more evident in lower-class neighborhoods than in middle-class ones.

The writer's subject is pollution. What is the pollution's action? Limply, the sentence tells us its "effects" are "evident." The following edited version makes pollution the agent that performs the action of a livelier verb, "fouls." The edited sentence is more specific—without being longer.

> *Pollution* more frequently *fouls* the air, soil, and water of lower-class neighborhoods than of middle-class ones.

Editing Practice

The following passage, about a plan for creating low-income housing, contains two weak sentences. In this case the weakness results from wordiness. (Note the overuse of vague nouns and prepositional phrases.) Decide for each sentence what the true subject is, and make that word the subject of the verb. Your edited version should be much shorter.

> As in every program, there will be the presence of a few who abuse the system. However, as in other social programs, the numbers would not be sufficient to justify the rejection of the program on the basis that one person in a thousand will try to cheat.

Choose Carefully between Active and Passive Voice

Active voice and passive voice indicate different relationships between subjects and verbs. As we have noted, ideas are usually clearest when the writer's true subject is also the subject of the verb in the sentence—that is, when it is the agent of the action. In the passive voice, however, the agent of the action appears in the predicate or not at all. Rather than acting as agent, the subject of the sentence *receives* the action of the verb.

The following sentence is in the passive voice:

> The air of poor neighborhoods is often fouled by pollution.

There is nothing incorrect about the use of the passive voice in this sentence, and in the context of a whole paragraph, passive voice can be the most emphatic way to make a point. (Here, for example, it allows the word *pollution* to fall at the end of the sentence, a strong position.) But, often, use of the passive voice is not a deliberate choice at all but rather a vague and unspecific way of stating a point.

Consider the following sentences, in which the main verbs have no agents:

> It *is believed* that dumping garbage at sea is not as harmful to the environment as *was* once *thought*.
>
> Ronald Reagan *was considered* the "Great Communicator."

Who thinks such dumping is not so harmful? Environmental scientists? Industrial producers? Who considered Reagan a great communicator? Speech professors? News commentators? Such sentences are clearer when they are written in the active voice:

> Some environmentalists believe that dumping garbage at sea is not as harmful to the environment as they used to think.
>
> Media commentators considered Ronald Reagan the "Great Communicator."

In editing for the passive voice, look over your verbs. Passive voice is easily recognized because it always contains (1) some form of *to be* (*is, was, were, will be, has been,* and so on) as a helping verb and (2) the main verb in its past participle form (which ends in *ed, d, t, en,* or *n,* or may in some cases be irregular: *drunk, sung, lain,* and so on).

When you find a sentence phrased in the passive voice, decide who or what is performing the action; the agent may appear after the verb, or not at all. Then decide if changing the sentence to the active voice will improve the sentence as well as the surrounding passage.

Editing Practice

1. The following paragraph from a student's argument needs editing for emphasis. It is choking with excess nouns and forms of the verb *to be,* some as part of passive constructions. You need not eliminate all passive voice, but do look for wording that is vague and ineffective. Your edited version should be not only stronger but also much shorter.

> Although emergency shelters are needed in some cases (for example, a mother fleeing domestic violence), they are an inefficient means of dealing with the massive numbers of people they are bombarded with each day. The members of a homeless family are in need of a home, not a temporary shelter into which they and others like them are herded, only to be shuffled out when their thirty-day stay is over to make room for the next incoming herd. Emergency shelters would be sufficient if we did not have a low-income housing shortage, but what is needed most at present is an increase in availability of affordable housing for the poor.

2. Select a paragraph of your own writing to edit; focus on using strong verbs and subjects to carry the main idea of your sentences.

Editing for Emphasis

When you edit for emphasis, you make sure that your main ideas stand out so that your reader will take notice. Following are some suggestions to help.

Emphasize Main Ideas by Subordinating Less Important Ones

Subordination refers to distinctions in rank or order of importance. Think of the chain of command at an office: the boss is at the top of the ladder, the middle management is on a lower (subordinate) rung, the support staff is at an even lower rung, and so on.

In writing, subordination means placing less important ideas in less important positions in sentences in order to emphasize the main ideas that should stand out. Writing that lacks subordination treats all ideas equally; each idea may consist of a sentence of its own or be joined to another idea by a co-ordinator (*and, but,* and *or*). Such a passage follows, with its sentences numbered for reference purposes.

> (1) It has been over a century since slavery was abolished, and a few decades since lawful, systematic segregation came to an unwilling halt. (2) Truly, blacks have come a long way from the darker days that lasted for more than three centuries. (3) Many blacks have entered the mainstream, and there is a proportionately large contingent of middle-class blacks. (4) Yet an even greater percentage of blacks are immersed in truly pathetic conditions. (5) The inner city black poor are enmeshed in devastating socioeconomic problems. (6) Unemployment among inner city black youths has become much worse than it was even five years ago.

Three main ideas are important here—that blacks have been free for some time, that some have made economic progress, and that others are trapped in poverty—and of these three, the last is probably intended to be the most important. Yet, as we read the passage, these key ideas do not stand out. In fact, each point receives equal emphasis and sounds about the same, with the repeated subject-verb-object syntax. The result seems monotonous, even apathetic, though the writer is probably truly disturbed about the subject. The following edited version that subordinates some of the points is more emphatic. We have italicized the main points.

> *Blacks have come a long way* in the century since slavery was abolished and in the decades since lawful, systematic segregation came to an unwilling halt. Yet, while many blacks have entered the mainstream and the middle class, *an even greater percentage are immersed in truly pathetic conditions.* To give just one example of these devastating socioeconomic problems, *unemployment among inner city black youths is much worse now than it was even five years ago.*

While different editing choices are possible, this version plays down sentences 1, 3, and 5 in the original, so that sentences 2, 4, and 6 stand out.

As you edit, look for passages that sound wordy and flat because all the ideas are expressed with equal weight in the same subject-verb-object pattern. Then single out your most important points, and try out some options for subordinating the less important ones. The key is to put main ideas in main clauses, and modifying ideas in modifying clauses or phrases.

Modifying Clauses   Like simple sentences, modifying clauses contain a subject and verb. They are formed in two ways: with relative pronouns and with subordinating conjunctions.

Relative pronouns introduce clauses that modify nouns, with the relative pronoun relating the clause to the noun it modifies. There are five relative pronouns:

that
which
who
whose
whom

The following sentence contains a relative clause:

> Alcohol advertisers are trying to sell a product *that is by its very nature harmful to users.*
>
> —JASON RATH (student)

Relative pronouns may also be implied:

> I have returned the library book *you loaned me.*

Relative pronouns may also be preceded by prepositions, such as *on, in, to,* or *during:*

> Drug hysteria has created an atmosphere *in which civil rights are disregarded.*

Subordinating conjunctions show relationships among ideas. It is impossible to provide a complete list of subordinating conjunctions in this short space, but here are the most common and the kinds of modifying roles they perform:

> *To show time:* after, as, before, since, until, when, while
> *To show place:* where, wherever
> *To show contrast:* although, though, whereas, while
> *To show cause and effect:* because, since, so that
> *To show condition:* if, unless, whether, provided that
> *To show manner:* how, as though

By introducing it with a subordinating conjunction, you can convert one sentence into a dependent clause that can modify another sentence. Consider the following two versions of the same idea:

> Pain is a state of consciousness, a "mental event." It can never be directly observed.

> *Since pain is a state of consciousness, a "mental event,"* it can never be directly observed.
>
> —PETER SINGER, "Animal Liberation"

Modifying Phrases Unlike clauses, phrases do not have a subject and a verb. Prepositional phrases and infinitive phrases are most likely already in your repertoire of modifiers. (Consult a handbook if you need to review these.) Here, we remind you of two other useful types of phrases.

Participial phrases modify nouns. Participles are created from verbs, so it is not surprising that the two varieties represent two verb tenses: present participles end in *-ing:*

> *Hoping to eliminate harassment on campus,* many universities have tried to institute codes for speech and behavior.

> The desperate Haitians fled here in boats, *risking all.*
>
> —CARMEN HAZAN-COHEN (student)

and past participles end in *-ed, -en, -d, -t,* or *-n:*

> Women themselves became a resource, *acquired by men much as the land was acquired by men.*
>
> —GERDA LERNER

> *Linked more to the Third World and Asia than to the Europe of America's racial and cultural roots,* Los Angeles and Southern California will enter the 21st century as a multi-racial and multicultural society.
>
> —RYSZARD KAPUSCINSKI

Notice that modifying phrases should immediately precede the nouns they modify.

An *appositive* is a noun or noun phrase that restates another noun, usually in a more specific way. Appositives can be highly emphatic, but more often they are tucked into the middle of a sentence or added to the end, allowing a subordinate idea to be slipped in. When used like this, appositives are usually set off with commas:

> Rick Halperin, *a professor at Southern Methodist University,* noted that Ted Bundy's execution cost Florida taxpayers over six million dollars.
>
> —DIANE MILLER (student)

Editing Practice

1. Edit the following passage as needed for emphasis, clarity, and conciseness, using subordinate clauses, relative clauses, participial phrases, appositives, and any other options that occur to you. If some parts are effective as they are, leave them alone.

> The monetary implications of drug legalization are not the only reason it is worth consideration. There is reason to believe that the United States would be a safer place to live if drugs were legalized. A large amount of what the media has named "drug-related" violence is really prohibition-related violence. Included in this are random shootings and murders associated with black market transactions. Estimates indicate that at least 40 percent of all property crime in the United States is committed by drug users so they can maintain their habits. That amounts to a total of 4 million crimes per year and $7.5 billion in stolen property. Legalizing drugs would be a step toward reducing this wave of crime.

2. Edit a paragraph of your own writing with an eye to subordinating less important ideas through the use of modifying phrases and clauses.

Vary Sentence Length and Pattern

Even when read silently, your writing has a sound. If your sentences are all about the same length (typically fifteen to twenty words) and all structured according to a subject-verb-object pattern, they will roll along with the monotonic rhythm of an assembly line. Obviously, one solution to this problem is to open some of your sentences with modifying phrases and clauses, as we discussed in the previous section. Here, we offer some other strategies, all of which add emphasis by introducing something unexpected.

1. Use a short sentence after several long ones.

> [A] population's general mortality is affected by a great many factors over which doctors and hospitals have little influence. For those diseases and injuries for which modern medicine can affect the outcome, however, which country the patient lives in really matters. Life expectancy is not the same among developed countries for premature babies, for children born with spina bifida, or for people who have cancer, a brain tumor, heart disease, or chronic renal failure. *Their chances of survival are best in the United States.*
>
> —JOHN GOODMAN

2. Interrupt a sentence.

> The position of women in that hippie counterculture was, *as a young black male leader preached succinctly,* "prone."
>
> —BETTY FRIEDAN

> Symbols and myths—*when emerging uncorrupted from human experience*— are precious. Then it is the poetic voice and vision that informs and infuses—*the poet-warrior's, the prophet-seer's, the dreamer's*—reassuring us that truth is as real as falsehood. And ultimately stronger.
>
> —OSSIE DAVIS

3. Use an intentional sentence fragment. The concluding fragment in the previous passage by Ossie Davis is a good example.
4. Invert the order of subject-verb-object.

> Further complicating negotiations is the difficulty of obtaining relevant financial statements.
>
> —REGINA HERZLINGER

> This creature, with scarcely two thirds of man's cranial capacity, was a fire user. Of what it meant to him beyond warmth and shelter, we

know nothing; with what rites, ghastly or benighted, it was struck or maintained, no word remains.

—LOREN EISELY

Use Special Effects for Emphasis

Especially in persuasive argumentation, you will want to make some of your points in deliberately dramatic ways. Remember that just as the crescendos stand out in music because the surrounding passages are less intense, so the special effects work best in rhetoric when you use them sparingly.

Repetition   Deliberately repeating words, phrases, or sentence patterns has the effect of building up to a climactic point. In Chapter 7 we noted how Martin Luther King, Jr., in the emotional high point of his "Letter from Birmingham Jail," used repeated subordinate clauses beginning with the phrase "when you" to build up to his main point: ". . . then you will understand why we find it difficult to wait" (paragraph 14, page 121). Here is another example, from the conclusion of an argument linking women's rights with environmental reforms:

> Environmental justice goes much further than environmental protection, a passive and paternalistic phrase. *Justice requires that* industrial nations pay back the environmental debt incurred in building their wealth by using less of nature's resources. *Justice prescribes that* governments stop siting hazardous waste facilities in cash-poor rural and urban neighborhoods and now in the developing world. *Justice insists that* the subordination of women and nature by men is not only a hazard; it is a crime. *Justice reminds us that* the Earth does not belong to us; even when we "own" a piece of it, we belong to the Earth.
>
> —H. PATRICIA HYNES

Paired Coordinators   Coordinators are conjunctions that pair words, word groups, and sentences in a way that gives them equal emphasis and that also shows a relationship between them, such as contrast, consequence, or addition. In grade school you may have learned the coordinators through the mnemonic *FANBOYS*, standing for *for, and, nor, but, or, yet, so.*

Paired coordinators emphasize the relationship between coordinated elements; the first coordinator signals that a corresponding coordinator will follow. Some paired coordinators are:

both _____ and _____

not _____ but _____

not only _____ but also _____

either _____ or _____

neither _____ nor _____

The key to effective paired coordination is to keep the words that follow the marker words as grammatically similar as possible. Pair nouns with nouns, verbs with verbs, prepositional phrases with prepositional phrases, whole sentences with whole sentences. (Think of paired coordination as a variation on repetition.) Here are some examples:

> Feminist anger, or any form of social outrage, is dismissed breezily— *not* because it lacks substance *but* because it lacks "style."
>
> —SUSAN FALUDI

> Alcohol ads that emphasize "success" in the business and social worlds are useful examples *not only* of how advertisers appeal to people's envy *but also* of how ads perpetuate gender stereotypes.
>
> —JASON RATH (student)

Emphatic Appositives   While an appositive (a noun or noun phrase that restates another noun) can subordinate an idea, it can also emphasize an idea if it is placed at the beginning or the end of a sentence, where it will command attention. Here are some examples:

> *The poorest nation in the Western hemisphere,* Haiti is populated by six million people, many of whom cannot obtain adequate food, water, or shelter.
>
> —SNEED B. COLLARD III

> [Feminists] made a simple, though serious, ideological error when they applied the same political rhetoric to their own situation as women versus men: *too literal an analogy with class warfare, racial oppression.*
>
> —BETTY FRIEDAN

Note that at the end of a sentence, an appositive may be set off with a colon or a dash.

Emphatic Word Order   The opening and closing positions of a sentence are high-profile spots, not to be wasted on weak words. The following sentence, for example, begins weakly with the filler phrase "there are":

> *There are* several distinctions, all of them false, that are commonly made between rape and date rape.

A better version would read:

> My opponents make several distinctions between rape and date rape; all of these are false.

Even more important are the final words of every paragraph and the opening and closing of the entire argument.

Editing Practice

1. Select one or two paragraphs from a piece of published writing you have recently read and admired. Be ready to share it with your class, explaining how the writer has crafted the passage to make it work.

2. Take a paragraph or two from one of your previous essays, perhaps even an essay from another course, and edit it to improve clarity, conciseness, and emphasis.

Editing for Coherence

Coherence refers to what some people call the "flow" of writing; writing flows when the ideas connect smoothly, one to the next. In contrast, when writing is incoherent, the reader must work to see how ideas connect and infer points that the writer, for whatever reason, has left unstated.

Incoherence is a particular problem with writing that contains an abundance of direct or indirect quotations. In using sources, be careful always to lead into the quotation with some words of your own, showing clearly how this new idea connects with what has come before.

Because finding incoherent passages in your own writing can be difficult, ask a friend to read your draft to look for gaps in the presentation of ideas. Here are some additional suggestions for improving coherence.

Move from Old Information to New Information

Coherent writing is easy to follow because the connections between old information and new information are clear. Sentences refer back to previously introduced information and set up reader expectations for new information to come. Notice how every sentence fulfills your expectations in the following excerpts from an argument on animal rights by Steven Zak.

> The credibility of the animal-rights viewpoint . . . need not stand or fall with the "marginal human beings" argument.

Next, you would expect to hear why animals do not have to be classed as "marginal human beings"; and you do:

> Lives don't have to be qualitatively the same to be worthy of equal respect.

At this point you might ask upon what else we should base our respect. Zak answers this question in the next sentence:

> One's perception that another life has value comes as much from an appreciation of its uniqueness as from the recognition that it has characteristics that are shared by one's own life.

Not only do these sentences fulfill reader expectations, but each also makes a clear connection by referring specifically to the key idea in the sentence before it, forming an unbroken chain of thought. We have underlined the words that accomplish this linkage:

The credibility of the animal rights viewpoint . . . need not stand or fall with the "*marginal human beings*" argument.

Lives don't have to be *qualitatively the same* to be worthy of *equal respect.*

One's perception that *another life has value* comes as much from an *appreciation of its uniqueness* as from the recognition that it has characteristics that are shared by one's own life.

One can imagine that the lives of various kinds of animals *differ radically. . . .*

In the following paragraph, reader expectations are not so well fulfilled:

We are presently witness to the greatest number of homeless families since the Great Depression of the 1930s. The cause of this phenomenon is a shortage of low-income housing. Mothers with children as young as two weeks are forced to live on the street because there is no room for them in homeless shelters.

While these sentences are all on the subject of homelessness, the second leads us to expect that the third will take up the topic of shortages of low-income housing. Instead, it takes us back to the subject of the first sentence and offers a different cause—no room in the shelters.

Looking for ways to link old information with new information will help you find problems of coherence in your own writing.

Editing Practice

1. In the following paragraph, underline the words or phrases that make the connections back to the previous sentence and forward to the next, as we did earlier with the passage from Zak.

The affluent, educated, liberated women of the First World, who can enjoy freedoms unavailable to any women ever before, do not feel as free as they want to. And they can no longer restrict to the subconscious their sense that this lack of freedom has something to do with—with apparently frivolous issues, things that really should not matter. Many are ashamed to admit that such trivial concerns—to do with physical appearance, bodies, faces, hair, clothes—matter so much. But in spite of shame, guilt, and denial, more and more women are wondering if it isn't that they are entirely neurotic alone but rather that something important is indeed at stake that has to do with the relationship between female liberation and female beauty.

—NAOMI WOLF

2. The following student paragraph lacks coherence. Read through it, and put a slash (/) between sentences expressing unconnected ideas. You may try to

rewrite the paragraph, rearranging sentences and adding ideas to make the connections tighter.

> Students may know what AIDS is and how it is transmitted, but most are not concerned about AIDS and do not perceive themselves to be at risk. But college age heterosexuals are the number one high risk group for this disease (Gray and Sacarino 258). "Students already know about AIDS. Condom distribution, public or not, is not going to help. It just butts into my personal life," said one student surveyed. College is a time for exploration and that includes the discovery of sexual freedom. Students, away from home and free to make their own decisions for maybe the first time in their lives, have a "bigger than life" attitude. The thought of dying is the farthest from their minds. Yet at this point in their lives, they are most in need of this information.

Use Transitions to Show Relationships between Ideas

Coherence has to be built into a piece of writing; as we discussed earlier, the ideas between sentences must first cohere. However, sometimes readers need help in making the transition from one idea to the next, so you must provide signposts to help them see the connections more readily. For example, a transitional word like *however* can prepare readers for an idea in contrast to the one before it, as in the second sentence in this paragraph. Transitional words can also highlight the structure of an argument ("These data will show three things: first . . . , second . . . , and third. . . ."), almost forming a verbal path for the reader to follow. Following are examples of transitional words and phrases and their purposes:

> *To show order:* first, second, next, then, last, finally
> *To show contrast:* however, yet, but, nevertheless
> *To show cause and effect:* therefore, consequently, as a result, then
> *To show importance:* moreover, significantly
> *To show an added point:* as well, also, too
> *To show an example:* for example, for instance
> *To show concession:* admittedly
> *To show conclusion:* in sum, in conclusion

The key to using transitional words is similar to the key to using special effects for emphasis: Don't overdo it. To avoid choking your writing with these words, anticipate where your reader will genuinely need them, and limit their use to these instances.

Editing Practice

Underline the transitional words and phrases in the following passage of published writing:

> When people believe that their problems can be solved, they tend to get busy solving them.
>
> On the other hand, when people believe that their problems are beyond solution, they tend to position themselves so as to avoid blame. Take the woeful inadequacy of education in the predominantly black central cities. Does the black leadership see the ascendancy of black teachers, school administrators, and politicians as an asset to be used in improving those dreadful schools? Rarely. You are more likely to hear charges of white abandonment, white resistance to integration, conspiracies to isolate black children, even when the schools are officially desegregated. In short, white people are accused of being responsible for the problem. But if the youngsters manage to survive those awful school systems and achieve success, leaders want to claim credit. They don't hesitate to attribute that success to the glorious Civil Rights movement.
>
> —WILLIAM RASPBERRY

PROOFREADING

Proofreading is truly the final step in writing a paper. After proofreading, you ought to be able to print your paper out one more time; but if you do not have time, most instructors will be perfectly happy to see the necessary corrections done neatly in ink on the final draft.

Following are some suggestions for proofreading.

Spelling Errors

If you have used a word processor, you may have a program that will check your spelling. If not, you will have to check your spelling by reading through again carefully, with a dictionary at hand. Consult the dictionary whenever you feel uncertain. You might consider devoting a special part of your writer's notebook to your habitual spelling errors: some students always misspell "athlete," for example, while others leave the second "n" out of environment.

Omissions and Jumbled Passages

Read your paper out loud. Physically shaping your lips around the words can help locate missing words, typos ("saw" instead of "was"), or the remnants of some earlier version of a sentence that did not get fully deleted. Place a caret in the sentence, and write the correction or addition above the line, or draw a line through unnecessary text.

Punctuation Problems

Apostrophes and commas give writers the most trouble. If you have habitual problems with these, you should record your errors in your writer's notebook.

Apostrophes

Apostrophe problems usually occur in forming possessives, not contractions, so here we discuss only the former. If you have problems with possessives, you may also want to consult a good handbook or seek a private tutorial with your instructor or your school's writing center.

Here are the basic principles to remember.

1. Possessive pronouns never take an apostrophe.

   his, hers, yours, theirs, its

2. Singular nouns become possessive by adding *-'s.*

   A single parent's life is hard.
   A society's values change.
   Do you like Mr. Voss's new car?

3. Plural nouns ending in *-s* become possessive by simply adding an apostrophe.

   Her parents' marriage is faltering.
   Many cities' air is badly polluted.
   The Joneses' house is up for sale.

4. Plural nouns that do not end in *-s* become possessive by adding *'s.*

   Show me the women's (men's) room.
   The people's voice was heard.

If you err by using apostrophes where they don't belong in nonpossessive words ending in "s," remember that a possessive will always have a noun after it, not some other part of speech such as a verb or a preposition. You may even need to read each line of print with a ruler under it to help you focus more intently on each word.

Commas

Because commas indicate a pause, reading your paper aloud is a good way to decide where to add or delete them. A good handbook will elaborate on the following basic principles. The example sentences have been adapted from an argument by Mary Meehan, who opposes abortion.

1. Use a comma when you join two or more main clauses with a coordinating conjunction.

   Main clause, conjunction (*and, but, or, nor, so, yet*) main clause.

   Feminists want to have men participate more in the care of children, but abortion allows a man to shift total responsibility to the woman.

2. Use a comma after an introductory phrase or dependent clause.

   Introductory phrase or clause, main clause.

   To save the smallest children, the Left should speak out against abortion.

3. Use commas around modifiers such as relative clauses and appositives, unless they are essential to the noun's meaning. Be sure to put the comma at both ends of the modifier.

   _____ , appositive, _____

   _____ , relative clause, _____

   One member of the 1972 Presidential commission on population growth was Graciela Olivarez, a Chicana who was active in civil rights and anti-poverty work. Olivarez, who later was named to head the Federal Government's Community Services Administration, had known poverty in her youth in the Southwest.

4. Use commas with a series.

   ____x___ , ___y___ , and ___z___

   The traditional mark of the Left has been its protection of the underdog, the weak, and the poor.

Semicolons

Think of a semicolon as a strong comma. It has two main uses.

1. Use a semicolon to join two main clauses when you choose not to use a conjunction. This works well when the two main clauses are closely related or parallel in structure.

   Main clause; main clause.

   Pro-life activists did not want abortion to be a class issue; they wanted to end abortion everywhere, for all classes.

   As a variation, you may wish to add a transitional adverb to the second main clause. The adverb indicates the relationship between the main clauses, but it is not a conjunction, so a comma preceding it would not be correct.

   Main clause; transitional adverb (*however, therefore, thus, moreover, consequently*), main clause

When speaking with counselors at the abortion clinic, many women change their minds and decide against abortion; however, a woman who is accompanied by a husband or boyfriend often does not feel free to talk with the counselor.

2. Use semicolons between items in a series if any of the items themselves contain commas.

$$\underline{\quad},\underline{\quad};\ \underline{\quad},\underline{\quad};\ \underline{\quad},\underline{\quad}$$

A few liberals who have spoken out against abortion are Jesse Jackson, a Civil Rights leader; Richard Neuhaus, a theologian; the comedian Dick Gregory; and politicians Mark Hatfield and Mary Rose Oakar.

Colons

The colon has two common uses.

1. Use a colon to introduce a quotation when both your own lead-in and the words quoted are complete sentences that can stand alone. (See the section in Appendix A entitled "Incorporating and Documenting Source Materials" for more on introducing quotations.)

Main clause in your words: "Quoted sentence(s)."

Mary Meehan criticizes liberals who have been silent on abortion: "If much of the leadership of the pro-life movement is right-wing, that is due largely to the default of the Left."

2. Use a colon before an appositive that comes dramatically at the end of a sentence, especially if the appositive contains more than one item.

Main clause: appositive, appositive, and appositive.

Meehan argues that many pro-choice advocates see abortion as a way to hold down the population of certain minorities: blacks, Puerto Ricans, and other Latins.

Grammatical Errors

Grammatical mistakes can be hard to find, but once again we suggest reading aloud as one method of proofing for them; grammatical errors tend not to "sound right" even if they look like good prose. Another suggestion is to recognize your habitual errors and then look for particular grammatical structures that lead you into error.

Introductory Participial Phrases

Constructions such as these often lead writers to create dangling modifiers. To avoid this pitfall, see the discussion of participial phrases earlier in this appendix. Remember that an introductory phrase dangles if it is not immediately followed by the noun it modifies.

Incorrect:

Using her conscience as a guide, our society has granted each woman the right to decide if a fetus is truly a "person" with rights equal to her own.

(Notice that the implied subject of the participial phrase is "each woman," when in fact the subject of the main clause is "our society"; thus the participial phrase does not modify the subject.)

Corrected:

Using her conscience as a guide, each woman in our society has the right to decide if a fetus is truly a "person" with rights equal to her own.

Paired Coordinators

If the words that follow each of the coordinators are not of the same grammatical structure, then an error known as nonparallelism occurs. To correct this error, line up the paired items one over the other. You will see that the correction often involves simply adding a word or two to, or deleting some words from, one side of the paired coordinators.

not only _____
but also _____

Incorrect:

Legal abortion not only protects women's lives, but also their health.

Corrected:

Legal abortion protects not only women's lives but also their health.

Split Subjects and Verbs

If the subject of a sentence contains long modifying phrases or clauses, by the time you get to the verb you may make an error in agreement (using a plural verb, for example, when the subject is singular) or even in logic (for example, having a subject that is not capable of being the agent that performs the action of the verb). Following are some typical errors:

The *goal* of the courses grouped under the rubric of "Encountering Non-Western Cultures" *are.* . . .

Here, the writer forgot that *goal,* the subject, is singular.

During 1992, *the Refugee Act of 1980,* with the help of President Bush and Congress, *accepted* 114,000 immigrants into our nation.

The writer here should have realized that the agent doing the accepting would have to be the Bush administration, not the Refugee Act. A better version would read:

During 1992, the Bush administration accepted 114,000 immigrants into our nation under the terms of the Refugee Act of 1980.

Proofreading Practice

Proofread the following passage for errors of grammar and punctuation.

The citizens of Zurich, Switzerland tired of problems associated with drug abuse, experimented with legalization. The plan was to open a central park, Platzspitz, where drugs and drug use would be permitted. Many European experts felt, that it was the illegal drug business rather than the actual use of drugs that had caused many of the cities problems. While the citizens had hoped to isolate the drug problem, foster rehabilitation, and curb the AIDS epidemic, the actual outcome of the Platzspitz experiment did not create the desired results. Instead, violence increased. Drug-related deaths doubled. And drug users were drawn from not only all over Switzerland, but from all over Europe as well. With thousands of discarded syringe packets lying around, one can only speculate as to whether the spread of AIDS was curbed. The park itself was ruined and finally on February 10, 1992, it was barred up and closed. After studying the Swiss peoples' experience with Platzspitz, it is hard to believe that some advocates of drug legalization in the United States are urging us to participate in the same kind of experiment.

CREDITS

Text Credits

MATTHEW CONOLLY, "Euthanasia Is Not the Answer" from a speech delivered at the Hemlock Society's Second National Voluntary Euthanasia Conference, February 9, 1985. Reprinted with permission of the author.

ANGELA J. GRELLHESL, "Mediating the Speech Code Controversy." Reprinted by permission of the author.

SIDNEY HOOK, "In Defense of Voluntary Euthanasia," *The New York Times.* Copyright © 1987 by The New York Times Company. Reprinted by permission.

MARTIN LUTHER KING, JR., "Letter from Birmingham Jail." Reprinted by arrangement with the Heirs of the Estate of Martin Luther King, Jr., % Writers House as agent for the proprietor. Copyright © 1963 by Martin Luther King, Jr.; copyright renewed 1991 by Coretta Scott King.

MICHAEL LEVIN, "The Case for Torture," *Newsweek,* June 7, 1982. Reprinted with permission of the author; "A Case Against Civil Rights for Homosexuals," *Feminism and Freedom.* Copyright © 1987 by Transaction Publishers. Reprinted by permission of the publisher. All rights reserved.

WILLIAM F. MAY, "Rising to the Occasion of our Death." Copyright 1993 Christian Century Foundation. Reprinted by permission from the 7/11/93 issue of *The Christian Century.*

MARGARET LIU MCCONNELL, "Living with Roe v. Wade," *Commentary,* November 1990. Reprinted with permission of the author.

WILLIAM MURCHISON, "Should Dallas Drop Ban: City Shouldn't Ignore Morality," from *The Dallas Morning News' Viewpoint,* January 17, 1992. Reprinted with permission of The Dallas Morning News.

ANNE MARIE O'KEEFE, "The Case Against Drug Testing." Reprinted with permission from *Psychology Today Magazine.* Copyright © 1987 Sussex Publishers, Inc.

ANNA QUINDLEN, "Public and Private; Making the Mosaic," *The New York Times,* November 20, 1991. Copyright © 1991 The New York Times Company. Reprinted by permission; "Mother's Choice" from *Ms. Magazine,* February 1988. Reprinted by permission of the author.

ROGER ROSENBLATT, "How to End the Abortion War." Copyright © 1992 by The New York Times Company. Reprinted by permission.

JOEY SHANKS, "An Uncomfortable Position." Reprinted by permission of the author.

JUSTIN SPIDEL, "Who Should Have the Right to Marry?" Reprinted by permission of the author.

CINDY TARVER, "An Appeal to Prejudice." Reprinted by permission of the author.

ELLEN WILLIS, "Abortion: Whose Right to Life Is It Anyway?" Copyright © 1985 by Ellen Willis. Reprinted by permission of the Charlotte Sheedy Literary Agency.

AMBER YOUNG, "Capital Punishment: Society's Self-Defense," reprinted with permission of the author.

Photo and Illustration Credits

Page 153 Silver Jeans, Peace on Earth, Christmas 1993 campaign U.S. by permission of Brainstorm; page 154, courtesy of Department of Defense; page 155, photograph by Barbara Alper by permission of Stock Boston; page 156, photograph by Richard Pasley by permission of Stock Boston; page 157, by permission of Jim McCloskey; by permission of Mike Luckovich and Creators Syndicate.

INDEX

Boldfaced numbers indicate page on which term is defined.

active voice, 256–257
advertising, 43, 152–154
allusions, 24
American Psychological Association (APA)
    style, 229–242
analogies, 45, 92–93
analysis
    and critical reading, 20–22, 32–35
    evidence, 35
    for inquiry, 53–56, 58–59
    theses, 22, 31–32, 90–91
APA style. *See* American Psychological
    Association (APA) style
apostrophes, 268
appeals. *See* character appeals; emotions;
    reason, appeal to; style
Appeal to Prejudice, An (Tarver), 58–59
appositives, 260, 263
argument, aims of
    defined, **3–4, 13**
    overview, 4–8
    summary, 8
    See also convincing; inquiry; negotiation;
    persuasion
argument, defined, **3**
Aristotle, 9
assumptions
    and convincing, 76–77, 82
    and inquiry, 44–45, 49–50
    and negotiation, 178–180
    and persuasion, 115, 131
audience, **13**
    commonalities with, 116
    for convincing, 74, 76–77, 82, 87–88,
        90, 91, 96
    critical reading, 21
    and inquiry, 42
    for persuasion, 114–116, 131–132, 135,
        141–142, 144, 145–146
    See also rhetorical context
author's background. *See* rhetorical context

behavior, influencing. *See* persuasion
belief systems, 91

bias, 45, 217
bibliographic information, 215–216
bibliographies, 211
    annotated, 228–229
    works-cited/reference lists, 235–242
body paragraphs, 102–104. *See also*
    evidence; reasons
brief preparation, 84–105, **84–85**
    audience, 87–88
    drafts, 100–105
    evidence, 98–100
    position establishment, 85–87
    reason selection/ordering, 95–97
    reason sources, 91–95
    and research, 218
    thesis analysis, 90–91
    thesis development, 88–89

Capital Punishment: Society's Self-Defense
    (Young), 36–40
card catalogs, 207
cartoons, editorial, 156–158
Case against Drug Testing, The (O'Keefe),
    78–81
Case for Torture, The (Levin), 46–48
case strategy, **75**–77, 101. *See also* case
    structure
case structure, **75,** 84–85, 97. *See also* brief
    preparation; case strategy; structure
cause and effect, 93–94
character appeals
    and negotiation, 200
    and persuasion, 6–7, 114, 134–135,
        143–145
    and rhetoric, 9
City Shouldn't Ignore Morality
    (Murchison), 56–58
claims, **31**–32. *See also* theses
class discussions, 71–73
coherence, **264**–266
collaboration, 161, 184
colons, 270
commas, 268–269
common ground, 116, 135, 144